Jumana Bayeh is a Senior Lecturer at Macquarie University, Australia. She has held research fellowships at the University of Toronto, the University of Edinburgh and the Lebanese American University in Beirut. She is the author of numerous articles on Arab diaspora fiction, is the co-editor of a special journal issue on 'Arabs in Australia' and has published on the relationship between diaspora and world literature.

THE LITERATURE OF THE LEBANESE DIASPORA

Representations of Place and Transnational Identity

Jumana Bayeh

I.B. TAURIS

LONDON • NEW YORK • OXFORD • NEW DELHI • SYDNEY

I.B. TAURIS
Bloomsbury Publishing Plc
50 Bedford Square, London, WC1B 3DP, UK
1385 Broadway, New York, NY 10018, USA

BLOOMSBURY, I.B. TAURIS and the I.B. Tauris logo are
trademarks of Bloomsbury Publishing Plc

First published in Great Britain 2015
Paperback edition first published 2019

Cover design: Eleanor Rose
Cover image © Vince Cavataio/Getty Images

A catalogue record for this book is available from the British Library.

ISBN: 978 1 78076 998 1
PB: 978 1 78831 534 0
eISBN: 978 0 85773 617 8

A full CIP record is available from the Library of Congress

Typeset in Garamond Three by OKS Prepress Services, Chennai, India

To find out more about our authors and books visit
www.bloomsbury.com and sign up for our newsletters.

CONTENTS

Acknowledgements   vii

Introduction: Diaspora Literature and Place   1

Part I   War and the City

1. The Urban Space: Beirut at War   33
2. The Destruction of West Beirut in Tony Hanania's
   Unreal City   43
3. Undermining the Christian City in Rawi Hage's
   De Niro's Game   69

Part II   Home, Mobility, Immobility

4. Domicile and Diaspora: Women Write the Home   99
5. Stasis and Domesticity in Nada Awar Jarrar's
   Somewhere, Home   109
6. Home and Movement in Alia Yunis' *The Night Counter*   139

Part III   Contesting the Nation-State

7. Nation, State and Diaspora   171
8. One Land or Two? Israel and Palestine in Amin
   Maalouf's *Ports of Call*   183

Conclusion: Place and Diaspora Literature   207

Notes   214
Bibliography   255
Index   271

ACKNOWLEDGEMENTS

This book explores the unconventional and unique representations of place found in Lebanese diaspora fiction. In writing it I was supported by many people and institutions. Helen Groth provided critical and insightful feedback on numerous chapter drafts, which were invaluable to the completion of this book. I am also grateful for her continued professional support and guidance.

Most of this work was completed at Macquarie University and I would like to thank colleagues in the Modern History, Politics and International Relations department as well as the English department for their support over the years. The late Andrew Vincent was unwavering in his enthusiasm for the cross-disciplinary nature of this work, while John Stephens and Geoffrey Hawker ensured that such an approach would be accommodated. Sections of this book were completed while I was away from my university. In 2007, 2011 and 2013 I held research fellowships at the Lebanese American University in Beirut, the University of Copenhagen and the University of Edinburgh. I am indebted to Paul Tabar, Sune Haugbolle and Anthony Gorman for supporting my applications to their institutions, their willingness to discuss the finer points of diaspora and Lebanese politics with me, and integrating me into their seminars and classes. At the University of Edinburgh I was also generously supported by its Institute for Advanced Studies in the

Humanities, which was the perfect environment for undertaking the last revisions of this work. Financial assistance from Macquarie University and the Arab Australian Chamber of Commerce and Industry made these research periods abroad possible.

I am immensely grateful to Bill Ashcroft, Saree Makdisi and Lindsey Moore who read and commented on an earlier draft of this book in its entirety. I would like to thank John Keane for his insightful feedback on the political aspects of this work as well as lending me his house while away in Berlin. Thanks to the artists Joana Hadjithomas and Khalil Joreige who gave permission to use one of the images from their *Wonder Beirut* series for the cover. I am indebted to Azmina Siddique, my editor at I.B.Tauris, who was enthusiastic about this book from the start, and to Allison Walker and Sarah Plant for their copy editing assistance. Of course special thanks must go to David Pritchard, whose constant support and care makes everything possible.

Finally, if this book has anything new to say or, as the maxim goes, if I have seen a little further than others it is because I stood on the shoulders of giants. Those giants are my father, Hanna Bayeh, and my uncle, Youssef Bayeh. Although they are not aware of this, the diasporic sensibility I write about here is derived from my observations of these two longstanding migrants to Sydney, Australia. My father and uncle taught me from a very young age that the events that take place in the world, especially the Middle East, are much more complex than what is represented in the Orientalist portrayals of the region, especially in the mainstream media. While I can hardly say we agree on all aspects of Middle Eastern politics and culture, what I am certain of is that their unsettling, non-conformist and sometimes abrasive views can be traced back to every page of this book.

INTRODUCTION

DIASPORA LITERATURE AND PLACE

In the novel *Unreal City* (1999) by the Lebanese-British writer Tony Hanania, the unnamed protagonist stands in the centre of war-riven Beirut and describes the ruined city that surrounds him:

> As I rested against the parapet I noticed the faint outline of keyhole arches behind my head and painted lozenges and stellae over the crumbled ceilings, and it was only then I realized where I was standing. This had once been the most famous restaurant in all the city where we had sometimes come as a treat on those dreary Sunday afternoons in the years before the war, the tables laid out as if on either side of a souk, each with its centrepiece of beets, white plums, almonds in ice, my mother always in a simple cream slip-dress and an extravagant hat, my father slapping my hands as I flicked pistachios over at the politicos on the other tables.
>
> The street above must have been partially cleared in an earlier truce, and the going was easier through the following three blocks, the peeling yellow paintwork of the Fattal Building rising over the painted façades; across the grassed-over square the upper storey of what was once the Rivoli Cinema, the faded lettering of the billboard still advertising a film from the mid-seventies, *The Divorced with Jack Lemmon and ...*[1]

While this particular passage focuses on Beirut, oscillating between its pre-war elegance and decimated present, it is exemplary of the fixation with place found in Lebanese diaspora fiction. Alongside Beirut, which is a key site of interest in most Lebanese diaspora novels, other places like the domestic dwelling, the homeland and the nation-state are afforded similar attention.

This book attends to this question of place and how it is represented by several writers who are geographically displaced from their Lebanese homeland. In doing so it focuses on a key aspect that has, according to Avtar Brah, been repeatedly overlooked within diaspora studies. Brah claims that while diaspora is closely linked to a "politics of location", its "strong association [. . .] with displacement and dislocation means that the experience of *location* can easily dissolve out of focus".[2] The association of diaspora with dislocation is not inaccurate, but what is troubling is the resulting marginalisation of location and place within studies of dispersal. Both place and displacement are crucial to diaspora because it is in the "contradictions of and between" these two elements that "diasporic positioning" and experience emerges.[3] Lebanese diaspora literature's preoccupation with place draws attention to this lacuna within diaspora studies and challenges many of the underlying principles associated with it. By examining a number of Lebanese diaspora novels and the representations of place contained within them, this book illustrates how literature broadens our under-standing of diaspora and encourages us to rethink the ways that the term has been theorised.

One of these ways involves exploring the seemingly converse relationship between diaspora and place. While place, associated with home, homeland and nation, is geographically located, diaspora is often thought of in terms of dislocation and displacement. The antithetical relationship between these two terms is strongly, even if unwittingly, asserted in William Safran's "Diasporas in Modern Societies: Myths of Homeland and Return".[4] In this article, a text that has become foundational within the field of diaspora studies, Safran centralises the notion of displacement and suggests that the only place dispersed communities are collectively anchored by is a past homeland. This is evident in five of the following six characteristics of diaspora that Safran identifies. According to Safran, all diasporas are: (1) dispersed from an original centre, (2) share a collective memory, vision or myth of the homeland, (3) experience alienation from the host society, (4) possess a desire to return to the ancestral homeland, (5) express a commitment to the maintenance or restoration of the homeland, and (6) maintain a relationship with or connection to the homeland.[5] Of these six, only the third criterion makes reference to a place – the host society – that is not the primary homeland and very little is said about host societies in the remainder of the article.

What underpins Safran's ridged views of dispersal and place is the fact that his model is based almost exclusively on the Jewish experience. He writes that while "we may legitimately speak of Armenian, Maghrebi, Turkish, Palestinian, Cuban, Greek, and perhaps Chinese diasporas at present and of the Polish diaspora of the past [. . .] none of them fully conforms to the 'ideal type' of the Jewish Diaspora".[6] Safran, however, is not alone in conceptualising diaspora in terms of the Jewish example. Gérard Chaliand and Jean-Pierre Rageau indicate in their introductory remarks to *The Penguin Atlas of Diasporas* that "dispersion seems to be the hallmark of the Jewish people".[7] Various diasporas, such as the Lebanese, Palestinian, Gypsy and African, are described in separate chapters of Chaliand and Rageau's book but the first chapter, approximately one-third of the book, is dedicated to the Jewish case. Robin Cohen's text *Global Diasporas: An Introduction* seeks to transcend the Jewish tradition in its opening chapter, but in doing so it implicitly sets up the Jewish experience as foundational.[8] Even though the subsequent chapters of his book discuss other diasporas, Cohen's examples, as Floya Anthias points out, "are drawn from the experience of Jews as the proto-typical form".[9]

In light of these examples, and others, Michele Reis has argued that in the "absence of a suitable theoretical framework for analysing contemporary diaspora, a sizeable body of literature exclusively makes reference to the Jewish case, thereby establish-ing it as the archetypal diaspora".[10] Just because displacement and return are the hallmarks of Jewish dispersal, this does not mean they are the features of all other diasporic groups. In fact Reis goes on to state that what is assumed as the "normative" (Jewish) model needs to be abandoned in order to achieve less "problematic" definitions of the term.[11] Differences between diasporas abound and one significant feature relates to the historicity of a particular community's dispersal. Reis, for instance, is careful in her article to designate the Jewish diaspora to the "Classical Period, associated primarily with ancient diaspora".[12] Moreover, not all diasporas are determined by religion. This is why James Clifford, in his seminal essay "Diasporas", criticises Safran's model for its monotheism and notes the need for a "more polythetic definition [...] than Safran's [which] might retain his six features, along with others".[13]

Safran's first characteristic of diaspora communities involves "dispersion from a specific original 'centre' to two or more 'peripheral', or foreign, regions".[14] This notion of dispersion is embedded in the etymology of diaspora. The term has its roots in the ancient Greek verb *speirō* "to scatter" and the preposition *dia* "through or over". Judith Shuval echoes the dispersal sensibility of diasporas and insists that it is intrinsic to diaspora theory. She argues that "a critical component" in most definitions of diaspora includes "a history of dispersal" and a "collective [...] cultural memory of the dispersion".[15] Such explanations of diaspora assume that all diffusions occur from a particular place or originary point. However, as Clifford asks, to what "extent does [or should] diaspora, defined as dispersal, presuppose a center" and in turn assume a teleology of return to that centre?[16] The centring of diasporas in this way subverts what Clifford refers to as the "diasporic social form". Rather than stress dispersion from a centre and a return to it, Clifford outlines diasporic subjectivity as being formed through networks that are decentred.[17] Such networks are based in acts of travel and negotiated through multiple modes of communication. These decentred networks of travel and communication connect several communities of transnational people without necessarily referencing a single place "over there".[18] In fact, as Clifford argues, such "connections may be as important as those formed around a teleology of origin/return".[19]

This characteristic of dispersion is closely linked to Safran's fourth feature, which argues that diasporans "regard their ancestral homeland as their true, ideal home and as the place to which they or their descendants would (or should) eventually return".[20] Safran has the Jewish experience in mind here where the creation of Israel in 1948 made return possible.[21] This criterion, however, allows little room for the ambivalence as expressed by Jewish anti-Zionists, like Ephraim Nimni, Ilan Pappé and Tanya Reinhart, who are critical of teleologies of return.[22] Beyond the Jewish experience, Amitav Ghosh shows that members of the Indian diaspora do not always emphasise return to the homeland. Instead, they are more focused on the recreation of Indian culture within their various places of settlement. Through writers like V.S. Naipaul and A.K. Ramanujan it is argued that India, via cultural expression, has been "infinitely reproduced" outside of its centre.[23] Similarly, Paul Gilroy describes the forced transportation of black British, African-American and Caribbean subjects from Africa through the Middle Passage as constituting a "black Atlantic" diaspora.[24] This example complicates the notion of return – where would today's African-Americans return to? – as well as Safran's sixth feature of diasporas being oriented by continuous cultural connections to a single homeland.

An insistence on return is, as Stuart Hall suggests, a very "closed" way of thinking about diaspora, especially when dispersed communities frame their return in terms of going back to the "true" home of their original culture.[25] The Jewish centredness of Safran's model means actual return is seen as an achievable feature even if, as he later outlines, Jewish return is extremely particular and was driven by a utopian project that was set against the dystopian experiences of racism.[26] Another view of diaspora illustrates that it need not simply "refer us to those scattered tribes whose identity can only be secured in relation to some sacred homeland to which they must at all costs return".[27] Diaspora defined in this way is deeply flawed simply because it assumes that all dispersed communities can go back to their places of origin. In the case of the Lebanese diaspora the idea of return is a complex one where the possibility for a nostalgic return to the homeland was complicated by war. Lebanon experienced a prolonged and severe period of civil unrest from 1975 to 1989. Many Lebanese left during this time with few returning at the end of the hostilities. The civil war erased any possibility of a return to the projected and heavily romanticised days of pre-war Lebanon, because the state was altered so much and scarred so deeply. Had Safran taken a broader view of diasporic experience he would have recognised that a return to roots for diasporic communities, although desired, is not always attainable.

Despite this negation of return, roots remain an important aspect of the diasporic imagination and should not be marginalised in favour of "routes". Even Clifford, who has devoted himself to the study of movement and itinerancy, argues for the retention of "roots" and a balanced approach to "routes and roots".[28] This, however, is not the approach of the Lebanese diaspora writer Amin Maalouf. In his memoir *Origins* he writes:

> I don't like the word [roots], and I like even less the image it conveys. Roots burrow into the ground [. . .] they hold trees in captivity from their inception and nourish them at the price of a blackmail: "Free yourself and you'll die!" [. . .] Trees are forced into resignations; they need their roots. Men do not.[29]

Alternatively, routes emphasise movement, travel and journeys, which is what Maalouf sees as the object of his memoir – that is, to uncover his paternal family's journey from Lebanon to America and Cuba. A study and search for routes is of course part of any diaspora project, but doing this at the expense of roots can be a deeply flawed and dangerous venture. Karl Marx's analysis of capitalism theorises the concept of commodity fetishism, where products appear in the market completely disconnected from the very process of their genesis. Thus, as Ghassan Hage argues, "those who celebrate rootlessness seem to celebrate a form of human fetishism in which humans themselves [. . .] appear on the capitalist market as if they are totally detached socially and emotionally from the spaces and the socio-historical processes that made them into what they are".[30]

Clearly, then, any representation that emphasises one form of roots/routes to the detriment of the other presents an inaccurate picture of what diaspora entails. In his discussion of Gilroy's *The Black Atlantic*, Russell Potter offers an alternative view by illustrating the necessary oscillation between "roots" and "routes" in diaspora theory. Through the example of music, Potter highlights how black musicians are inspired by their African origins and their travels across the Atlantic. Music in the black diaspora

> serves as a force of continuum, reaching back to draw from African melodic and rhythmic *roots*, even as it is shaped by its own transatlantic *routes* of transmission, as when American R&B traveled to Jamaica and was reborn as Ska, which in turn gave rise to rock steady, Reggae, and dancehall.[31]

Such oscillation between roots and routes is also reflected upon in Hall's important essay "Cultural Identity and Diaspora". Hall begins by acknowledging the significance of the lure of the homeland, which in this case is represented by the Caribbean. He concedes that there always exists a relentless and

> endless desire to return to "lost origins", to be one again with the mother, to go back to the beginning. Who can ever forget, when once seen rising up out of that blue-green Caribbean, those islands of enchantment. Who has not known, at this moment, the surge of nostalgia for lost origins, for "times past"?[32]

At the same time Hall cautions against unchecked nostalgia, stressing that any return to the beginning "is like the imaginary in Jacques Lacan – it can neither be fulfilled nor requited".[33] Thus, embedded within the definition of the modern black diaspora is the oscillation, or ambivalence, between roots and routes.

Even Maalouf, despite seeming to opt for routes, reflects a similar ambiguity:

> Does [...] [my distaste for roots] mean I do not miss my [ancestral home in the Lebanese] Mountains? Of course I do – as God is my witness! There are love affairs like this; they thrive on absence and distance. So long as one is elsewhere, one can curse the separation and sincerely believe that one need only get together to be happy [...] Distance preserves love; abolish distance, and you run the risk of abolishing love.[34]

The alterity that Maalouf displays between his love of roots and his marked rejection of them is, as Hage argues, a typical feature of the Lebanese diaspora and points to the double consciousness inherent within the diasporic condition.[35] Thinking about diaspora in this way differs, as Anthias explains, from the way Cohen or Safran have constructed and used diaspora as a descriptive typological tool.[36]

So far I have outlined several concerns with how diaspora has been defined with its centring of return to purer places or times and its use of Jewish dispersal as archetypal. It is obviously not the intention of this work to reconstruct that kind of definition. Rather what this book will provide is an alternative and more "open" way of conceiving of diaspora. This entails thinking of dispersal in the way that Lily Cho, Floya Anthias and James Clifford conceive, where it is described as a subjective condition, a social condition and a diasporist mode of thinking and acting.[37] The work of these scholars advocates for a notion of diaspora that is less proscriptive. Loosened or prized away from strict definitional criteria and "ideal-types", what is revealed is a diasporic aesthetic or sensibility. Ambiguity, as seen in Maalouf, is one important characteristic of this sensibility but other aspects have increasingly become signifying features. This includes, as Khachig Tölölyan points out, diaspora's interaction "with a larger semantic domain that includes words like immigrant, expatriate, refugee, guest-worker, exile".[38] Such semantic elasticity does not compromise the uniqueness of the term but suggests that diaspora can be conceived in the alternate manner that Cho, Anthias and

Clifford describe. When viewed as a lived or subjective condition, diaspora provides new and innovative ways to understand the predicament of dislocation.

An element of the diaspora sensibility recognises that loss is an intrinsic aspect of the experience. The move in recent scholarship from Nico Israel and Hamid Naficy to distinguish diasporic consciousness from the exilic form has been used to circumscribe and establish the uniqueness of the former. Naficy, in reference to film production, argues that:

> diasporic consciousness is horizontal and multisided, involving not only the homeland but also the compatriot communities elsewhere. As a result, plurality, multiplicity, and hybridity are structured in dominance among the diasporans, while among political exiles, binarism and duality rule.[39]

Israel notes a similar difference between the two terms. Exile "tends to imply both a coherent subject or author and a more circumscribed, limited conception of place and home" while diaspora "aims to account for hybridity or performativity that troubles such notions of cultural dominance, location, and identity".[40] As Cho points out, however, it is wise to be cautious of claims that situate diaspora as being less concerned with loss and displacement than exile is. This is because by endowing exile with more loss, the importance of past places, past homes and roots are negated in the case of diasporic peoples. For Cho a diasporic subject condition, like the exilic form, is *"marked* by the contingencies of long histories of *displacements* and genealogies of *dispossession"*.[41]

As a result of this loss, Samir Dayal suggests that diasporans harbour a "double consciousness" which reveals a state of being that is always and everywhere aware of inconsistencies and contradictions. This means that they are able to "read" one culture through another and undertake erudite forms of transcultural critique.[42] Dayal's "diasporic double consciousness" is reminiscent of Edward Said's numerous theorisations of exile. In his Reith lectures Said argues that the "exile sees things both in terms of what has been left behind and what is actual[ly] here and now [which] means that an idea or experience is always counterposed with another".[43] Without being reductive it is crucial to recognise that exile and diaspora both involve a "rhetoric of displacement" and concurrently "present two overlapping ways of describing the predicament of displacement".[44] Although they can be imbued with various distinctions, separating "diaspora" from "exile" should not entail weakening the crucial feature of displacement.

Diaspora as it is conceived of here is not just about geographical displacement but also involves a "*diasporic* sensibility" that is defined by a "deterritorialized critical consciousness". A displaced critical or double consciousness necessitates, as Dayal explains, a "rethinking of diaspora beyond the state-centrist model of allegiance to the host vs. the home country".[45] In fact "doubleness" works to destabilise conventional notions of cultural homogeneity and recognises subjectivity as fractured and multiple. Diasporic double consciousness reveals "another way of framing the [. . .] relationship between culture, place and identity".[46] This exposes diaspora's capacity to disrupt many normative ideas about place, as expressed through homes, homelands and nation-states, and challenges the earlier described "closed" definition of the term. If, as Hall suggests, a diasporic sensibility oscillates between "now and then" temporalities or "here and there" spaces, then it becomes increasingly difficult to not realise that the "diaspora experience [. . .] is defined not by essence or purity, but by the recognition of a necessary heterogeneity and diversity".[47] It is this aspect of the diasporic condition, its very uncertainty and instability, that confronts the concept of place and disrupts its seemingly fixed character.

Place: Home, Homeland, Nation

Conservatively speaking, places are thought of as being static self-contained units, "as settled, coherent worlds of their own" and as unique and internally generated spaces.[48] However, modern processes of economic globalisation, the mass movement of people and the speed of communication have produced "feeling[s] of disorientation, a sense of fragmentation of local cultures and a loss, in its deepest meaning, of a sense of place".[49] The increased mobility of people through migration and the compression of time and space through telecommunications, email, social media and the internet have made distances between places seem less vast and communication across space instantaneous. These phenomena have produced, as Doreen Massey suggests, a greater sense of insecurity and unsettledness.[50] Likewise, Tim Cresswell points out that it is "commonplace in Western societies in the twenty-first Century to bemoan a loss of a sense of place as the forces of globalization have eroded local cultures".[51] What is often emphasised in these complaints is the anxiety surrounding the erosion of "pure places" that are seen to belong to a past "era when places were (supposedly) inhabited by coherent and homogenous communities".[52] In response to this what emerges is a reactionary emphasis on the need to reclaim place so that the "search after the 'real' meaning of places, the unearthing of heritages and so forth, is interpreted as being [...] a response to the desire for fixity and for security of identity in the middle of all this movement and change".[53] Advocates of this reactionary process seek to reconstruct place in its "authentic form" without realising the difficulties in taking such an approach. Massey draws on two such complications: "One is the idea that places have single, essential, identities. Another is the idea that the identity of place – a sense of place – is constructed out of an introverted, inward-looking history based on delving into the past for internalized origins."[54]

Writing against these two examples and demonstrating something quite different about place are scholars like Bill Ashcroft and, most prolifically, Doreen Massey. In their work they show how place is not static at all, but a site that is always "becoming" and is always in the process of being made. Ashcroft, writing within a post-colonial discourse, argues that "Place is never simply location, nor is it static [...] place is a continual and dynamic state of formation, a process intimately bound up with the culture and identity of its inhabitants".[55] Ashcroft draws on Massey's conceptualisation of place as the intersection of social relations. For Massey space is composed "in terms of the articulation of social relations which necessarily have a spatial form in their interactions with one another". Such relations "stretch beyond [a single place], tying any particular locality into wider relations and processes in which other places are implicated too".[56] In order for the character of a place to be understood, particular attention must be paid to the "rhizomic network", that is the interrelations and interactions with-in and with-out place, which underscores the place's emerging and changing identity.[57] Thinking of "places in this way implies that they are not so much bounded areas as open and porous networks of social relations".[58]

Based on the literature concerned with place, the most referenced example of it is that of home. The influential human geographer Yi-Fu Tuan, who first theorised the concepts of space and place, defines place by immediately associating it with home: "Place is security, space is freedom: we are attached to the one and long for the other. There is no place like home. What is home?"[59] Presumably the affinity between the terms stems from the similar characteristics that are associated with the two, such as safety, security and a sense of attachment or belonging. Cresswell notes that places are spaces that people have made "meaningful".[60] If this is the case then such meaning or significance is derived from the security and identity individuals and families feel when they are "at home". In similar fashion, Douglas J. Porteous draws a clear link between security and identity, arguing that "the security of the home allows personal identity to flower".[61] Home, in both Tuan and Porteous' work, is neatly defined by security and seen to buttress a sense of well-being.

These constructions marking place as home are universalised by Tuan when he suggests that "Home-bases are intimate places to human beings everywhere".[62] As Doreen Massey and Gillian Rose have demonstrated, however, such constructions of home are culturally masculine and assert a logic of place that is essentially feminine.[63] In fact according to Rose "Place is represented as Woman, in order that humanists can define their own masculinist rationality".[64] Subsequently, when place is associated with home it is "understood in the same terms as a maternal Woman [...] characterized in terms of a relationship with the (m)Other".[65]

Naturalising the notion of home in this way explains why it is the most readily referenced example of place, constructed by the masculine subject as the feminine object in order to give "him" comfort and security. Not surprisingly this version of place does not take into account how such cosiness can slide into fear and terror. Homes are also the scene of domestic violence, practiced against the very women with which place is equated. Domestic violence undermines the safety and security that is associated with home. In addition it highlights, especially when taking into account Porteous' argument that the personalisation of home "is an assertion of identity and a means of ensuring stimulation", the disturbing connotations that underpin the male-centred construction of the domestic space.[66]

Complicating this masculinist tradition, but departing slightly from Rose and Massey, is the work of African-American feminists like bell hooks and Toni Morrison. Their work illustrates that home can become a liberating and empowering space simply because it represents a secure place from the outside world. bell hooks, in *Yearning: Race, Gender, and Cultural Politics*, argues that the meaning of home in a context of oppression should be differentiated from more conventional understandings. For those who are subjugated, home is indeed a nurturing place, a space free from the dominating force of the oppressor. In relation to the black American community in the period of slavery, hooks argues that home was essential for freedom:

> We could not learn to love or respect ourselves in the culture of white supremacy on the outside; it was there in the inside, in that "homeplace" most often created and kept by black women that we had the opportunity to grow and develop, to nurture our spirits.[67]

In the specific case of the Lebanese diaspora, home is just as useful and can guide what Ghassan Hage refers to as the practice of home-building in the host country.[68] Hage explains that nostalgic feelings of past and originary places of residence are sought by migrants as a mode of feeling at home in the present. This longing for home in a migrant context is often interpreted "to be the exact opposite of home-building: a refusal to engage with the present, and a seeking of an imaginary homely past as a hiding place from the present time and space".[69] In an attempt to create homely feelings by remembering the past Hage, using the example of food, shows how the nostalgic sentiments of migrants can in fact be progressive. Within the Lebanese diaspora the fantasy of being fed a "mother's mouthful", *lu'mit 'umm* in Arabic, "is among the most powerful gendered structuring themes of yearning for *lib-blehd* or *blehdna*, the national home".[70] He cites an example where Lebanese migrants to Sydney were finally able, after several years of resettlement, to source the Lebanese variety of cucumbers at a local grocer. Their first instance of consuming these cucumbers in Sydney is celebratory to the extent that it induces singing and dancing at the kitchen table. Rather than seeing this as an expression of wanting to go back, Hage argues that such events allow migrants to "foster homely imitations so as to provide a better base for confronting life in Australia" away from their Lebanese home.[71] While home can indeed be a closed and repressive concept, it also serves as a useful and empowering guide in the case of oppressed and migrant subjects.

In light of this, home, while being structurally located in place, is also a concept that is flexible. As Diana Brydon comments, "Paradoxical as it seems, home is a mobile and unsettled concept".[72] Brydon draws on the example of Canadian writers like Margaret Atwood, Tessa McWatt and Yann Martel because their texts distinctively illustrate home's mobility. This is evident in Atwood's literary essay "Approximate Homes" where she states that "Home was not a place but a trajectory [...] Home was something that was constantly being approached but never reached [...] *Here we are, home at last!* They would say; though home had no location, only direction: homeward".[73] Likewise, for those in the diaspora, home must also contain connotations of mobility. Roger Rouse's example of Mexican migrants highlights how the terms that designate a group of people into a cohesive community, such as "mother tongue", "cultural identity" and "home", must be recast in light of the new social spaces that are created by that community in the process of migration. If one looks for "the raw materials for a new cartography [...] in the details of people's daily lives" what becomes evident is the emergence of new forms of understanding home.[74] Thus, for the Mexican migrants who relocate across the border to America, home is no longer just a rural township left behind but a place of community that is created in the multiple and changing links between "here" and "there". Home for these migrants is moveable and multiple or, to employ Angelika Bammer's terms, it is "plurilocal" – a distinct community located across a range of sites.[75]

Such plurilocality, as conceived of by Bammer, points to a slippage between the personal sphere of the home and the communal realm of the homeland. Eric Hobsbawm argues that "home in the literal sense, *Heim, chez soi*, is essentially private. Home in the wider sense, *Heimat*, is essentially public".[76] This private and public split between *heim* and *heimat* reflects a necessary ambiguity between the concepts of "home" and "homeland" with the latter often expressed in the contemporary era as "the nation".[77] In this respect parallels between nation and home work on a number of levels where both, as Bammer points out, are "fictional constructs" that rely on myth-based narratives.[78] These narratives categorise the nation in intimate and personal terms, like fatherland, motherland or homeland, and highlight that domesticity, family and nation are inseparable concepts.[79] In contrast the discourse of diaspora studies seeks to complicate this assumed compatible relationship between home and nation or between *heim* and *heimat*.

The nation-state, with its subtexts of home and family, is the most referenced example of place in diaspora-related texts and literature. Examples from two sources substantiate this. Firstly, Sudesh Mishra in *Diaspora Criticism* argues that of "the many supplementary terms that swirl in the orbit of diaspora criticism (hybridity, *décalage*, discontinuity, multilocality, nomadism, double conscious-ness and so on)" transnationalism and nationalism feature as the most prominent.[80] Secondly, Jana Braziel and Anita Mannur contend that the nation is a key component in what they refer to as the practise of "theorising" diaspora.[81] However, considering that diasporas predate the nation-state it seems odd that the latter should be so integral to the former. According to John Hutchinson and

Anthony D. Smith, the nation-state is a contemporary occurrence. They argue that "Many historians would agree that [. . .] nationalism became prevalent in [. . .] the latter half of the eighteenth century".[82] Diasporas, in contrast, have existed for millennia. Why then this obsession with the nation in theorisations of diaspora?

The answer to this can be traced to the timing of the emergence of diaspora studies as opposed to diaspora communities. According to Ato Quayson and Girish Daswani, the "establishment of the journal *Diasporas* by the Armenian American Khachig Tölölyan in 1991 [meant that] the field progressively acquired scholarly coherence with a visible set of debates and practitioners".[83] From this point, as Braziel and Mannur contend, "debates over the theoretical, cultural, and historical resonances of the term [diaspora] [. . .] proliferated in academic journals devoted to ethnic, national and (trans) national concerns".[84] In other words, diaspora scholarship is a relatively contemporary field of inquiry. Nation-states highlight that "dispersions, while not altogether new in form, acquired a different meaning by the nineteenth century, in the context of the triumphant nation-state".[85] The appeal of the nation-state in the past several centuries has not waned and, according to Massey, there has been an intense reconsolidation of the nation-state since the 1980s. This is evident in the rise of exclusivist claims to places, especially in the form of reactionary nationalisms opposed to new migrants and processes of globalisation.[86] Such claims of exclusivity are even further pronounced in a post-9/11 milieu where states have strengthened their own powers in terms of homeland and border security in a bid to curtail the influx of undesirable and supposedly threatening outsiders. Thus, the displacement of people, especially in a context where the nation-state is being reconsolidated, means that diaspora studies needs to be understood as interacting with and even defining itself against nationhood.

The particular aspects of nationalism that diaspora scholarship actively engages with can be difficult to identify. This is partly because the nation-state is a concept that has been so overly theorised that it is virtually impossible to point to a single agreed-upon meaning of the term. In fact, Hutchinson and Smith argue that "finding an adequate [. . .] definition" is the "central difficulty in the study of nations and nationalism".[87] According to Stephanie Lawson, the only definition of nationalism in which scholars concur involves the rather vague notion that the nation-state is "a species of collective identity grounded in some notion of culture".[88] This explanation of nationalism, however, overlooks two important aspects. The first is the territorial dimension that is embedded within the latter half of the compound term nation-state and the second is that a nation's "notion of culture" is generally one that is homogenously defined. While this latter point is certainly regressive, it continues to permeate definitions of nationalism. Michael Shapiro, for instance, writes that "a nation embodies a coherent culture" and Anthony D. Smith suggests that what binds the members of a nation-state is their shared "language, religion, race [and] ethnicity".[89] Diasporas, however, can challenge such normative depictions of nationalism because, as "the exemplary communities of the transnational moment", they can transcend the homogeneity and territoriality of nation-states.[90]

In the first and most obvious instance, diasporas expose the fallacy of a culturally homogeneous nation. Nations are not comprised of single or common cultures. This is evident in the fact that in the majority of countries today different languages are spoken in households alongside the national language. There is also an ever-increasing availability of a variety of multicultural food in many cities across the globe. The preoccupation with security and border protection laws designed to guard the contours of the nation highlight the porosity of nation-states. These examples illustrate how the "other" has crept into the discourse of the nation and in some racist constructions is seen to pollute the imagined purity of the state. However, as Brian Axel claims, it is not the diasporic constitution that is to blame for rupturing cultural homogeneity.[91] Rather it is the conceptualisation of the nation with its fantasy of "cultural oneness" that spawns a problem within nationalism itself. In other words, the impossibility of fulfilling this fantasy of "one nation, one people" is a problem of the nation that is generated, ironically, by the nation. It is through a diasporic consciousness that cultural diversity is uncovered as an already-inherent aspect of nation-states.

Julia Kristeva's work on foreigners and the Freudian uncanny in *Strangers to Ourselves* is helpful in demonstrating how this is so. Kristeva's strategy to interpret social affiliations within the nation-state from the position of the foreigner explores how this figure is "the one who does not belong to the state in which we are, the one who does not have the same nationality".[92] Her project complements Homi Bhabha's work, which deals with the narrative of the nation from "the perspective of the nation's margin and the migrants' exile".[93] Bhabha, while criticising Kristeva for romanticising exile, does note the importance of this approach. He suggests that "it is from those who have suffered the sentence of history – subjugation, domination, *diaspora, displacement* – that we learn our most enduring lessons for living and thinking".[94] Diasporic communities, perceived as foreign and marginal to the nation-state, fracture the imagined unity of the national body. Turning to Sigmund Freud's discussion of the uncanny, both Kristeva and Bhabha expose the threat of the margin – from foreigners, feminists, diasporans – to the perceived homogeneity of national identity.

Freud's semiotic examination of *das unheimlich*, the unhomely or uncanny, reveals "that among its different shades of meaning the word '*heimlich*' exhibits one which is identical with its opposite '*unheimlich*'".[95] The term *heimlich* belongs to two sets of ideas which place it in this ambiguous state: "on the one hand it means what is familiar and agreeable, and on the other, what is concealed and kept out of sight".[96] What Freud demonstrates here is that *heimlich* is closely tied to its opposite *unheimlich* because that which is "friendly", "familiar" or "comfortable" can also signify that which is "concealed", "deceitful" and "repressed". This association of *unheimlich* with its antonym means that the "uncanny is in reality nothing new or alien, but something which is familiar and old-established in the mind and which has become alienated from it only through the process of repression".[97]

Kristeva notes that the political issues surrounding foreigners and xenophobia, which are the central concern of *Strangers to Ourselves*, are not mentioned by Freud in his *unheimlich* essay. Nonetheless it is through Freud that one learns of the otherness that inhabits the subject from within and that the "strange(r)" projects from inside the familiar. This is why the notion of the uncanny points to a disruption of the insider versus outsider dynamic that operates within the nation:

> With the Freudian notion of the unconscious the involution of the strange in the psyche loses its pathological aspect and integrates within the assumed unity of human beings an *otherness* that is both biological *and* symbiotic and becomes an integral part of the *same*. Henceforth the foreigner is neither a race nor a nation.[98]

The experience of the uncanny not only exposes the unsettling recognition of a national community's internal "strangeness", but it also forces that community to renounce its imagined subjective unity because it recognises that there exists a "foreignness [. . .] within" and that "we are our own foreigners, we are divided".[99] So when Kristeva provocatively argues that the foreigner exists within and "when we flee from or struggle against the foreigner we are fighting our unconscious" foreignness, she highlights that to reject the foreigner is to repress "our" disintegrated national self and inappropriately persist in maintaining a solid national "us".[100] Given this, it becomes clear that the diasporic sensibility indeed lends itself to be understood in terms of an uncanny consciousness. Defined by alterity, double consciousness and a fragmented identity, the diasporic condition, like the figure of the foreigner, accepts the dis-integrated subjectivity of the self and in turn exposes the nation-state's own internal heterogeneity.

Part of the reason why the diasporic condition can achieve this is due to its deterritorialised state. Deterritorialisation here is not meant to indicate that which lies outside or beyond territory but rather how national identity is aligned with a necessary claim to land. In that regard diaspora "questions the nation by fundamentally puncturing the notion that territorial association or land and cultural affiliation are natural sources of identification".[101] Nationality in a diaspora context is not derived from land-based affiliation. Many diasporic groups are deterritorialised "because their collective claims to an identity do not depend upon residence on a particular plot of land".[102] Lebanese migrants residing in Australia or the United States, the European continent or Latin America do not gain a sense of their culture by living in Lebanon but rather through a process that Benedict Anderson refers to as "long-distance nationalism" which is a form of "nationalism that no longer depends as it once did on territorial location in a home country".[103]

Gilles Deleuze and Félix Guattari's work on minor literatures further demonstrates how literary production from deterritorialised writers questions ideas that tie identity to territory. As they explain, minor literatures do not belong to the literary canon of "great" Western literature, and for this reason such texts are always concerned with centres of power. This highly politicised literature is associated with a collective consciousness and "finds itself positively charged with the role and function of collective, and even revolutionary, enunciation". The collective or national consciousness is rewritten through revolutionary enunciation because "the writer is in the margins or completely outside his or her fragile community". It is this kind of marginalised positioning that "allows the writer all the more the possibility to express another possible community and forge the means for another consciousness and another sensibility".[104] Lebanese diaspora authors are concerned with the very political underpinnings of exclusion and inclusion within the body politic of the nation-state. But in the Lebanese context this is not, as might be initially assumed, simply confined to stories about exclusion and marginalisation in the host country. A great deal of these writers are anxiously concerned with the national story of Lebanon, with its own troubled narratives of exclusion of various communal "others" in a state based on sectarian lines of identification. Rawi Hage's *De Niro's Game* (2006), discussed later in Chapter 3, is a clear example of this. It writes back to the fraught national story of Lebanon by highlighting the early years of the civil war and the involvement of the protagonist, Bassam Al-Abyad, and his best friend, George Al-Faransawi, in a conservative Christian militia. The massacre of

Sabra and Shatila in 1982 compels Bassam to leave Lebanon for Paris as he cannot participate in the extermination, the ultimate form of exclusion, of the Palestinian and predominately Muslim other.

Another aspect of Deleuze and Guattari's minor literature "is that in it language is affected with a high coefficient of deterritorialization".[105] Through the example of Franz Kafka writing in Prague German, Deleuze and Guattari illustrate how language can be appropriated for strange and minor uses just like "blacks in America today are able to do with the English language".[106] As argued earlier, the concept of diaspora that concerns this book is marked by displacement and double consciousness. In that regard the strain of ambivalence, of the double, of existing "in a median state, neither completely at one with the new setting nor fully disencumbered of the old" means that the diasporic writer is not only compelled to speak two or more languages but also to negotiate and translate between them.[107] This resonates with Kristeva's work on foreigners, where she argues that once deprived of the attachments to the mother tongue, the individual who learns a foreign language is able to enunciate the most unpredictably daring, bold or audacious statements in the newly-acquired means of verbal communication. For diaspora writers, like the Lebanese, this entails a negotiation of "the contradictory strains of languages *lived* and languages *learned* [which] has the potential for a remarkable critical and creative impulse".[108] Several of the novels examined in this book draw on Arabic and Lebanese idioms that are literally translated into English and refuse syntactic compromise. In addition, some Arabic words are left untranslated mid-sentence, transliterated into their English pronunciation, with the idea that the context will reveal the meaning to a non-Arabic speaker. Such an interesting use of linguistic hybridity is not necessarily novel. Mikhail M. Bakhtin's work on the subject published in the 1970s, later translated as *The Dialogic Imagination: Four Essays* in 1981, reveals that such a linguistic strategy, although not entirely original, is especially significant to the migrant or displaced writer.[109] This is because for many displaced authors there is a lack of fit between language and place. According to Ashcroft, "this gap, between the experienced place and the language available to describe it, lies at the heart of the experience of [. . .] displacement".[110] Theodor Adorno, displaced from his native Germany after relocating to America, shows that for "a man who no longer has a homeland, writing becomes a place to live".[111] For the displaced writer, then, place is "much more than the land [. . .] place *is* language, something in constant flux, a discourse in process".[112] The diasporic Lebanese authors that are the subject of this book write in a language that is not their mother tongue and are therefore twice displaced, both geographically and linguistically. As a result these writers are compelled to re-construct a language that might better suit their experiences, not just in the new society they have migrated to, but as a way to represent the plurality, the fragmentation and the hybridity of place.

Such new experiences that oscillate between the "old home" and the "new home", between the "here" and "there", the "then" and "now" disrupt linear approaches to time where the past, present and future cannot always be understood in a chronological order. As Clifford suggests the "co-presence of 'here' and 'there' is articulated with an anti-teleological [. . .] temporality. Linear history is broken, the present constantly overshadowed by the past".[113] This is echoed by Cho, who argues that "understanding the temporality of diasporic subjectivity [. . .] [includes] that which is profoundly out of joint, neither before nor after a particular experience, haunted by the pastness of the future".[114] Within the black Atlantic, the formative event of the Middle Passage marks a "recurring break where time stops and restarts" within diaspora consciousness where in "syncopated time, effaced stories are recovered".[115] In Lebanon's modern history, the start of the civil war in 1975 captures that moment where time stops and restarts for the Lebanese. The formative nature of this moment is reinforced by Michael Humphrey, who argues that the contemporary use of the phrase "Lebanese diaspora and its present self-consciousness was brought into existence by the displacement of people by the Lebanese war".[116] If enslavement and exploitation constitute the pattern of black experiences after the Middle Passage, then in the Lebanese case "diasporic experience is the product of national disintegration and the [. . .] experience of resettlement and migration".[117] War and migration, then, are two features that profoundly shape the Lebanese diaspora and, as this book contends, Lebanon's diaspora literature. In order to fully appreciate the impact of these features on diaspora fiction it is necessary to outline Lebanon's war history and the nature of the Lebanese people's dispersal.

The Lebanese Diaspora

The migration of people from the area that is today known as Lebanon has been prominent since the latter half of the nineteenth century. Kemal Karpat and Michael Suleiman note that a number of economic and socio-political factors contributed to the migration of a substantial number of people from the 1860s through to World War I. By the time of the oil boom in the Gulf in the 1960s and 1970s, 10,000 Lebanese per year had relocated to oil-producing countries. Despite this, it was not until 1975 and the onset of the 15-year civil war that a dramatic acceleration of migration took place. Dalia Abdelhady suggests that 990,000 Lebanese, 40 per cent of Lebanon's population, migrated in the period from 1975 to 1989.[118] While 1989 is the presumed end of the civil war – it is the year that the peace treaty known as the Ta'if Accords was signed – the war continued for approximately two more years. Between 1989 and 1991 the surge of violence among various Christian militias compelled more Lebanese to look for stable conditions abroad. In addition, the failure of the Ta'if Accords to guarantee peace "led many Lebanese to think of their presence outside of Lebanon as less of temporary exile and more in terms of permanent settlement".[119] The contemporary occurrence of these events explains why Gabriel Sheffer classifies the Lebanese diaspora as recent rather than historic. Sheffer goes on to list the various places the Lebanese have migrated to – Syria, Egypt, the Persian Gulf, Argentina, Brazil, Venezuela, Mexico, the USA, France, Australia and West Africa – highlighting the vastness of their dispersal.[120] So when Michael Humphrey argues against the homogenisation of this dispersed community, suggesting that the expression "Lebanese diaspora" is reductive, he does so because the "Lebanese emigrants who constitute the present diaspora are the product of quite different migrations with their own very distinct relationships to societies [they settled in] and to contemporary Lebanon".[121]

Part of this specificity stems from the political organisation of Lebanon which, after gaining independence from France in 1943, was established as a consociational democracy.[122] The foundation of the initial political arrangement, the National Pact, stressed a form of power-sharing between representatives of the Christian and Muslim political elite. Positions in the state, from the president down, were allocated by religious affiliation. In a state that has 18 recognised confessions, emphasising identity within the political structure has proven extremely precarious. Various scholars of Lebanese politics, such as Theodor Hanf, Michael Hudson, Samir Khalaf, Kamal Salibi and Fawaz Traboulsi, generally concur that Lebanon's sectarian-based political system is the main source of its unrest and instability. Despite the fact that the Ta'if agreement stipulated the urgent need for the deconfessionalisation of Lebanese politics, this has not occurred. Within Lebanon this means that political identity remains tied to confession. While this is hardly unexpected in Lebanon, it is surprising that members of the diaspora are also party to this kind of sectarian identification. As Humphrey points out, the Lebanese diaspora is indeed confessionalised and this confessionalisation "is only extended by the failure of the Ta'if Accords to reconstruct and reconcile the Lebanese within a new moral community".[123] This explains why Lebanese diaspora communities remain unable to "conceive of the 'imagined present' or 'past' in the same way".[124]

The inability of the Lebanese government to implement Ta'if and to deal with issues of sectarian identification has manifested itself in the suppression of Lebanon's recent bloody past with a grand attempt to skip over the issues that produced such an embattled history. This attempt is what Saree Makdisi refers to as a "narrative" that insists with "fanatical conviction that there can be historical progress, that there can be redemption, that the war can be said to have reached blissful fulfilment".[125] Such a narrative is partly constituted by the project to physically reconstruct a particular section of Beirut, referred to as the Downtown, by the Solidere company.[126] The entire thrust of this project is to rebuild an area that is economically viable and profit driven. This is why the new Downtown resembles very little of its pre-war past. It is an area dedicated to the latest styles and fashions, with high-end brands a dominating feature. That same area prior to the war, not then known as the Downtown, was, however, markedly different and reflected the character of city with more integrity. It was, to draw from Makdisi's description,

> extremely heterogeneous, unevenly and discordantly combining fruit and vegetable stands, fish mongers, gold markets, clothing stores, and Beirut's famous red light district; mixing together the clean and unclean, the ugly and the beautiful, the smelly and the perfumed; and expressing what Montalbán has referred to in a not dissimilar context as the "legitimate disorder of life".[127]

The Downtown of today is not, as Makdisi would argue, authentic at all but has created a spectacle of authenticity. It has done this by both burying the remnants of the war and incorporating elements of Lebanese history that suit Solidere's commercial interests, rather than partaking in "a genuine engagement with and acknowledgement of historical processes" and events.[128] In this regard, what the Solidere project epitomises is the historical amnesia that is emblematic of post-war Lebanon. In fact, Lebanon is so unwilling to engage with the past that it has been unable to produce an historical narrative that is informative about the war in all its complexity. As a supplement to the war that the Lebanese state has chosen to ignore, the glorified days of the pre-war era and the projected glory of the post-war future have become the focus of the national narrative, with little mention of Lebanon's unresolved issues and the marked sense of injustice felt by many.[129]

The lack of engagement with the recent past is an extremely precarious aspect of post-war Lebanon and is exacerbating the domestic turmoil characterised by the ongoing ill will between various sects. Attempts by Solidere to build a new Downtown are producing a city centre that lacks authenticity and this, by extension, implicates the construction company in the narrative of amnesia that dominates contemporary Lebanese politics and society. Thankfully, such amnesia is countered by another more accurate assessment of Lebanon in its post-war fiction. Lebanon's post-war novels reflect in many ways an attempt to write back to the history and pain of the civil war, both from authors residing in Lebanon and those producing texts in the diaspora.[130] This book focuses on the latter group of writers whose stories mirror what Humphrey isolates as key elements of Lebanese diasporic experience. The first relates to the unresolved events of the war and addresses Lebanon's suppressed narrative of civil turmoil. Novels characteristic of this group are *Unreal City* (1999) by Tony Hanania and *De Niro's Game* (2006) by Rawi Hage. The second is more concerned with the difficulties of migration, settling into a new society and finding ways to negotiate between past and present homes. The texts that engage with issues of migration include *Somewhere, Home* (2003) by Nada Awar Jarrar, *The Night Counter* (2009) by Alia Yunis and *Ports of Call* (1999) by Amin Maalouf.[131] What is common to all these texts, despite their differing emphases, is how the diasporic condition of the authors – a sensibility that is doubled, decentred and dislocated – actively reconstructs and contests essentialist definitions of place.

This book is divided into three parts in order to reflect this complex engagement with place. Part I: War and the City begins with a chapter that outlines the urban theory developed by the German and Chicago Schools. What is noteworthy about these two schools is how the former, dominated by Max Weber and George Simmel, stresses economic issues and the evolution of the city in relation to the progress of capitalism while the latter, which includes Robert Park and Louis Wirth, emphasises how the character of a city is shaped by its human inhabitants. Chapter 1 finishes by addressing the specificities of Beirut's history and, most importantly, its division during the war into West Beirut, the Muslim sector, and East Beirut, the Christian quarter. This is relevant because the two urban novels that are examined in the subsequent two chapters, *Unreal City* and *De Niro's Game*, are alternately set in the Muslim West and the Christian East. The urban theories that are explored are equally significant because they underpin how each novel depicts Beirut. In Chapter 2

Unreal City is examined in relation to Weber and Simmel's theories. It focuses on the ways in which the narrative addresses issues of urban development in economic and capitalistic terms. Alienation is a key theme here, and in Hanania's novel the war economy exacerbates the protagonist's sense of estrangement and induces his recruitment into a militant Islamic movement in South Lebanon. In Chapter 3 the theories advocated namely by Park are used to analyse Hage's East Beirut novel. *De Niro's Game* delves into the insular and isolated world of the Christian metropolis and illustrates how a cityspace is determined by its inhabitants.

Part II: Home, Mobility, Immobility turns its attention to the domestic sphere. Chapter 4 reviews opposing theories on domesticity and movement, highlighting that while home is often thought of as grounded and immovable, it is increasingly considered to be a concept based on mobility. This is especially the case within diaspora studies where the bias for routes and itinerant homes is most pronounced. This, however, is not always reflected in fiction by diaspora writers, as Chapters 5 and 6 illustrate. Chapter 5 examines the novel *Somewhere, Home*. It argues that while this novel is critically lauded for its female-centred domestic narratives and its supposedly non-essentialist views of domesticity it actually, in a rather subversive manner, reinforces a particularly conservative and static image of home. Part of the reason for this stems from the novel's rural setting and the fact that the narrative revolves around a house that is located in a mountainous region of Lebanon. Similarly, the novel addressed in Chapter 6, *The Night Counter*, also contains a house in rural Lebanon. And yet, despite its looming presence, the house in Yunis' text does not bolster the idea that home must be fixed and specifically located. Rather what this novel exposes, through various literary techniques, is that the concept of domesticity is in fact inherently mobile.

In the final section, Part III: Contesting the Nation-State, the notion of the nation-state is introduced. Chapter 7 focuses on the relationship between nationalism and diaspora, examining how and why each concept is integral to the other. The terms that constitute the compound phrase "nation-state" are individually analysed. As the discussion reveals, "nation" is often represented by various theorists of nationalism as culturally exclusive, while "state" is related to land and territory. The theories are consequently applied specifically to Israel illustrating that cultural exclusivity and territoriality are vital components of the Jewish state. The reason for this concentration on Israel relates to the text that is the subject of the Chapter 8, *Ports of Call*. This novel is predominately concerned with the years that precede the establishment of Israel in 1948, and is narrated by a character who works tirelessly to subvert the possibility of separation between Jews and Arabs. *Ports of Call* does not succumb to the mutilating logic of segregation but instead focuses on the coexistence of Jews and Arabs. It does this by highlighting coexistence as an historical fact and emphasising the common Levantine heritage that these two peoples share. By stressing the valency of coexistence in this manner, Maalouf's text contests the central precepts of the nation-state and argues for a bi-national state where Jews and Arabs cohabit, as they have for centuries, in the same land.

Unlike the previous two parts, which examine two novels, this final part deals with one. This is because *Ports of Call* differs dramatically from the oeuvre of contemporary Lebanese diaspora literature. In contrast to the narratives that Hanania, Hage and Jarrar offer, where Lebanon or Beirut feature heavily, or Yunis presents, where America dominates, Maalouf does not overwhelmingly concentrate on his homeland or his place of migration but instead turns his attention to the Israel–Palestine question. This does not mean that Maalouf's *Ports of Call* is any less diasporic than the other novels or that the author should not be described as a Lebanese diaspora writer. Rather, what Maalouf demonstrates through his novel is how the diasporic sensibility can be applied to situations or contexts that do not immediately concern the writer's homeland or place of migration. Indeed, if the diasporic condition is defined by its ability to disrupt the assumed cultural homogeneity of nation-states, then Maalouf's criticism of the partition of Israeli-Jews and Palestinians is not surprising.

Finally, in the conclusion, I return to the relationship between place and diaspora literature. I revisit some of the foundational ideas that are framed in the introduction and the analysis presented throughout this book. In doing so I identify principles that allow a novel to be read and defined as a form of diaspora writing that extend beyond an author's own diasporic status. A key principle is undoubtedly the notion of place and, as the novels examined in this book reflect, diaspora literature complicates this notion. This is because diaspora fiction seeks to establish new ways of thinking about a range of places – cities, homes, homelands and nation-states – and eludes the use of traditionally restrictive terms. While some of the novels examined in this book are more brazen and successful at this than others, they all attempt to promote a view of place that is both plural and heterogeneous.

PART I

WAR AND THE CITY

CHAPTER 1

THE URBAN SPACE:
BEIRUT AT WAR

If, as Iman Khalil claims, a "distinctive part of literature on war and warfare is the narration of civil war experiences" then it is no surprise that so many Lebanese authors continually write about the civil violence that shattered Beirut in the 1970s and 1980s.[1] According to Jad Tabet, when the war first broke out in 1975 it quickly settled in the heart of the capital city, and even though the war seeped into peripheral parts of the country, Beirut remained the major focal point of destruction.[2] Thus, the significance of Beirut, both the place and its character, cannot be underestimated in the two civil war narratives examined below. Both *Unreal City* and *De Niro's Game* reveal the complex nature of "place", particularly when the place in question is a city subject to war and war's various side-effects. In light of the specificity of the city within these novels, this chapter will examine various theories of the city and consider how the war-riven urban space of Beirut relates to them.

Much of the contemporary scholarship on urban development notes that cities in the past three centuries have changed dramatically due to a proliferation of inhabitants and an exponential increase in geographical size.[3] Until the late 1700s urban studies maintained a traditional approach, laid out in ancient philosophy and carried through to the Middle Ages. Accordingly, the city was merely seen as "the image of society itself, and not some special, unique form of social life".[4] However, with the onset of the Industrial Revolution in the late 1700s social commentators, such as Henry Mayhew (1812–87), Charles Booth (1840–1916) and Friedrich Engels (1820–95), reconsidered the complex and specific social dynamics taking place within the cityscape. Focusing on nineteenth century London, the main hub of the Industrial Revolution, these writers concluded that in "both its ecology and its class relations, [the] 'classic' city was a product of the Age of Capital, whose internal dynamics could be specified".[5]

The study of urban culture in the twentieth century was dominated by German theorists like Max Weber (1864–1920) and George Simmel (1858–1918). Building on the scholarship of their predecessors, who saw the role of capitalism as a central feature of urban development, this group, collectively referred to as the German School, perceived alienation and marginalisation as key aspects of urban life. Weber argues that the metropolitan space is underpinned by a concept of cosmopolitanism and that cosmopolitan culture is a necessary corollary of urbanism. Weber's theories of the city are shaped by the concept of "difference". Difference is, according to Weber, a necessary feature of a cosmopolitan society because it allows for coexistence to thrive in societies that contain a diverse range of peoples. By taking this concept of cosmopolitanism and applying it to his discussions of urban life Weber, as Richard Sennett explains, perceived the city as a "social form which permits the greatest degree of *individuality* and *uniqueness* [...] [and includes] the set of social structures that encourage social individuality and innovation".[6] This Weberian "ideal-typical" definition of the city did not conform to the nineteenth and twentieth century urban space mainly because, as Weber and many of his contemporaries thought, industrialised centres took on a uniform mould and were unable to develop a unique character or culture.[7] As a result, cities were intensely impersonal places which lacked "the reciprocal personal acquaintance of the inhabitants, elsewhere characteristic of the neighbourhood".[8] Furthermore, the modern city could only ever amount to a primitive, underdeveloped space because it failed to fulfil the promises of individuality, uniqueness and innovation. This failure was connected to the force of modern capitalism which, because of its rationalism and intense bureaucracy, had produced a cold and less than civilised urban environment. Concentrating on the economic activity within the industrialised town, whose "inhabitants live primarily from commerce and the trades [. . .] [and whose] local population satisfies an economically significant part of its everyday requirements in the local market", Weber argues that the city "is always a market center".[9]

George Simmel, one of Weber's contemporaries, viewed the city in similar terms but advocated that its chief elements should be psychological rather than economic. His argument was that the "eighteenth century found the individual in oppressive bonds which had become meaningless – bonds of a political, agrarian, guild, and religious character".[10] Liberation from these bonds meant that individuals "now wished to distinguish themselves from one another" and to emphasise their "qualitative uniqueness and irreplaceability".[11] The struggle, then, to achieve real freedom and develop a sense of individuality was to be located in the modern city: "It is the function of the metropolis to provide the arena for this struggle."[12] Despite the stress placed on the opportunities that may prevail in the city, Simmel's work was consistent with the assumptions laid out by the German School, namely that the metropolis was the paradigm of an inhuman social environment that was entirely impersonal and governed by an excess of rationality.[13]

If the subsequent group of theorists, like Robert Park (1864–1944) and Louis Wirth (1897–1952), sought to build on the work of Weber and Simmel, they did so by taking a divergent position with regard to the assumptions the Germans had established. Collectively known as the Chicago School, these social scientists emerged in the aftermath of World War I and were interested in the internal character of the city. Perhaps the most influential essay to appear among this second generation of scholars was Robert Park's "The City: Some Suggestions for the Investigation of Human Behavior in the Urban Environment".[14] Park took the view that the city was more than a physical artefact, a collection of individuals and administrative devices. Rather, the city is "a state of mind, a body of customs and traditions, and of the organized attitudes and sentiments that inhere in these customs and are transmitted with this tradition".[15] By studying the nature of the urban space through "human ecology" Park was able to stress "that the city is rooted in the habits [. . .] of the people who inhabit it".[16] So, unlike his German counterparts, Park refused to privilege the physical organisation of a city in shaping its culture over and above the role of humanity. It is the interaction of the physical and moral aspects of the city that mould the city space in Park's work.

Park's discussion of segregated areas within the urban environment reflects the importance of this interaction. He argues that "the isolation of [. . .] racial colonies of the so-called ghettos and areas of population segregation tend to preserve and, where there is racial prejudice, to intensify the intimacies and solidarity of the local neighborhood groups".[17] The segregation of the city therefore enacts, or embodies, a politics of race in two ways: first, it encourages sentiments of racial prejudice to develop within the wider community towards the ghettoised population, and second it strengthens racial solidarity within each isolated community. Given the highly sectarian nature of Lebanon, it is possible to extend Park's emphasis on racial communities to include religious segregation. During the war Beirut became a city divided along religious lines. The Christian community increasingly congregated on the city's Eastern side, while the Muslim community was more concentrated on its Western front. This physical division resulted, first, in the connection between territorial space and sectarian identity and, second, not unlike Park's assertions regarding segregated racial communities, it intensified and exacerbated religious prejudices.

Beirut and War Amnesia

The reduction of Beirut into these two sectarian quarters is a clear reflection of the city's particular historical development. Beirut, until modern times, was a very modest settlement. According to Samir Kassir, in his magisterial study of Lebanon's capital, Beirut prior to 1840 was a walled medieval town with a population of approximately 15,000.[18] The influx of Maronite Christian refugees from Mount

Lebanon, due to the civil strife in 1860 between rural Maronite and Druze communities, saw Beirut increase in size and density. After this crisis the rural exodus was relentless. Within 36 years, by 1896, Beirut's population had risen dramatically to 120,000 and by 1930 the city became the permanent residence of one quarter of Lebanon's population.[19] This rapid spike in inhabitants did not immediately produce an increase in construction activity and urbanisation. In fact it was not until the 1950s that real evidence of urbanisation began to emerge. At this stage Beirut began to expand vertically with high-rise buildings and apartment blocks disturbing the city's once horizontal and even skyline.

By the mid-1970s, shortly before the outbreak of hostilities, 70 per cent of Lebanon's population inhabited the cities, with Beirut alone absorbing almost 45 per cent. By this period the city was comprised of all the sectarian communities that inhabited the country.[20] However, despite this rapid and intense urbanisation Beirut failed to embrace or develop a sense of "urbanism".[21] The research of Samir Khalaf, Fuad Khuri and John Gulick reveals that urbanism as a way of life did not accompany urbanisation due to the endurance of kinship ties, communal loyalties and confessional affinities.[22] The level of communal trauma associated with Beirut's urban development, starting with the mass influx of rural-based Christians in the 1860s, explains why kinship and confessional affinities remained strongly intact within the urban setting.[23] If these traditional attachments worked their way into Beiruti society, however, they did so not in spite of urbanisation but because of it. As Mike Davis explains, urbanisation and the major demographic changes that accompany it pit different groups in direct competition for contested and scarce resources.[24] This is especially prevalent in a developing and multi-confessional country like Lebanon, where the necessary fault-lines of the competition are organised primarily around sectarian loyalties.

The endurance of confessional loyalties within the city space conforms to an assertion put forward by the Chicago-based scholar Louis Wirth. He argues that cities are formed by an ongoing process of growth and that, correspondingly, urban spaces "should not be [expected] [...] to wipe out completely the previously dominant modes of human association".[25] This is one reason why the Lebanese urban experience has maintained the imprint of rurally-based sectarian relations. The particular and peculiar Lebanese political system encourages its citizens, especially Beirutis who are at the centre of this system, to maintain their confessional affinities. In other words, it is not simply the case that Lebanon's rural migrants are unable to shed their cultural practises and primordial formations when they move into the urban environment. Rather, their reliance on rural primordial relations is compounded by the Lebanese political system of consociational democracy. Consociationalism, as defined by Arend Lijphart, reflects a political arrangement of power sharing that can accommodate diverse ethnic and sectarian societies. For Lijphart, consociationalism is the preferred model of democracy in plural societies where "government by elite cartel [is] designed to turn democracy with a fragmented political culture into a stable democracy".[26] Since the National Pact of 1943, the Lebanese system has privileged confessionalism as the organising principle of political identification, thereby forcing Lebanese nationals "to group themselves into their sectarian communities as a precondition for becoming vocal and effective within the Lebanese polity".[27] So rather than promote a sense of "urbanism" as a way to undo confessional affiliations, city life in Beirut strengthens and ratifies old kinship relations.

Consequently, in the mid-1900s, Beirut was not a site that embraced the forces of social modernisation and urbanism − rather it reflected "an environment that [was] always already structured around primordial formations".[28] When rural folk moved away from their village homes, for whatever reason, they entered this environment and maintained or solidified their religious codes of affiliation. The short-lived civil war of 1958, commonly seen as a "dry run" for the civil war "proper", was fuelled by sectarian tension within the urban context of Beirut.[29] This was similarly the case in the subsequent civil war that embedded itself within the urban space and physically divided it. The demarcation point was referred to as the Green Line because of the greenery that grew along the buffer zone after buildings and roads were destroyed and abandoned. As the

Green Line emerged in stages it is probably more accurate to describe it by the Arabic phrase *khoutout al tammas*, which translates in the plural as "confrontation lines". The first front in 1975 stretched between the predominately Shi'a Muslim neighbourhood of Shayah in south Beirut (an impoverished community that migrated from rural South Lebanon) and the adjacent Maronite Christian area of Ain al-Rummaneh in the Eastern sector of the city. By the 1980s the Green Line had expanded and exacerbated the cantonisation of the urban centre. Even areas that were once relatively mixed by Lebanese standards became increasingly homogenous as residents moved across the dividing line to their appropriate side of the city. According to Ester Charlesworth:

> the number of Muslims living in "Christian" East Beirut, who had made up 40 per cent of the 1975 population, dropped to just 5 per cent of the 1989 population. A similar redistribution occurred in West Beirut, where the Christian population dropped from 35 per cent of the total in 1975 to 5 per cent in 1989.[30]

In the post-civil war era, where the East/West divide no longer officially exists, Beirutis have been unable to transcend the "mental geography" of the city's protracted division.[31] Michael Davie notes that in the post-war era ideas continue to "persist that 'West Beirut' is Muslim, fundamentalist, overrun by terrorists, under the control of foreign renegade countries, disorganized, dangerous, and that 'East Beirut' is Christian, prosperous, organized, pro-Western, tolerant, and safe".[32] The persistence of the Green Line as a mental and cultural referent of separation is now accompanied by other layers of division. These new divisions, while not as formally demarcated as the wartime Green Line, are based on issues related to security and class. In regard to the former, Mona Fawwaz, Mona Harb and Ahmad Gharbieh argue that post-war Beirut contains conflicting security systems and equally conflicting perceptions of what constitutes a threat. Hezbollah, whose security system is largely unchallenged in Beirut's southern suburbs, perceive local right-wing politicians allied to a foreign agenda, namely a US-driven neo-liberal one, as a threat.

Conversely, those conservative politicians, who dominate the security system of the Solidere area, view Hezbollah's security system as a national threat.[33] While these rival security zones are geographically-based, they also "work to entrench socio-spatial divisions and shape the daily experiences of [city] dwellers".[34] In terms of class, Esther Charlesworth's interviews with a number of Beirut's poorer residents reveal a sense of exclusion from the city's affluent centre. These residents suggest that an informal "red line" is being drawn around the Solidere area and constitutes an even harsher boundary than the old Green Line. In fact some "architectural and political commentators have suggested that Beirut is now [...] far more polarized than it was just after the war in 1991".[35] Thus, Beirut, from its earliest development to the present day, is a pertinent example of a city that is physically organised around the cultural and historical experiences of its inhabitants.

These new tiers of division are strongly associated with the reconstruction project and the mode within which it has been conceived. In the introduction I suggested, following Saree Makdisi, that the Solidere programme for the Downtown was a kind of "narrative" suppressing Beirut's rich but also recent bloody history. From Solidere's perspective, as Miriam Cooke points out, the war years are "the hiatus between 'days of glory' and the [glorious] future" to come.[36] Solidere's motto captures this sentiment well: "Beirut: Ancient City of the Future." In that regard not all history is being suppressed, but the history that is chosen is carefully selected and often distorted. In *Beirut Reborn: The Restoration and Development of the Central District*, a text that contains the details of the Solidere Master Plan for restoration, authors Angus Gavin and Ramez Maluf do note that in a place as old as Beirut any collective sense of "city memory" is a product of countless layers of history.[37] They go on to make a direct and explicit link between Beirut's historical record and its capacity to participate in the global economy: "The preservation of Beirut's unique cultural and historic identity will reflect favourably upon the city's status as it competes against others in the Middle East and the Eastern Mediterranean for an international role and prominence."[38] In order for Beirut to compete as an international city it needed more history, and history in the context of the Downtown project meant reverting to the ancient Phoenician past in order to marginalise the recent war past. By appropriating Lebanon's archaeological record, Solidere has chosen to focus on the 4,000-year-old Phoenician society precisely because this society's imagery "symbolizes a linkage between Lebanon's ancient seafaring inhabitants, who once controlled Mediterranean commerce, and today's Lebanese, who, according to Solidere, are united by their commercial instincts and entrepreneurial spirit".[39] Every piece of history that is incorporated into the new Downtown, those ancient artefacts that have been carefully retained in the building process, points to the commercialisation of Downtown's place identity.[40]

This kind of historical appropriation is not just limited to Solidere's vision for the Downtown but is symptomatic, first, of the government's official denial and, second, of society's widespread denial of the country's recent past. In the first instance, the governing body has done little to process the war's causes and consequences. Apart from proving unable to produce an historical account of the civil war, many of the current bickering politicians emerged from the war years. Even though their activities during the war as militia heads and factional leaders are questionable, these politicians continue to haunt the present scene because, in a bid to consolidate the official line that the "war is over", the state granted an amnesty for all war crimes. In doing this the government has repeatedly denied its citizens an open avenue to pursue "critical and honest vision based on the acknowledgement of the vicissitudes and pitfalls of this history".[41] In the second instance, widespread historical amnesia has filtered through to the popular conception of the prosperous and glorious days before the war in the 1950s and 1960s. Saree Makdisi's discussion of postcards in Lebanon highlights the danger of romanticising Lebanon's "golden age". Almost all the cards available today were printed long before the civil war and depict

the city in its former glory, presenting [...] images of Martyrs' Square [a site that is part of the contemporary Downtown] bustling with cars and people in the 1950s, of the gleaming

Phoenicia Hotel in its heyday in the 1960s or the crowded streets in the commercial center before the war.[42]

These out-dated representations of Beirut suggest that the city's current and disappointing state has been contained by images that reflect an "authentic" Beirut that once existed. In actual fact these images, which are completely irreconcilable with contemporary Beirut, function as mere substitutes.[43] Again, not unlike the government's decree of amnesty, such images do not encourage any real engagement with the war years, as painful as that may be, and simply take the role of replacing the distress left by the war.[44] Failing to process the injustices of the civil war has meant that the Lebanese have been unable to move beyond the physical and confessional divisions that tarnished their society prior to and during the period of unrest. The persistence of these divisions exposes the danger of ignoring and suppressing the war's unresolved issues. What makes matters worse in this context is the selective raiding of both Lebanon's ancient record and "glorious" pre-war past to produce an inauthentic history that has various blind spots – the most obvious being the civil war.

The texts to be discussed in the two subsequent chapters are novels that directly connect with the civil war and render a history that is at odds with what is currently happening in Lebanon. These novels refuse to glorify Beirut's ancient and pre-war commercial successes and instead paint a vivid picture of a period that Lebanon has too quickly forgotten. Focusing on the impact of war in an urban setting, the following discussion of Tony Hanania and Rawi Hage's novels will include the formative discourse of city culture outlined by Weber, Simmel, Park and Wirth. Hage's *De Niro's Game* tends to stress the internal character of Beirut, as is Park's preference, and reflects this character through its human inhabitants. In other words, the physical structure of Beirut – its war-ravaged buildings, roads and homes – is a consequence of a war carried out through human action. While war remains an important theme in *Unreal City*, it is capitalism's exploitative nature and how capital and war effect city-dwellers that is examined. This novel tends to emphasise the position taken by the German School, where the protagonist's alienation is depicted as a consequence of capitalism.

CHAPTER 2

THE DESTRUCTION OF WEST BEIRUT IN TONY HANANIA'S *UNREAL CITY*

Hanania's novel has been labelled as a text that predominately deals with the Lebanese civil war where "personal and national tragedies [are] intertwined".[1] The nameless narrator, who is "nearly always out of his head" due to severe drug abuse, experiences this war at a distance.[2] He is insulated from it at its inception and is sent to a private boarding school in London. There are, however, periodic visits back to his homeland even as the violence intensifies in the 1980s. By this stage he has secured jobs in London and Madrid, at the Tate gallery and Sotheby's. His passage to England is guaranteed not only by his education but also his mixed cultural heritage. His late mother is Palestinian-English and was educated in North Yorkshire. Her father was the governor of Haifa in Palestine during the mandate period. This is where the narrator's maternal grandfather met his Palestinian wife.[3] The narrator's father is a Lebanese university professor at the American University of Beirut. While in Lebanon before the war the family spent the academic year in West Beirut and the summer months in their ancestral village in South Lebanon. Thus, the narrator is highly educated, belongs to a privileged economic class and is steeped in both Eastern and Western cultures.

Despite this, what readers learn about the narrator in the initial pages of the novel stands in stark contrast to the image described above. Written as a retrospective "testimony" covering events from the pre-war years to July 1990, the narrator reveals that he is preparing himself for a suicide mission. The target is a renegade Muslim writer residing in London who "had mocked the customs of his fathers, and aped the manners of his conquerors, and betrayed the religion of the Prophet".[4] Though never mentioned by name, it can be assumed that the writer is Salman Rushdie and that the narrator, who becomes a member of a Muslim brotherhood, is responding to the *fatwa* issued against Rushdie in 1989. What then, asks Vinten, "has happened to this louche, educated [and secular] man to turn him into a killer?"[5]

For Vinten the novel does not provide any adequate answers to this question – the narrator's story is merely a "thin wisp of hashish smoke" where "characters flit across the pages [. . .] silent and without substance".[6] However, what Vinten fails to remark upon is the emergence of the urban space as a central character in this novel. Indeed, *Unreal City* contains vivid and rich urban description which makes Beirut just as much a character as the narrator who roams its streets. Given this, part of the answer to Vinten's original question lies in recognising the novel's urban disposition and its capacity to marginalise the narrator. As discussed in the previous chapter, urban sociologists, like Weber and Simmel, assume that the city space is harsh and alienating. Their concentration on the large and impersonal nature of urban spaces as explanations for the isolating tendencies of city culture are only reinforced by Beirut's wartime conditions. Indeed, the metropolis in this novel is alienating and the narrator's specifically Beirut experience of estrangement is determined by the chaos of the war, the distorted capitalistic black economy that develops during this period, and the feminisation of the city through the narrator's fallen lover, Layla. It is this environment that shapes the narrator's decision to become a killer because, as Michel de Certeau suggests, "spatial practices in fact secretly structure the determining conditions of social life".[7]

While the title *Unreal City* signals the importance of the urban space in Hanania's novel, it also intimates how the city will be characterised. Hanania draws on a phrase from T. S. Eliot's *The Waste Land* to introduce readers to a war-ravaged Arab city. With this reference to the "unreal city" of Eliot's poem an intertextual relationship is set up to grasp the nature of urban decay that Hanania's novel explores. Richard Lehan suggests that *The Waste Land* poem casts London as "one of the several cities caught in the process of rise and fall".[8] This is especially evident in the following lines: "Falling towers/Jerusalem Athens Alexandria/ Vienna London/ Unreal".[9] Eliot's rather bleak modernist illustration of the city space is, according to Lehan, drawn from the poet's belief "that as the city lost touch with the land, with the rhythms and the psychic nourishment of nature, a spiritual meaning was lost".[10] Losing touch with the land by moving to the city is similarly linked to a loss of nature and spirituality in *Unreal City*. Abu Musa, the narrator's neighbour in South Lebanon, in his "peasant whisperings" claims that:

A young shabb [man] who goes into the city is as one who drinks from the water that no longer flows.
He is the caravan that follows the mist-lights on the marshes.
The rat who visits the wicker basket in the cellars of the Bey [the chief or local leader].[11]

Associating those who have left for the city with rodents and whose urban lives have lost their sources of nourishment, Abu Musa's words echo Eliot's views on the city. In that respect Hanania's Beirut is like the fallen cities listed in Eliot's poem as, through its civil war experience, it too underwent a process of urban decay.

Beirut as Wasteland

The depiction of Beirut as a wasteland in *Unreal City* emerges in two interconnected forms. The first is reflected in the text's concern with the development of a distorted economy driven by a market of illicit trade. While Eliot's London becomes "exhaust[ed] from within as its inhabitants succumb to the secular ends of profit and loss", in

Beirut the role of the economy in its urban decay is intensified by the war.[12] Hanania's Beirut is driven by wartime entrepreneurs, such as characters like Jaffer, who manipulate the black market by trading in drugs and looted goods in order to accumulate wealth. The second approach that the text uses to explore urban entropy is through gender and the progressive feminisation of Beirut. The narrator's lover, Layla, embodies images of the seductress, mistress and prostitute whose final fall from grace is closely aligned to the degradation and decay of Beirut.

With regard to the former, the role capitalism plays in the development of modern Lebanon is explored in the novel through domestic architecture. Akram Khater observes, in his examination of residential dwellings in late nineteenth and early twentieth century Lebanon, that houses could be differentiated according to the socio-economic status of their owners. Furnishings and property location allowed one to discriminate between the houses of the upper and lower classes. The houses of the poor were sparsely furnished and generally found at the village's periphery, while the wealthier residences contained more fixtures, such as beds as opposed to simple mattresses, and were centrally located.[13] In the last 30 years of the nineteenth century, however, houses were not just distinguishable based on the objects contained within them or their location; they were also visually altered to conform to new architectural trends and interior design. This period was marked by Lebanon's contact with capitalism and its integration into the world economy through migration and silk farming.[14] The narrator in *Unreal City* conveys these sorts of distinctions in architecture in relation to his ancestral village in South Lebanon, juxtaposing the residences of the poor with the houses of the wealthy.

The focus on domestic architecture takes place in one of the novel's earliest chapters and commences with details of the poorer houses. It is the village's exploited *fellahin*, farmers or peasants, who own these residences. They live in a separate quarter of the village in low-rise tenements "no more than a single room, with quilt and mattresses over the floor, a paraffin-stove against the rear wall, in the small yard a donkey or chickens, and plastered-mud vats for grain, meal and straw".[15] The wealthiest member of the village, the *Bey* or local leader, lives in a much less modest dwelling that is, as the narrator reports, highly modern and Westernised. The *Bey* "gradually excises all traces of the Orient from within itself, the traditional Ottoman manzuls and receptions shifting into the café-rococo of the corridors".[16] The study is filled with copies of *Punch* and *Country Life* magazines alongside scuffed leather armchairs. Inside the house it "feels like England in a heat wave; a scent of dead flies and horsehair, of things coming unstuck".[17] For the narrator, the *Bey*'s effacement of all "traces of the Orient" from his home is indicative of his abandonment of local culture. Perceiving himself as above his own community, speaking "grandiloquent" English and having attended Cambridge University, this *Bey*, like his predecessors, exploits the *fellahin* around him.[18]

One such example of this exploitation takes place when the elder *Bey* dies. This elder *Bey* had kept Abu Musa as his trusted *murafiq* (companion) and, following tradition, appoints Abu Musa's son, Musa-al-Tango, to the post. Musa-al-Tango, loyal like his father to the *Bey*'s family, "had worked as a rat-catcher in the cellars of the old Bey before taking his place as a murafiq at the doors of the great diwan".[19] His allegiance to the *Bey*'s household is further demonstrated as he participates in election planning, is one of the three followers who travels to Beirut to receive the elder *Bey*'s son upon his return from Cambridge, and is among the group of men to accompany the *Bey* to parliament.[20] Despite this loyalty and service, the new *Bey* marginalises Musa-al-Tango and appoints Fawzi-from-the-mountains as his *murafiq*. This act not only disregards the traditional line of succession but is also an unprecedented transgression. It leaves the inhabitants of the village confused as to why, as "the old Bey lay dying in the university hospital, his son had appointed Fawzi-from-the-mountains and his cousins to the household".[21]

Fawzi represents a preference for a more contemporary *murafiq* who overpowers not only Musa-al-Tango but also the entire village. Fawzi's reckless and domineering approach results in the most extraordinary forms of persecution against the peasants. During the war, without censure from the *Bey*, "Fawzi-from-the-mountains and his followers [. . .] had set up tolls on the paths through the orchards, looted food and clothing from those fellahin families who remained".[22] Furthermore, as Abu Musa and Musa-al-Tango's stories reveal, this *Bey*'s acceptance of his *murafiq*'s thuggish behaviour at the expense of the peasants is not unprecedented. Musa-al-Tango tells of his father's experience of the severity of the famine that gripped Lebanon during the Great War. It drove "one farmer [to sell] his entire olive grove to the [elder] Bey for a single lemon; another his house and ass for three sacks of wheat; fellahin were sold for single pails of milk".[23] And yet, during that same period of extreme starvation, Abu Musa "worked [. . .] in the cellars of the old Bey [. . .] wading thigh deep in the horded grain as the villagers starved down in the valleys".[24] What Musa-al-Tango reports to the narrator illustrates that previous local leaders, just like the incumbent, exploit the peasants' suffering as a way to maximise their own gains. The narrator is informed in his youth by Musa-al-Tango's wife "of the old village belief that the last of the beys would redeem the crimes of all his forefathers".[25] Initially this knowledge is of little consequence to the narrator until it is revealed that the *Bey* "in a codicil [. . .] had named [. . .] [the narrator] as his true son and the entailed". The narrator's inheritance of "Swiss bonds [. . .] held in a private bank in Basle" are derived from "the revenues [. . .] [of] the final rents and harvests" from land that had been confiscated or forcibly obtained from the peasants.[26] This inheritance allows the narrator, safely located in Europe, to maintain a regime of "high living" but it also implicates him in the suffering the peasants experienced at the hands of his forefathers.

The relationships between these generations of local leaders and the poorer villagers illustrates that the rural environment and society in Lebanon are shaped by the onset of capitalism and modernity. The powerful *Bey*s are able to exploit the impoverished classes and as a result of these circumstances many people of the village choose to immigrate to the city and abroad.[27] The urban scenes within the novel depict capitalism in similarly grave terms, particularly as they contribute to the narrator's isolation and withdrawal from society. Hanania, as he reveals in an interview, subscribes to the notion of urban alienation. He sees himself as an exile from Lebanon and explains that "Through the idea of Lebanon, through Lebanon as an idea, I explore exile as alienation".[28] Given these comments, it is no surprise that the alienating tendency of the urban environment is emphasised in his novel.

How Hanania examines the isolation of the protagonist is tied in with the transformative consequences of the war. The narrator's observations of the changes taking place in Beirut are a register of nostalgia for the lost city of his youth. He recalls spending many afternoons as a child in the homes of his father's bridge partners, in "the most fashionable strip of rue Hamra, the row of marble-porched mansion buildings with staggered cream terraces like the decks of an ocean liner".[29] As an adult, however, he walks down the same road only to find that refugees from the south of the country now populate the area. What was once a series of "show-windows of boutiques and jewellers" has been transformed, by the squatters, into "fruit and poultry stalls".[30] Despite being able to identify with the squatters when he hears the familiar "southern" accents of "Marjayoun and Nabatiyeh and of [his] own village", these stalls nevertheless betray the narrator's memories of Beirut and alienate him from the city.[31]

This is one face of the transformation, one that emphasises the poverty of certain urban dwellers. The other side draws attention to the uneven distribution of wealth. By taking advantage of the chaos, certain Beirutis, unlike the impoverished squatters, are able to reap large financial rewards. The calculated destruction of Beirut's Ottoman villas is an instance where the vested interests of real estate developers ensure these buildings are strategically targeted:

> the higher modern blocks had not taken so many direct hits, but these listed palazzos had been deliberately targeted by the gunners in the hills on the orders of property speculators who were already dreaming of the new city they would build over the ruins.[32]

The destruction of abandoned buildings at the orders of property speculators expresses the level to which the war fostered the development of a black market economy. According to Salim Nasr, the growth of this parallel economy commenced with the outbreak of hostilities in 1975.[33] Smuggling, extortion, private taxation, drug and ammunition sales proved to be lucrative activities in Lebanon's war period. As the war progressed, illegal trade within the black economy rose exponentially. Between 1975 and 1982 such clandestine transactions represented a maximum of 20 per cent of the economic activity of Lebanon. After 1982, with the siege of Beirut and the exit of the Palestinian leadership from the capital, the number rose to more than 50 per cent.[34] In monetary terms the collective sum of the black economy between 1975 and 1990 is estimated to be US$900 million.[35]

The character Jaffer, one of Musa-al-Tango's sons, is most implicated by the narrative in this pursuit of economic opportunism. He is depicted as a Hollywood-inspired thug with "sideburns that he had copied from the gangster films [...] dark glasses, his billowing shirt open to the waist, the sheen of his platforms boots flickering in the sinking sun".[36] Taking over an apartment in Hamra Street, he fills it with looted goods such as Quranic inscriptions taken from shelled mosques or treasures taken from the wealthy like "a warped salver that had once hung in the Bey's manzul".[37] By this stage few of Beirut's inhabitants remain in the city, having left because of the war. Those who remain are, according to the narrator, like Jaffer "typical country boys on [their] spree in town".[38]

It is within this environment of chaos, looting and illegal trade that the narrator becomes increasingly estranged from his childhood city. Having spent seven years abroad in London, his return home is to a place that is unfamiliar. Selling loot from the ruins of the war or trading in Bekka opium might be profitable for Jaffer, who eventually becomes "as rich as a glazier", but for the narrator these are not viable options.[39] In fact he distances himself from Jaffer's thuggish lifestyle: "Along rue du Rome he [Jaffer] began calling at the Christian girls in their tight jeans, waving, making the gesture of the thumb and palm, and I lagged behind him not wishing to seem part of it."[40] The narrator's isolation is further exacerbated when he refuses to leave his Beirut residence and relies on Jaffer to deliver food supplies. He realises that he could only risk "an expedition to the stalls on the days Jaffer came" to the house, an indication that "the streets must be passable".[41] By this stage the command of the city that the narrator once enjoyed has become the province of disreputable figures like Jaffer who can successfully negotiate the streets of the new, war-riddled capital. Thus, it is through the development of the black market economy in Beirut that readers witness the intensity of the narrator's alienation from the city.

The stress on Beirut's drive for capital gain is also closely tied to the depiction of the urban space as woman. An example of this association is explored toward the end of *Unreal City* just as the narrator is recruited into the militant Islamic party, *Jihad al-Binaa*. Inside the bombed house of the *Bey* the narrator finds a map of Beirut that reduces the city's size and focuses on its recreational precincts. On this map the city consists merely of "water skiers among the ruffles of the waves, minarets and umbrella pines inland, belly-dancers marking the night club districts, plump waiters in fezzes [marking] the famous restaurants of the day".[42] It is a selective record of Beirut that incorporates only those places that the likes of the wealthy *Bey* can enjoy. Despite providing Beirut with its labour force, the "lower districts of the city, the southern suburbs and the hinterland of Shiyah, had been omitted from the map".[43] What the *Bey*'s map incorporates in place of these are all of the city's "principal boulevards [that] fell in broad lubricious glissades between each pleasure zone".[44] The reference to Beirut's pleasure zones and the map's concentration on them captures not only the city's commercial aspects but also, from within the *Bey*'s male view, depicts the city as an erogenous and feminised space. This feminisation of Beirut, much like the development of capitalism in the urban space, extends the narrator's sense of isolation.

The feminisation of Beirut is not unique to *Unreal City*. Angelika Neuwirth and Brigit Embalo have identified that it is a trope within Arabic literature. Neuwirth explains that in Arabic literary culture the city is subtly feminised so that it is hidden "underneath the image of a female figure".[45] In *Unreal City* it is Layla, a Palestinian refugee from the Shatila camp, who embodies images of the seductive mistress and prostitute that Beirut hides behind. As a seductress, the narrator holds Layla responsible for luring him back to the city. Having "strung her [Layla] along for three summers with gifts and visions and promises" the narrator expresses a sense of retrospective guilt for leaving her behind.[46] During his annual trips to Lebanon he refuses all of Layla's pleas to be taken to England "before the war came down on the camps again".[47] Back in the safety of London the narrator hears of the massacres in the residential area of Sabra and the Shatila refugee camp. He writes to Layla's brothers, Asad and Harun, "via the Red Crescent offices in Holborn, but my letters seemed never to get through; my enquiries about Layla unanswered".[48] Fearing that she has perished in the war he returns to Beirut to search for her. This return compels the narrator to blame "no one else [but her] for reeling me back into this underworld".[49] Layla's capacity to "reel" the narrator back to Beirut indicates the extent to which she controls him, even in her absence.

Part of Layla's supposed power over the narrator stems from the sexual temptation that is derived from the seductive power of the female body. Embalo, adding further nuance to the trope of feminisation, argues that female seduction is one key way that this trope is expressed. Within what she refers to as "city-writing", Embalo suggests that the "analogy/identification of woman and city operates on the level of the female body [...] Her body is the vanishing point of longing and of fear at the same time".[50] Hanania develops the connection between Layla and Beirut by focusing on the ways this female character uses her body. The narrator's abandonment of Layla means that she is left to fend for herself in the increasingly violent city and is forced into prostitution. When the narrator learns of Layla's affair with his childhood friend, Jaffer, he does not relate her betrayal to his neglect but instead associates her transgression with his fear of the urban space. As he states: "I needed to hold her betrayal close to me. If I lost my fear the city had trapped me."[51] Failing to reclaim Layla or, more to the point, to reclaim her body from Jaffer and other lovers connects what seem to be two disparate ideas in the narrator's mind – the city and the female body. Ultimately, it is only Layla's sexual infidelity that liberates the narrator from the city.

Layla's infidelity is not her only act of disloyalty. She also betrays her own Palestinian community through an affair with a Maronite militiaman. In this instance Layla's sexual transgression is politically charged because this Christian militiaman collaborated with the Israelis. She is therefore aligned with the two groups responsible for the massacre of the Palestinians in 1982. Her own brother, Asad, is so ashamed and emotionally wounded by her act that he denies her very existence. As he informs the narrator, "It is as if she was never born".[52] Alongside her family's rejection, Layla is also openly ostracised by the female members of her community who "spit at her and kick the dirty water in her face" as retribution for her unforgivable act.[53] Neuwirth claims that behind the overt imagery surrounding, the female figure in Arabic literature "*al-Madīna* [the city] [. . .] occupies the very center of an allegorical subtext".[54] In this regard Layla's fall from grace functions as an allegory of Beirut's betrayal of the Palestinian cause. This is another well-established trope in Arabic literature, evident in poems by Mahmoud Darwish or Nizar Qabbani, where figures like Layla are held responsible for the duplicity of Beirut and the betrayal of its refugee population. Like Hanania, Darwish in his poem "*Qasidat Beirut*" or "Ode to Beirut" (1982) personifies Beirut as a woman called Layla. Embalo argues that in this poem Beirut is imagined as the idyllic landscape of Palestinian and Arab liberation.[55] Indeed, Darwish's poem depicts Beirut as "our [i.e. Palestinian] tent/our last star, our tent/our only star" for the Palestinian revolution while the rest of the Arab world is portrayed as a hopeless and devastated landscape.[56] However, the 1982 massacre poignantly highlights Beirut's betrayal of the Palestinian cause and extinguishes the possibility that Beirut can ever be a site for such liberation struggles.

The extent of urban decay and degradation is fully realised when the narrator ventures into the city to look for Layla. This journey is significant because it is the narrator's final one before undergoing his religious conversion within the Islamic militant party. By this stage he is aware of Layla's prostitution and is told that she is stationed in the brothel district in the Bourj city centre, referred to in the novel as Sahat al-Burj. This journey takes the narrator through such heavily destroyed parts of Beirut that he is almost unable to recognise the area or to note any past familiarity. Despite having frequented as a child "the most famous restaurant in the city [...] as a treat on those dreary Sunday afternoons in the years before the war" it takes him some time to realise where he is.[57] He is finally able to discern several formerly prominent buildings that in the pre-war era signified a modern and cosmopolitan Beirut. Their decimated state is symbolic of Beirut's decay and also foreshadows the extent of the city's deterioration that the narrator is about to discover through his encounter with Layla.

In Sahat al-Burj the narrator is directed by the "old women wearing platinum wigs; short, threadbare coats above their shiny skirts" to follow a woman and a soldier "walking through a fallen wall into the [...] single corner-building rising like an anvil above the wilderness".[58] The building is comprised of several rooms each occupied with "soldiers reclining with their water-pipes as the women bend over them".[59] In the final room the narrator finds a girl standing at

the window, her back to the door, a silk shawl over her skinny shoulders, a girl with a dyed-blond bob looking down at the few lit streets in the eastern sector [...] I call her [Layla's] name again, and she turns [...] a girl of no more than fourteen, her gown open, the garters loose over her thin thighs; her lips bruised, the kohl smudged under her eyes.[60]

Even though the girl he encounters is not Layla, the narrator remains profoundly disturbed by the child prostitution he is exposed to and assumes that Layla has assimilated into this world. The ruined sites he recognised earlier are juxtaposed with the brothel district, stressing that the cosmopolitan city of his childhood is transformed, much like Layla, so that it no longer maintains its idealised status.

Through this feminisation of Beirut, Hanania's text places the burden of the degradation of the city on the woman. As Embalo points out, the metaphorical transformation of the city into a woman might be a common feature in contemporary Arabic literature, but this "is of course only possible in a male dominated view".[61] It is not surprising, as the scholarship of Embalo and Neuwirth suggests, that the image of the lustful or seductive city-woman that dominates Arabic urban literature has been produced by male poets like Qabbani and Darwish. By leaning heavily on the female figure, that is by connecting Layla's demise with Beirut's decay, Hanania maintains a tradition borne in Arabic literature. Consequently, he gives a rather distorted view of the male/female relationship by substituting the roles of victim and victimiser. This is exemplified by the male narrator who believes that it is he, not Layla, who has become a victim of the city. In turn both Layla, a stateless and impoverished Palestinian, and Beirut, the destroyed city, are held responsible for their own demise. Despite his efforts to circumvent his role in Layla's fall and Beirut's destruction, the narrator is eventually overcome by guilt at his neglect of both. He seeks to redeem his reputation first through the act of narration and second through a suicide mission.

Redemption

The novel's opening pages make explicitly clear that the protagonist is recording his own "testimony" – a quasi-autobiographical account of his life, from his childhood years to his adulthood. Neuwirth explains that one of the major archetypal images found in Arabic literature is the act of "'narrating' for the sake of the narrator's 'redemption' and liberation".[62] By recording and narrating his own story the protagonist is, according to the conventions of Arabic literature, ensuring that he will be absolved of his life's many misdeeds which include deserting Layla, turning his back on Beirut and maintaining his complicity in Lebanon's oppressive class. What structures his account, apart from the temporal division of the day into "daybreak", "noon" and "nightfall", are the novel's three books, "Sidon", "Dark Star" and "Homecoming". Within these books the Adonis myth and the theme of rebirth are often invoked. It is not surprising that the narrator is drawn to this particular myth because its preoccupation with rebirth provides the appropriate narrative frame for him to imagine his redemption.

The myth of Adonis has traditionally been associated in Western literature with Modernist writers and with ideas of fertility and rebirth. This is evident in the work of Eliot, especially in his *Waste Land* poem, where he acknowledges the use of anthropological material related to the Adonis myth. His two sources are Jessie L. Weston's *From Ritual to Romance* which, Eliot claims, "will elucidate the difficulties of the poem [*The Waste Land*] much better than my notes can", and Sir James George Frazer's *The Golden Bough*.[63] Weston deals with the Adonis myth by examining its relevance to ideas associated with vegetation and fertility:

> The woes of the land and the folk are set forth in poignant detail, and Tammuz [the Semitic name for Adonis] is passionately invoked to have pity upon his worshippers, and to end their sufferings by a speedy return. This return [...] was effected by the action of a goddess [...] who, descending into the nether world, induced the youthful deity to return with her to earth [...] Tammuz is not to be regarded merely as representing the Spirit of Vegetation; his influence is operative, not only [...] as a Spring god, but in all [his] reproductive energies [...] he may be considered as an embodiment of the Life principle.[64]

The "life principle" mentioned by Weston is of central concern to the Adonis myth and is contingent upon the rebirth of the deity. His rebirth instigates vegetation in the land and, in that respect, Adonis can also be associated with fertility. In fact, according to Frazer, the principle of life and fertility in the Adonis myth are "one and indivisible".[65] In this context Eliot's engagement with this myth is understandable. The London of his poem is a wasteland, a "desert [...] cut off from the redeeming water, the mythic impulses of life", and a myth that is concerned with vegetation and rebirth provides a fitting counterbalance.[66] As Saddik Gohar points out, this is why Eliot, writing in a post-World War I milieu, used this myth as a way to respond to the stagnant and crumbling conditions which surrounded him.[67]

In the Arab world Adonis, better known as Tammuz, was popularised in the 1950s by poets like Badr Shaker Al-Sayyab, Abdul Wahhab Al-Bayati and Ali Ahmad Said Asbar. Asbar even went so far as to adopt "Adonis" as his professional name. These poets, according to Gohar, "responded passionately to [. . .] *The Waste Land*, establishing an analogy between the stagnant situation in the Arab world in the aftermath of WWII and the wasteland myth in Eliot's poem".[68] Similar to Eliot, who experienced and wrote about the implications of World War I, his Arab counterparts responded to various catastrophic events like the loss of Palestine and the emergence of harsh local regimes. As a result "Eliot's discourses about a fallen civilization [were] appropriated and recycled [in post-World War II Arabic poetry] to fit into local political contexts".[69] It is through Eliot, then, that Arab poets connected with the Adonis/ Tammuz myth and it is also Eliot, more so than any other English writer, who was able to "exert so deep an influence on Arabic poetry" that "he almost cut it entirely from its roots".[70] After this point, Adonis/Tammuz became so influential that poets like Al-Sayyab and Al-Bayati "initiated the so called 'Tammūz-movement' [. . .] reviving [mythical] figures like 'Ishtār and primarily Tammūz to act as protagonists in their peculiar recast of reality in terms of drought and fertility, death and resurrection".[71]

According to Frazer there are several myths of Adonis that stem from different geographical spaces such as Greece, Syria and Iraq. It is widely assumed that the worship of Adonis originated in ancient Greece but, in actual fact, the earliest civilisation to have venerated Adonis was the Phoenician. As Frazer explains the "worship of Adonis was practiced by the Semitic people of Babylonia [Iraq] and Syria, and the Greeks borrowed it from them as early as the Seventh Century before Christ".[72] Frazer asserts that Adonis' true name is Tammuz, the name that is most likely prevalent in the Lebanese collective consciousness, and that "Adonis" simply relates to the Greek word "Adon" meaning Lord.[73] While there are slight differences between the Syrian, Greek and Babylonian myths, generally all versions include the wounding of Adonis/Tammuz by a wild boar on the mountainside near a river. In the Syrian version this river is specifically *Nahr Ibrahim* (Abraham's River) which is located in the district of Mount Lebanon. The deity's blood dyes the river and the anemone flowers red. After his wounding Adonis remains trapped in the underworld until his lover, Ishtar, rescues him. During the period of Adonis and Ishtar's seclusion in the underworld, the natural world becomes barren and is only rejuvenated when the lovers return. This is repeated annually and, as Issa Boullata explains, marks the turning of the seasons: "Tammuz has to be killed by the wild boar and suffer the darkness of the underworld before he returns to the wasteland in spring, filling it with abundance and fertility."[74]

Unreal City makes use of the Adonis myth several times and it is appropriated by the characters to narrate their particular concerns. Layla is the first to recount the Adonis story: "In the spring, for one or two weeks, the earth turns crimson with wild anemones [. . .] When we walked here together Layla used to tell me the flowers were dyed with the blood of Adonis, seeping up from the underworld."[75] Abu Musa is the next character to mention the myth to the narrator but, in this instance, it is recounted as if it were an actual occurrence in recent history: "Abu Musa had heard the tale of a handsome young hunter gored on the mountain by a wild boar and of the river to the north which still ran crimson with his blood every spring."[76] Abu Musa's appropriation of the myth memorialises the past and locates the myth within his and the narrator's village. The mountains and river he refers to were "less than seventy years ago" overgrown with trees – firs, junipers, holm-oaks and vines.[77] Stripped bare by the Turks so they could construct railway lines, it is only the *fellahin* who can remember the once fertile woods. Finally there is Harun, Layla's brother, who aligns the myth with the local history of Sidon, a key port city in southern Lebanon. According to Harun every

> spring when the hills were scarlet with anemones the Sidonians drew their god through the orchards in effigy to the sea, and to the springs, and drowned him, and as his lover Ishtar had once wept the women wept and rent themselves and covered their hair with earth and waited for the return of their loves from the waters.[78]

In this final rendition the myth is spatially recast and Adonis is depicted as a local figure from Sidon. Both Harun and Abu Musa rework the myth, making it identifiable with South Lebanon despite ancient sources that indicate that Adonis was central to Byblos, closer to the north of the country, where King Cinyras dedicated an ancient sanctuary to the god.[79]

The novel utilises this myth as a structuring device, emphasising the seasonal turns and juxtaposing barrenness with vegetation. The first book, "Sidon", focuses on the narrator's youth, where he travels between England to attend school and Lebanon for the summer. As he spends the summer months at home among family and friends the narrator associates London with the "cold exile of boarding school".[80] The timing of his so-called exile is marked by the seasonal changes within Lebanon itself: "Today we [the people of his ancestral village] have seen the first clouds drifting up from the south, high, dark, lonely, like weather balloons [...] it is almost time for me to leave again."[81] As in the Adonis myth, the winter months in this novel are depicted as harsh and cruel. The narrator views his own "parting [as] a harbinger of the hard winter to come" and, in that respect, parallels his exile with the underworld exile of Adonis.[82]

"Book II: Dark Star" reflects the darkness the narrator increasingly experiences. His infrequent trips through Beirut as he searches for Layla, Asad and Harun convey the city's desolation:

> [winding] down past the derelict casinos into the ruins of the city, the streets around the crossing so grown over with creepers and bushes I had not recognized the way, pitch-dark canyons where once stood teeming avenues and squares, across the bay the half-moon through the hollow façades.[83]

The greenery of the city's public parks, like the Senayegh Gardens, quickly become another casualty of the war. Used by the refugees fleeing the south for shelter, they are "soon stripped of their remaining trees for firewood and building purposes".[84] This lack of vegetation is further exacerbated when the narrator likens the city's gardens to those tended to by the patients in an asylum. As a child on summer holiday before the war he recalls trips to "Ashrafieh asylum in the pine hills above the city" with his father who was a trustee on the hospital's board.[85] He "would sit [...] and watch the patients walking in the garden with watering-cans between tidy rows of bright shrubs and flowerbeds".[86] These gardens, as he eventually learns, were "made out of paper, the leaves from streamers, the rocks from paper mâché, the blooms from crepe and tinted foil. As the patients poured from the watering-can, a fine white powder covered the coloured paper like icing sugar."[87] Reflecting on this event as an adult, the narrator recalls his childhood fear and how he ran away from the building with his eyes shut and locked himself in his father's vehicle. In the novel's present, the paper gardens of the asylum extend throughout the entire city:

> Driving through the city that winter I saw many such gardens. Along the ruined avenues where the blasted palms and planes had been stripped away stood trees of discarded water-containers with fronds of plastic sheeting, groves of stacked tyres and twisted piping where once there had been lemon orchards and mulberry terraces.[88]

By association all of Beirut had become like an asylum, a "dark star into which those blindly falling could send back no returning signals".[89] This recalls the period of Adonis' own descent into the underworld which, as Frazer describes, signifies "the land from which there is no returning, to the house of darkness, where dust lies on the floor".[90]

"Dark Star" is predominately set in winter, where the bleakness and desolation of the city is constantly reinforced through the mention of rain. The narrator's arrival at Beirut airport is marked by "torrential rain".[91] Even though he remains in Beirut through the summer months, very little is made of the warmer weather. Throughout there are descriptions of the relentless wet weather: "When it rained hard I waited for Jaffer"; "With the last of the winter rains"; "It is raining hard."[92]

The final book departs from the coldness of winter and darkness of Book II and instead focuses on lightness and rebirth. The very first page of "Book III: Homecoming" signals a return of vegetation: "across the lawns below the lines of pepper and acacia trees, buddleia and lilac, the lower reaches turned over to the villagers to grow tobacco and zucchini".[93] By this stage in the novel the narrator has fled Beirut and has taken residence in the *Jihad al-Binaa* complex in South Lebanon. His association with *Jihad al-Binaa* reflects the predominance of rejuvenation in this section. *Jihad al-Binaa* literally translates as the "Struggle for Construction" and represents a division within Hezbollah dedicated to the construction of housing and public infrastructure both in rural and urban areas that are densely populated by Shi'a Muslims. The complex, apart from housing young Shi'a men like the narrator, functions as a warehouse where materials like "water-tanks, mobile generators, bore tripods for drilling artisan wells" are stored for Hezbollah's reconstruction projects.[94] Unlike the Solidere reconstruction programme which focuses on the revitalisation of commercial Beirut, *Jihad al-Binaa*'s motivation has been to provide welfare to its impoverished followers in the form of housing, electricity and water supplies.[95] In joining this group, the narrator rejects his privileged background and aligns himself with a partisan political ideology that has a religious and welfare focus.

As suggested earlier, the narrative's structure is centred on seasonal motifs of winter, darkness, rain, light, sterility and vegetation. This, in keeping with the conventions of Arabic literature, is one of the modes by which the narrator seeks redemption. As his testimony is produced in narrative form, however, the only absolution he can possibly gain is from those who read the text after his death. In order to complete a religious and culturally-specific redemption the narrator adopts the ideology of Shi'a Islam. An important aspect of this religious ideology is its tendency to emphasise a core sense of injustice that is derived from the martyrdom of Imam Hussein. Hussein is the grandson of the Prophet Muhammad and the child of the Prophet's most trusted companion, Ali. According to the teachings of Shi'a Islam, Ali was the closest blood-relative of the Prophet and his natural successor. Despite this connection, three Caliphs prevented Ali from succeeding the Prophet. Ali's thwarted leadership aspirations and his assassination combine to "present the first major event in the history of Islam which caused the development of an initial sense of injustice" among Shi'a Muslims.[96] The subsequent killing of Ali's followers and family, including his son Hussein, in Karbala compounds the Shi'a sense of being treated unjustly. Shi'a followers worldwide commemorate Hussein's martyrdom annually, over a period of ten days. This event is known as *Eid al-'Ashura* and is celebrated in *Muharram*, the first month of the Islamic calendar. Participation in *'Ashura* includes the re-enactment of Hussein's plight, the performance of the martyr plays, and a public procession where men strike their breasts, display their wounds and women weep loudly as the death of the martyr is retold.

Eid al-'Ashura in *Unreal City* is documented by the narrator as a communal celebration within his ancestral village where all households, rich and poor, mark the event by erecting banners and joining the evening processions.[97] The narrative then shifts focus from the collective experience to the narrator's discovery of a personal injustice. On the tenth evening, at the culmination of the festival, the narrator notices a "figure staggering out into the alley, wiping his mouth with the back of his hand, his shirt unbuttoned [...] his aubergine flares dragging on the wet cobbles. Jaffer walked quickly, without looking around."[98] Jaffer's activities that night remain ambiguous but the narrator suspects that he has slept with Layla. While learning of Layla's betrayal physically sickens the narrator – "I had not eaten since the morning, and when I retched the trail was watery" – this scene also foreshadows the discourse of martyrdom that the narrator is attracted to soon after.[99] The appeal of *'Ashura* and the narrative it showcases relates to what Zeina Maasri describes as "its interpretative power".[100] Through interpretation and appropriation, the narrative of Hussein's martyrdom is "effectively put to use" by Shi'a Muslims globally to explain various contemporary struggles.[101] In the case of Shi'a Muslims in Australia, Paul Tabar's research highlights that *'Ashura* and its subtext of injustice have been transformed by Shi'a migrants so as to respond to their current and local circumstances.[102] In the context of Hanania's novel, the strategic narrative framing of Layla's dishonesty alongside the text's detailed discussion of the *'Ashura* event connects the larger

Shi'a sense of injustice with the narrator's own personal feelings of betrayal and injustice. In that sense Hanania appropriates the significance of this annual commemoration and applies it to the protagonist, firmly locating aspects of *Unreal City* within a particular Shi'a Muslim aesthetic.

The appeal of this Shi'a discourse for the narrator is further realised when Ali, the son of Musa-al-Tango and Jaffer's brother, recruits him into *Jihad al-Binaa*. Unlike his brother, Ali does not embrace a thuggish lifestyle in order to exploit the poor during the war. He instead opts for a religious approach and is portrayed throughout the text as a dedicated Muslim. In his adolescence Ali segregates himself from the other young men in the village, who lead relatively secular lives, and elects to sit "in the same place [. . .] his legs crossed, his Qur'ān open on his lap".[103] His religious incantation continues to develop to the point where he begins to mimic the "reedy Persian accent" of the Iman who visits the village periodically: "I [the narrator] had found Ali's talk increasingly difficult to follow. He had begun to affect a Persian accent. He spoke in riddles [. . .] I did not like to look at the wispy hatchings on his cheeks and chin."[104] The significance of Ali's Persian intonation reflects the centrality of post-revolutionary Iran as a spiritual guide for Shi'a Muslims in the Arab world. Although the narrator is initially unable to identify with Ali, preferring his own secular lifestyle, he eventually comes to accept the highly fundamentalist views Ali espouses. In terms of narrative sequence, the turning point for the narrator is drawn from his discovery of Layla's prostitution which, as previously discussed, completes his alienation from the city of his youth. The remorse and isolation he now feels is accompanied by the realisation that his privileged status allowed him to escape the war. Indeed, he is not a victim of the war like Harun, Asad or Layla, and is not exposed to the possibility of an "honourable" death like "the former students of [his] father [. . .] who died defending the strongholds in Tyre and Beaufort Castle" in South Lebanon.[105]

The narrator is further ostracised for his privileged status after the *Bey* names him as his biological son. In London at the Ealing *Husseinya*, a communal hall Shi'a Muslims congregate in and where the narrator eventually resides before his mission, he finds his room and belongings vandalised by the other male residents whose "families had suffered under the beys".[106] Initially, before joining the brotherhood, the narrator attempts to placate his feelings of guilt and to substitute the painful nostalgia he feels for his previously peaceful home city by becoming an expert in the "discipline of forgetting".[107] In this pre-religious stage, he uses women, sex and drugs as a way to suppress his remorse and nostalgia. However his "brief and barren affairs" with several society girls in London and Madrid do not appease the narrator for long: "I held up a mirror to their frivolous vanities, but their illusions were too shallow for a man to drown in."[108] As a result the narrator notes a growing sense of self-disgust and becomes absorbed within the structure of the Muslim brotherhood.

His assimilation within this group introduces readers to the second way that the novel explores redemption, specifically through the suicide mission the narrator undertakes against a renegade writer in London. By targeting this writer the narrator chooses to die in the name of protecting Islam and, in that respect, elects to become a martyr. According to Abul Ezzati, the concept of martyrdom (*shahada*) in Islam can only be understood within the context of the Islamic principle *jihad*, or Holy War.[109] Mentioned in both the Qur'an and the *hadith* (the sayings of the Prophet), the principle of *jihad* is seen as a collective duty of all Muslims and represents the sixth pillar of Islam. Maher Jarrar, in his article on Arabic literary representations of Holy War, suggests that Muslim scholars have categorised *jihad* in two forms – smaller and greater. The first "takes the form of war" while the latter involves "the struggling with oneself against oneself and one's sins".[110]

The novel depicts the narrator's acceptance of *jihad* as if it were "written", even suggesting that his "own conversion has been the only child of fate".[111] In his youth the narrator constantly questions Ali about the "crimes of the old beys" but is told that all will be revealed "on the appointed day".[112] After his conversion he is informed for a second time, in this instance by Musa al-Tango, how "it was written that the last of the beys [i.e. the narrator] would redeem the crimes of all his forefathers".[113] It is true, as Syrine Hout argues, that the narrator's conversion is a response "to what he now perceives to be his call of duty" but this is not, as she goes on to suggest, aimed at rescuing his "suffering nation".[114] If the narrator was motivated by a sense of national duty why, then, assassinate a writer who lives, as Hout notes, "thousands of kilometres from Lebanon"?[115] For Hout the answer lies in the narrator's newly-found allegiance to Ali and the religious discourse Ali represents. In order to present a complete analysis of the narrator's need to redeem himself through a specific Islamic theology, I suggest that it is not the narrator's sense of duty to his ailing nation that drives him toward *jihad*, nor a result of sense of loyalty to Ali. The expected response in both these instances would be for the narrator to undertake his mission inside Lebanon, perhaps by participating in the war Hezbollah maintained with Israel well after civil hostilities ceased in Lebanon. This would represent an example of smaller *jihad* but would not absolve the narrator entirely for his immoral, drug-riddled and sexually promiscuous life. Rather, the narrator's target of the writer, thought to be Salman Rushdie, is an example of greater *jihad*, a struggle against the self.

In a divine vision, the now deceased Ali reveals to the narrator the location of Rushdie's residential dwelling:

By the sign of the pebbles, and the sign of the fallen trees, he [Ali] had shown this house of the writer to be a cursed and unclean house [. . .] In this house the writer had mocked the customs of his fathers, and aped the manners of his conquerors, and betrayed the religion of the Prophet, and forgotten the tongue of his people. The fruit of the groves and orchards of his fathers was lost in the sweet vapours of his pipe, and the labours of the fellahin and aghas on the lands of his forefathers spent in forgotten nights of pleasure, and among his company of flatterers and revellers he was reckoned the sleekest pig in the sty, and when his lands were wasted he had lived from the coining of base jests and by making an entertainment of the sufferings and foibles of his people, and as his people were hunted down like rats and the world turned its back he had hidden himself in the study of idols and painted illusions, and when his groves and orchards were felled by his enemies he had abandoned himself to the kayf [bliss] [. . .] of his pipe, and as his city burnt he lost each night in dancing and his days in idle reveries.[116]

While suggesting that these are the sins of the writer, the narrator shifts to describe his own immoral acts. For example, in the above passage he registers his guilt toward the *fellahin* who worked the land of his forefathers while he revelled in the vapours of the pipe. During his time in Madrid in 1982, working in a gallery at the height of the war, he looks away from the newspapers that report the atrocities taking place in Beirut and Lebanon, preferring to immerse himself in "painted illusions". Rather than defend his city as it burned, he spent his nights dancing and his days in "idle reveries". The narrator's identification of his own immoral acts with those of the blasphemer Rushdie illustrate that his final act of redemption, his suicide mission, reflects a commitment to greater *jihad* which will reconcile his guilt and personal transgressions.

The narrator's attack on Rushdie constitutes the final scene of the novel and moves the narrative from the penultimate scene in South Lebanon to London. Despite closing the narrative within an urban environment in England, the significance of Beirut — that "unreal city" that is the subject of Hanania's text — is hardly diminished. On the contrary, the retreat to England returns to what the novel's London-based opening establishes, which is the important intertextual relationship between Eliot's London, as depicted in his *Waste Land* poem, and Hanania's Beirut. Both Eliot and Hanania write in a post-war milieu where the cities they depict are severely decimated. In addition to this war connection, Hanania's use of London to frame his narration of the Lebanese civil war recalls the important theme of alienation that Eliot explores in his poem. As Long suggests, *The Waste Land* has not only been "adopted as English Modernism's definitive report on the city", it also casts a negative verdict regarding city-life, one that is characterised by inhumane conditions and social isolation.[117]

Conclusion

Unreal City's depiction of the urban experience is reflected in the earliest sociological work that deals with the urban environment. Scholars like Weber and Simmel have demonstrated close connections between urban experience and alienation. Cities are presented as cold and deeply impersonal spaces by these early German researchers precisely because of their function as a market centre. Hanania's novel echoes these sentiments, illustrating how the development of a distorted capitalist market in wartime Beirut underscores the narrator's alienation. The text, through the narrator's "testimony", registers a relentless interest in Beirut's over-determined capitalism. This is especially true in the final period of the narrator's life when he becomes a member of the *Jihad al-Binaa* movement. The novel's concentration on the particular work of *Jihad al-Binaa*, which stresses the composition of vital infrastructure in order to improve the daily conditions of Lebanon's more impoverished citizens, posits a subtle yet powerful critique of another post-war reconstruction project driven by Solidere. For Solidere, the reconstruction of post-war Beirut is geared towards commercial and financial interests, not social infrastructure. In that regard, Hanania's *Unreal City* offers a reading of the cityscape that reflects on such economic issues and how the capitalist market, distorted by the war, further destroys the city and its inhabitants. Rather than emancipate the individual, the Beirut of Hanania's novel alienates and destroys the individual.

The alienating tendency of the urban environment, particularly one that is marked by violence and civil unrest, is also a feature of Rawi Hage's *De Niro's Game*. It is the protagonist, Bassam Al-Abyad, who experiences a heightened sense of estrangement and isolation within his home city. When his mother is killed during intense fighting, Bassam is left in East Beirut devoid of family. The only relationship that closely resembles that of a familial connection is with George Al-Faransawi (George the Frenchman), his childhood companion and a brother of sorts. Even this relationship is strained, however, when the two friends select divergent paths in order to negotiate their survival in the war-torn city – George, who joins the local militia, prefers to remain while Bassam, who avoids incorporation into the militia, registers an unrelenting desire to leave. Through the two friends' contrasting choices the novel both depicts and undermines the undeniable Christian milieu of East Beirut. In that regard, Hage's *De Niro's Game*, like Hanania's *Unreal City*, is just as concerned with urban culture, only this time the emphasis is on the role of the metropolis' human inhabitants in framing or resisting that culture.

CHAPTER 3

UNDERMINING THE CHRISTIAN CITY IN RAWI HAGE'S *DE NIRO'S GAME*

As a "slush pile discovery at House of Anansi Press" Hage's debut novel was certainly an unlikely contender for the lucrative International IMPAC Dublin Literary Award.[1] Yet despite being rejected by various publishers and only just rescued from the dustbins at Anansi, Hage went on to win the Dublin-based prize. Chosen by a panel of eight international judges from a list of more than 100 nominated novels, part of its wide-ranging appeal, according to judge Eibhlín Evans, is its "eloquent, forthright and at times beautifully written" style.[2] For the panel of experts, Hage's first novel rang "with insight and authenticity" especially as it demonstrates how "war can envelope lives [...] where there are no winners, just degrees of survival".[3] The struggle to survive the day-to-day ravages of civil war Beirut certainly preoccupies the city's predominately Christian residents of this novel. Characters are forced to endure many hardships, from the absence of water, food and electricity to the random loss of loved ones during indiscriminate air raids. Hage's protagonist scatters throughout his first-person narration many references regarding the adversity that grips the city. Residents are compelled to wait in "long lines for bread", are at the mercy of the city's power supply "because in Beirut [...] the electricity came and went as it pleased" and, like Bassam's mother who plunges "her entire upper body [...] into the [neighbour's water] metal tank" with a bucket in hand, are forced to steal water when the pipes run dry for countless days.[4]

Such hardships produced by the war are the focus of various reviews of Hage's book. As the above quotation from the IMPAC judge reveals, part of the panel's decision to award Hage the prize stems from his representation of the general senselessness of war. Indeed, at the novel's culmination there are no victors, only ample evidence of suffering, torture and death. This is why Daniel Campi writes that "*De Niro's Game* is a denunciation of a world gone mad on the drug of violence".[5] Campi grounds the text within a broader discussion of war by summarising its story as one "that could have taken place in any of those savage, out-of-control parts of the world, from Baghdad to Darfur".[6] Likewise Syrine Hout, despite emphasising the impact of the civil war in terms of the distorted masculinity it produced and the militarism it encouraged among male Lebanese youth, maintains that the text's representation of violence is one that has global reach. She argues that this universal quality is evident in the book's title – *De Niro's Game* – which not only references George's *nom de guerre* of De Niro but also establishes the book's connection to Robert De Niro and the 1978 film he stared in called *The Deer Hunter*. This film, which tracks the friendship of two America soldiers during the Vietnam war, was popular when it was screened in Lebanon during the civil war era. Hage's selection of "*De Niro's Game*" was, as Hout's discussions with the author reveal, a deliberate one because he wanted a title that was not "directly referential to Arabic culture".[7] This initiates what Najat Rahman describes as Hage's mediation of the Lebanese civil war through the "representation of *other* wars".[8]

Reading these several assessments of the novel, it would be logical to conclude that *De Niro's Game* simply provides a negative commentary on the subject of war, and given the comparisons to other war-riven places like Vietnam, Baghdad and Darfur that its commentary is general and even universally applicable. Very few reviews take note of its East Beirut context and the prevalent

Christian identity within that quarter. Even the author reflects an assessment of his novel that is more universal than particular. He claims that *De Niro's Game* is not necessarily limited to a representation of war in East Beirut but "could have applied exactly to West Beirut" and even "to the whole space, to the whole country".[9] Nouri Gana is, it seems, the sole reviewer who attempts to couch this text within an East Beirut, Christian frame. Given the limited length of his book review, he skirts around the issue's edges and only concedes that the novel is "Disturbingly confessional" and its perspective "particular[ly] [...] Christian".[10] Yet this only superficially engages with the "disturbingly" sectarian aspects of the novel and what insights and limitations its Christian perspective allows for. On the whole, Gana's review can be assimilated into the body of material that emphasises the novel's location in the broader discourse of war and survival.

Part of the reason why the several reviewers of Hage's novel underestimate the specificity and significance of the urban setting is because of the strong presence of the two male characters, Bassam and George, and their increasingly divergent positions regarding the war and the city. According to Salah Hassan, these two characters are central to the narrative because "Hage's representation of the civil war [...] negotiates the destruction of the Lebanese state through figures of the unstated".[11] It is these male characters that constitute Hassan's "unstated" figures because they challenge the political authority of the state through their thuggish behaviour. Bassam attests to his and George's violence in the first chapter during a rampage through the city on a motorcycle: "War is for thugs [...] like us, with guns under our bellies, and stolen gas in our tanks."[12] Despite their unethical and bullying behaviour, readers are nonetheless drawn into the story because, as Dina Georgis notes, "Hage's novel evokes empathy" for Bassam and George and "in doing so restores their humanity".[13] In addition to this, what becomes of George and his deepening involvement in the militia also engages the reader's curiosity. While he last appears in the narrative at the end of the novel's second section, completely drug-addled and displaying varying degrees of angst over his participation in a brutal massacre, it is not until the final pages of the novel that his fate and demise are fully revealed. In various assessments of the novel, the story of Bassam and George and how their relationship can survive a war that increasingly pulls them in differing directions is given primary importance. In doing this reviewers, perhaps unwittingly, relegate the setting of East Beirut as a mere stage for the novel's events.

Despite wanting to argue in favour of a place-based reading of *De Niro's Game*, the attention that is paid to the novel's characters is not unjustified. Bassam and George, their decisions and actions in the city, drive the plot of the novel. These characters cannot be reduced or marginalised as secondary to the significance of the environment they inhabit. One way to negotiate the importance of the urban space while maintaining the dominance of the role played by the characters is to recognise that it is through and because of these characters that a greater appreciation of East Beirut's complex culture can be realised. Robert Park, as previously noted, is an advocate of making sense of urban spaces through their human inhabitants. He argues that the city is not simply comprised of its physical structure, its buildings and streets for example, but is also a "structure [that] has its basis [. . .] in human nature, of which it is an expression".[14] To that end, the city is "involved in the vital process of the people who compose it" rather than a mere "artificial construction" devoid of any humanistic role. Initially Park concedes that "We are mainly indebted to writers of fiction for our more intimate knowledge of contemporary urban life", but he is also quick to note that "the life of our cities demands more searching and disinterested study than even Émile Zola has given us in his 'experimental' novels".[15] A social scientist by training, Park's bias for empirical research is not unexpected. Given that his field of enquiry is set by the parametres of 1920s and 1930s American urban life rather than a city subjected to war, he is at some liberty to advise students, as he did in 1927, to participate in "first hand observation" of urban spaces by sitting "in the lounges of luxury hotels and on the doorsteps of the flophouses [. . .] In short go and get the seat of your pants dirty in real research".[16]

While this suggestion from Park is an important one for scholars who wish to analyse the role of the "human inhabitant" in shaping the city's "state of mind" and its "customs and traditions", getting one's "pants dirty in *real* research" may not be entirely achievable for the social scientist or urban planner who is trying to reconstruct the trauma and devastation of wartime Beirut in the post-war period. Contemporary Beirut may have entered a much more peaceful era since the violence of the 1980s, but it remains a society deeply scarred by war. This lack of resolution is most certainly due to the collective amnesia that has engulfed Lebanese society since the war's end and has manifested itself in official state policies such as the amnesty decree and the inability of the state to produce an official history curriculum that includes the events of the civil war. Such amnesia is not limited to the realms of politics and education; it is also evident in Beirut's reconstruction plans. In fact Hashim Sarkis, a professor of urban architecture, states: "When it comes to architecture and urban planning, very little has been built or preserved to remind the Beirutis that a war has taken place on their streets."[17]

Maronites and Amnesia

The Maronite Christians, who are the subject of Hage's novel, have also failed to come to terms with their own recent history of violence, deliberately choosing, like remaining Lebanese, "amnesia [...] as a path out of the war".[18] One way to understand amnesia is to equate it with forgetting, but in reference to the Maronite Lebanese experience that idea does not adequately capture how Maronite Christians have also chosen to selectively remember certain aspects of the war. In that sense amnesia can also be thought of as a disturbance of memory. Samir Khalaf, in his work on the forging of identities within the contested space of post-war Beirut, reflects this ambiguous definition of amnesia. He argues that what exists in contemporary Beirut is a dual approach to the war where confessional groups attempt to "obliterate, mystify, and distance [themselves] from fearsome recollections of an ugly and unfinished war" while also preserving or commemorating them.[19] First, in their efforts to "preserve", the Maronite community is engaged in selectively commemorating aspects of the war by, for example, focusing on specific political leaders who were killed during that era. In a war as protracted as the Lebanese one, there are many slain Maronite *zuama* (political leaders) who continue to be honoured. However, for the supporters of two important Christian parties, the Phalange and the closely-affiliated Lebanese Forces (LF), it is the September 1982 assassination of the LF leader, Bashir Gemayel, that strikes a particular cord among a large portion of Maronites. On the streets of the eastern side of the city posters of Gemayel are still displayed and his death is commemorated annually, on 14 September, with public demonstrations and an official church service.[20] Second, where Khalaf talks about amnesia as a method of mystification and obliteration, the massacre of approximately 3,000 Palestinian refugees, from 16 to 18 September 1982, by LF and Phalangist soldiers as retribution for the assassination of Gemayel, has not been officially acknowledged by any of the contemporary Maronite leaders.[21] Despite the fact that the actual person responsible for the fatal bombing of Gemayel was not a militant Palestinian or Muslim – he was a Maronite and member of the Syrian Socialist Nationalist Party – no admission of guilt from the LF or Phalange has surfaced. In the 30 years that have elapsed since those violent acts at Sabra and Shatila, no official apology has been issued by Christian leaders and they have maintained their preference for repression and forgetting.[22]

This project to repress and even erase the carnage of Sabra and Shatila began in the immediate aftermath of the attacks. Bayan al-Hout, in her book *Sabra and Shatila: September 1982*, maintains that directly after the massacres when Bashir Gemayel's brother, Amin, assumed the presidency, official investigations into the conduct of the militiamen were obstructed by the state.[23] Amin Gemayel, drawn from the Phalange Party, had a vested interested in silencing critical voices and protecting the soldiers involved. Since then, well into the post-war era, no Maronite leaders involved in the massacres, figures like Samir Geagea or Elie Hobeika, have been brought to justice. In fact they have been incorporated into the post-war political system giving them, as Jim Quilty argues, "postwar legitimacy without accountability".[24] Geagea, after a decade in prison, has emerged as the triumphant leader and hero of the LF and Hobeika, accused by the

Israeli state in 1983 of leading the massacres, later became minister for the displaced in the 1990s.[25] Both of these men and the communities they represent have been protected by the state's amnesty on war crimes and, consequently, have not been forced to reassess their actions during the war. It is this that allows the Maronites to safely maintain a sense of righteousness, rather than remorse, and repress, rather than acknowledge, their role in the violence of the past.[26]

If the community and its leaders are not interested in resurrecting these confronting memories, preferring ignorance and repression, the city has also failed to force them to confront their past. As Hashim Sarkis mentions, very little has been done in the metropolis, in terms of its reconstruction project, to remind Beirut society that a brutal civil war took place within the city.[27] Solidere's restoration project focuses on Beirut's economic prosperity and is geared towards the creation of a commercial city-centre. It is certainly not interested in erecting reminders that showcase its recent war history. What Solidere hopes to create in Beirut is, as its motto states, an "Ancient City of the Future". By focusing, as Miriam Cooke notes, on "the regional [and ancient] past (Phoenician and Greek)" and the "new Beirut['s] global future", Solidere's motto succinctly captures how the project is actively engaged in erasing "the local past (the war)" from the urban landscape.[28] Given this, it is not surprising that there are so few state-sponsored public works, such as monuments or statues, that honour the many Palestinian civilians who perished in Lebanon, such as those who died in Tal el-Zaatar in 1976, in Sabra and Shatila in 1982, the War of the Camps in 1983, or the war in the Ain al-Helwi camp in 2007.[29] What this signifies for an architect and urban planner like Sarkis are the limitations of his profession. In his article "Beirut, the Novel", Sarkis indicates that he has lost a significant amount of faith in the capacity of urban architecture to find appropriate ways to commemorate or memorialise the war. As a remedy, Sarkis resorts to post-war literature and argues that authors like Rabih Alameddine and Elias Khoury are responsible for tapping "into the rich, horrific imagery of the war and [have] effectively salvaged this lengthy and exhaustive trauma in Lebanon's recent history from the looming amnesia of the post-war period".[30] In effect

Sarkis centralises literature, narrative and authors as a way to overcome what urban commentators cannot recover in the midst of the Beirut's efforts to obliterate, mystify and forget. In doing so, Sarkis restores scholarly "indebtedness" to "writers of fiction", thereby questioning Park's earlier claims that assessments of "contemporary urban life" require more "searching and disinterested" sociological approaches.

While Sarkis does not mention Rawi Hage specifically, his assessment of the post-war Beirut novel as being involved in a pro-active recovery of the nature of the city is applicable to *De Niro's Game*. Hage achieves this recovery by closely exploring the role of the city's inhabitants, namely Bassam and George, in shaping East Beirut's urban culture. In that respect Hage unwittingly preserves the importance of Park's approach to urban analysis where city culture is not only determined by its physical structure or its economic orientation but also by its inhabitants. This is not to suggest, however, that the two male protagonists should be conflated with "real-life" urban dwellers. For example, it is thought that *De Niro's Game* provides a semi-autobiographical account of Hage's life in East Beirut that correlates with the experiences of the character Bassam.[31] As the author himself asserts, Bassam's journey is not parallel to his own even if the inspiration for the novel is drawn from his time in the war-torn city.[32] It would be more accurate to think of *De Niro's Game* as a fictive reconstruction of a city that is spatially divided by war and where the male protagonists allow Hage to explore and destabilise the insular Maronite disposition that dominates East Beirut. As George conforms to the militant Christian culture of the place, he symbolises what Edward Said has referred to as the "potentate [. . .] who must guard only one place and defend its frontiers".[33] Nowhere is this desire to defend the frontiers of the Maronite sector more acutely revealed than in George's recruitment by the Christian militia. As a potentate, then, George is positioned in this narrative to depict the various aspects that constitute Maronite culture. These aspects include the fear and hatred of the adjacent Muslims, not only in West Beirut but throughout the whole Muslim world, the belief that Lebanon is a Christian territory and the cultural contention that Maronites are not Arab. Bassam, however, attempts to transcend the orthodoxy that surrounds him. While he is by no means the polar opposite to George, he nonetheless registers a capacity to undertake what Said describes as the role of the "traveller", that is to maintain some kind of critical facility regarding all forms of power. Not only does Bassam "traverse territory" when he leaves Beirut for Paris, he also "abandons the fixed position" of East Beirut's religious culture by overtly questioning George's dogmatic loyalty to it.[34] It is this that leads Syrine Hout to describe the novel as possessing a "secularist" and "atheistic" ethos, arguing that its commitment to secularity "is expressed [...] through Bassam's 'contested' identity".[35] Unlike George, who demonstrates his Maronite Catholicism by becoming a member of a Christian militia, Bassam is an atheist who openly declares "God is dead".[36] Despite all of George's efforts to recruit him, Bassam not only refuses to join the militia but also exposes it as a corrupt and thug-riddled organisation.

Bassam's unfavourable appraisal of the Christian army is not the only way that the novel stages its resistance to the city's religiosity. While a more detailed discussion of militia violence follows, it is important to note here that Bassam's assessment of the army is couched within the text's broadly irreverent view of the dominance of Maronite Christianity within East Beirut society. Hage deploys two interrelated literary devices to advance what Nouri Gana refers to as the novel's "particular but unconsenting Christian perspective".[37] First, there is Bassam's first person narration which guides the reader through his vision of the city. At the start of the novel the intensity of the war is introduced in the first clause of opening sentence, "Ten thousand bombs had landed", only to be quickly followed by Bassam's alarmingly relaxed attitude to the destruction: "and I [Bassam] was waiting for George".[38] Displaying none of the panic that one would expect in such a life-threatening scenario, Bassam maintains his detachment from the violence in a subsequent paragraph as he looks out of his apartment window and describes the external setting. Rather than focus on the effects of the destruction, he points to the "Christian cats [who] walked the narrow streets nonchalantly, never crossing themselves or kneeling for black-dressed priests".[39] Bassam's remark reveals the degree to which Beirut is obsessed by religion – even its stray cats are ascribed membership to the dominant faith – but it also makes apparent the protagonist's criticism of that obsession. By referring to the cats as "Christian" and applying to them the human and very Christian-like attributes of kneeling and crossing themselves, Bassam signals how these acts are considered customary among the city's residents. The cats' disinterest and daring refusal of these customs ridicules East Beirut's residents for their religiously supplicant behaviour.

The use of a window to literally frame Bassam's observations provides an early clue to the second and much more subversive way the text undermines East Beirut's Christianity. Apart from exposing Bassam's first-person narration, this view from the window also reveals how the text positions or focalises the reader to adopt a highly critical lens when attempting to make sense of East Beirut. As readers are led by the protagonist and are privy to his inner thoughts, the kind of focalisation found in *De Niro's Game* is what Gérand Genette has referred to as internal focalisation. Of the three types of internal focalisation Genette provides, the one he describes as the *"fixed –* canonical example"* best applies to *De Niro's Game* because it implies that everything passes through one character.[40] To that end, readers are positioned to adopt a view of the city and its religious culture that approximates rather than rejects Bassam's. Even in instances when other characters engage in dialogue with the protagonist, where their alternate points of view are registered, it is almost impossible to find these characters' positions convincing. This is particularly the case in the several instances where George tries to assure Bassam that the militia is conducting a just campaign against the Muslims in West Beirut. The effect of the text's internal focalisation, however, is that while it seems permissible to sympathise with George as an individual, an orphaned and confused youth attracted to the power of the militia, it is impossible to validate his dogmatic Maronite Christian political views.

This is explicitly rendered when George explains to Bassam his reasons for joining the militia. George claims that the army's local commander, Abou-Nahra, has requested that he leave "for Israel [...] for some training. The forces are establishing relations with the Jews down south".[41] When Bassam urges George not to go, explaining that it would be a mistake to do so, George defensively insists he must and suggests that to do so is noble rather than mistaken: "No, Bassam, we are alone in this war, and our people [the Christians] are being massacred every day [...] We will unite with the devil to save our land. How are we to make the Syrians and Palestinians leave?"[42] In George's representation, the threat to the Lebanese Christians from their enemies is intense – not only are they compelled to guard themselves from the Muslims in West Beirut, but also Palestinians and Syrians who are allied with Lebanon's Muslims. Bassam is not at all persuaded by this argument and tells George "I am fleeing and leaving this land to its devils". When George accuses Bassam of harbouring a nihilistic attitude ("You [Bassam] believe in nothing") and deserting the Christians, Bassam instantly refutes George's logic. He reminds him that neither of them are in a position to claim faith in or commitment to a greater cause: "Thieves and thugs like us [...] since when have we ever believed in anything?"[43] In effect, Bassam exposes his and George's violence and lawlessness as criminal activity implying, through his use of the comparative phrase "like us", that there are other thugs in East Beirut. Those others include the militiamen under Abou-Nahra's command who claim, as George does, to be fighting for a noble cause. At this stage in the narrative the implications of Bassam's comments are not accessible to the reader simply because the degree of corruption within the militia has not been completely revealed. Consequently, the reader is subtly positioned to anticipate that George and his militia colleagues are not honest or gallant fighters virtuously driven to protect their community and territory, but corrupt thugs who terrorise the urban space.

While this exchange between Bassam and George primes the reader to adopt a negative view of the militia, another scene cautions the reader about Bassam's sceptical views towards religion. As already noted in the reference to the Christian cats, not only is East Beirut decimated by war it is also obsessively dominated by religion. In a later scene religion is further scrutinised when it is claimed that a "young girl [. . .] saw the Virgin Mary hovering in the sky. She [the Virgin] opened her robe and shielded us all from the Muslims' falling bombs. The girl's hands are secreting holy oil."[44] Bassam finds a crowd of faithful believers, namely "old ladies dressed in black beating their saggy chests", gathered at his local church.[45] Those assembled are fighting against one another for a sample of the holy oil, all the while uttering "low hymns [. . .] hysterical cries [. . .] [and] superstitious shrieks".[46] The church's frenzied atmosphere is only further compounded when Bassam reaches the altar and looks into the young girl's face. Rather than note her serene demeanour after having witnessed the apparition of the Virgin, all he notices are "her eyes [that] shone with madness and evasion [. . .] and [that] she looked hazy and eerie".[47] By focusing on the madness that pervades the church, Bassam signals that he is not seduced by the wonder of the miracle. His introspective questioning is soon revealed as overt scepticism when he grabs hold of a "woman who had touched the girls hands [. . .] [and holds] her fingers to smell".[48] The text's constant reminders of the miracle's implausibility compels the reader to adopt Bassam's critical stance. The miracle scene, then, positions the reader to harbour scepticism towards the city's religiosity.

Beyond these specific examples, the novel's capacity to influence the reader in this manner has broader implications. Not only does it undermine George's advocacy of the Christian cause, it also obstructs the reader's capacity to perceive, or fully grasp, just what it is that George is so keen to defend. In fact much of the individual experience and history that underpins George's, and other militiamen characters like Abou-Nahra's, distorted views regarding Muslims, Arabs, Lebanese and Maronite self-identity are absent from the novel. Why is it, for example, that the Syrians and the Palestinians need to be made to leave Lebanon so urgently? What is it about Israeli-Jews that is attractive to the Christians? On what grounds does George refer to the land as "our land", thereby claiming ownership of it for the Christians? These questions are not adequately addressed in the novel but their answers provide insights into the complex Maronite aesthetic that developed well before the civil war started. It is therefore necessary to contextualise the particular 1980s Maronite view and culture that is depicted in the novel within the longer history of the Maronite community.

Maronite Culture

One of the most important aspects of Maronite culture has been the continual insistence of their ethnic and cultural uniqueness. This distinctiveness was incorporated into the 1943 independence agreement, known as *al Mithaq al Watani* or the National Pact, which ended France's mandate over Lebanon. The Pact, an agreement between key Muslim and Maronite political elites, not only secured the Maronites the pre-eminent post of president, but it also attempted to solve the sensitive question of the state's post-independence national character; or, more specifically, to resolve the question of Lebanon's "Arabness". For the Maronites "the Arab issue" was central because this Christian community had sought to define themselves as culturally distinct through a refutation of Arab and Islamic heritage. This was clearly the case in the early 1940s when the Muslim and Christian political representatives met to discuss what would constitute the Lebanese republic's cultural orientation. Contrary to the Muslim view, which stressed Lebanon's geographic location and linguistic ties in the Arab world, the Maronites felt they had a varied ancestry that made it independent of Arab roots. The Pact was an attempt to balance these two conflicting nationalisms, but the negotiating parties failed to achieve little more than a weak compromise. It was decided that Lebanon would be neither Eastern nor Western in orientation but retain an "Arab face" and foster cultural and economic links with the Western world.[49]

Between 1943 and 1975 certain Maronite leaders, focusing on the Pact's description of Lebanon's "Arab face", strongly advocated a "process of dissociating [Lebanon] from the Arab East and adhering to the West".[50] If, for these Maronites, Lebanon merely possessed an Arab exterior, its heart or essence was certainly not Arab. The urgency of this latter point was clearly articulated in November 1975 by the members of the Maronite League and clergy in a memorandum to parliament: "Maronitism antedates the Arab conquest of Syria and Lebanon and [...] [the] Arabism [of Lebanon] is only a *historical accident*."[51] The idea that Lebanon's Arab culture, reflected in its use of the Arabic language and its proximity to the remainder of the Arab world, can be dismissed on the grounds that the Arab conquest in 634 AD was a misfortune of history forms the basis around which Maronites are able to refute all forms of connections with Arab and Islamic culture. To that end, it is even argued by Matti Moosa that the Arabic language was imposed on the Maronite community whose members, prior to the Umayyad and Abbasid conquest of Lebanon in the eighth century, probably communicated in Syriac-Aramaic.[52]

Entangled within the issue of the Maronites' non-Arab status is the perception that Muslims, particularly since the Arab conquest, are a threat to their existence. Assessing the history of Christian–Muslim interaction, Ghassan Hage argues that "regardless of what else the conflicts between Maronites and Muslims in the last four or five centuries have been about, there is no doubt that a large majority of Maronites have experienced those conflicts as a struggle for their very survival".[53] Walid Phares, a Lebanese-American professor of politics and author of several texts on the Maronites and Christians in the Middle East, uncritically subscribes to the idea that Maronites have long been subject to attack. He argues that the Maronites have always faced an insecure existence due to Islamic aggression and provides historical "evidence" to prove that the civil war did not really start in 1975 but actually "began thirteen centuries ago". The Christian–Muslim confrontations

> began with the Arab conquest and continued with the Umayyads and the Abbasids and the Mamlouks and the Ottomans and the Iqta' and evolved with the Arab Nationalists and the Nasserites, until it reached the Palestinians. All of these represented in the Christians' eyes an expansionary intention which aimed at eradicating their free and independent and sovereign presence.[54]

Phares' work not only classifies the Muslims as a threat to Christians since the Arab conquest but it also, in the Maronite imagination at least, highlights that all Muslims, across geographical and temporal space, are motivated by the marginalisation and eradication of the Christians.[55]

This fear of marginalisation forms part of the long-standing Maronite insistence that Lebanon must exist as a Christian safe haven. Maronite yearning for a sustained and autonomous existence is not a contemporary desire that was forged after Lebanon was founded by the French in the 1920s or achieved independence two decades later, but one that "can be documented as far back as the fifteenth century".[56] In that regard, as Salibi explains, Maronite communal subjectivity, defined in part by its besieged status, actually gave shape to the idea of "Lebanon" as a Christian territory: "Lebanon already existed in the Maronite imagination before it became a political reality."[57] This position regarding Lebanese territory as exclusively Christian and as a place where Christians can practise their faith and culture freely, was best expressed during the civil war by Bashir Gemayel:

> we want to stay in this East so that our churches' bells can keep ringing when we want them to [...] We want to be able to baptise as we please; we want to be able to practise our traditions and rites, our faith and our convictions, as we please.[58]

According to Gemayel, the capacity for Christians to practise their rites and faith on their own terms is contingent upon the existence of Lebanon. This is even more clearly asserted when Gemayel says that "maybe if we [Maronites] were in Egypt or in Syria, we wouldn't have the right to rebuild or restore any Church that might be falling into ruins".[59] Referring to a plundered church in the Christian town of Damour, Gemayel argues that despite the desecration of this holy site by Palestinian militants, the Lebanese Christians will be able to restore it precisely because they are in Lebanon rather than in Egypt or Syria where Christian minorities are seen to have much less autonomy.

What I have outlined above are certain historically-determined features that underpin Maronite identity and culture. These features include claims that Lebanon is a Christian territory, that Lebanon's Christians face an existential threat from the surrounding Muslim countries, and that Maronites are not Arabs. In *De Niro's Game* it is through George and his fellow militiamen that readers are exposed to these features and understand that the militia's role in the city is to guard the frontiers of the East Beirut Christian enclave. This mode of guarding, however, does not only entail the militaristic protection of the city's borders but also involves the language that the militiamen deploy as part of a discursive defence strategy. An exchange between two of Bassam's colleagues, Said and Chahine, reflects this clearly. Chahine, closely affiliated with the militia, begins by expressing his discomfort with his mistreatment of Arab Muslim labourers. When one worker is left to die in freezing conditions over night, Chahine concludes that he can no longer exploit these men. He observes the deceased's grief-stricken co-workers and decides that these Muslims have, like the Maronites, "a *ruh* (spirit), as well".[60] Said, however, not satisfied with Chahine's humanisation of the Muslims, aggressively asks his colleague "I want to see how they will treat you in Egypt if you went to work there. You are a Christian. Look at the Copt and other Christians. How are they treated in these Muslim countries?"[61] By raising this question Said not only reminds Chahine of the ill-treatment Christians are supposedly experiencing in Arab states; he also, very much like Gemayel, implies that Lebanon must exist as a necessary safe haven for Christians. What both Said and Gemayel's words advocate is a sense that without Lebanon the Maronites would not enjoy a free existence with the right to practise their faith openly and to publically erect their religious symbols. In this scene Hage uses dialogue to build the defensive position of the Maronites.

Another instance where the register of dialogue frames the defensive position of the Maronites relates to the overwhelming threat of the surrounding Muslims. This is apparent in a conversation between George and Bassam where the former discusses his recent experiences on the front line. George begins his rendition of these events by referring to the enemies he encounters not simply as

Muslims from West Beirut, or other Arab Muslims from surrounding states, but by suggesting that a Muslim "nation" has mobilised against the Christians. He tells Bassam that "There are fucking black Somalis fighting with those Palestinians [...] The whole *ummah* is against us."[62] The Arabic word *ummah* does not necessarily mean "nation" and can also be understood as "community". Certainly within Islam it generally signifies the latter, most evident in the Quranic use of the phrase *ummah wahida*, which connotes "one community" or a community that is united through a common religious creed. The glossary in *De Niro's Game*, however, settles any ambiguity that George's use of the term may have and insists upon a definition that classifies *ummah* as nation.[63] In doing this Hage highlights how the Muslims are perceived, within George's Maronite view, as an organised group united not simply by their common faith but by a sense of nationalist and expansionist solidarity. George intensifies his claims against this united Muslim front when he tells Bassam how, on a secret ten-day mission, he was confronted by a range of enemies: "They are coming from all over the world to fight us, Bassam, here in our land. Palestinians, Somalis and Syrians – everyone has a claim on this land."[64] As a Christian potentate who can champion only one dogmatic stance, it is not surprising that the several fighters George encounters on his training mission are registered as evidence of a united Islamic nation that is aiming to drive the Christians out of Lebanon.

Undermining the Maronite Perspective

Apart from the two examples examined above, the novel does not provide much more varied evidence or in-depth explanations of the Maronite community's insular disposition. Due to the dominance of Bassam's point of view, a position that is sympathetic to the Maronite cause is minimally and weakly represented. What is strongly presented, however, is the undermining of the Maronite Christian culture which characters like George advocate. Led by Bassam's first-person narration, Hage draws on other literary devices in order to cast doubt on various aspects of the Maronite position.

His construction of the Maronite "potentate" stance exercises language in a particular way so that the need to guard the Christian enclave is not only evident militarily but also in the text's discourse. Ironically, in his mode of deconstructing that position, Hage's language selection conveys the shortcomings of the Maronite view. When depicting the destruction of the city, for example, Hage demonstrates East Beirut's historically-grounded cultural diversity. An often-repeated mantra in Hage's novel is that of "ten thousand falling bombs" which rupture the city and open up spaces to reveal Beirut's rich heritage. For archaeologists and urban planners, Lebanon's war destroyed many ancient monuments but it also brought to the surface other hidden artefacts.[65] Similar to the effect of bombs and the historical layers they expose, Bassam's descriptive language gives expression to connections between various historical epochs. This is evident in the following passage where Bassam ventures "down the main streets [of East Beirut] where bombs fell" and notes that this now destroyed metropolis is also the same site "where ancient Greeks had danced, Romans had invaded, Persians had sharpened their swords, Mamlucks had stolen the villagers' food, crusaders had eaten human flesh, and Turks had enslaved my grandmother".[66] In the midst of the destroyed city, the protagonist's descriptions of it demonstrate the historical multiplicity of the Eastern sector. In effect, Hage's novel points to evidence that destabilises the assertion that Lebanon is the exclusive territory of the Maronites.

Beyond the capacity of descriptive language to destabilise the Maronite claims of Christian exclusivity, the novel's narration of violence exposes that the Christian militia is not fighting a noble war in the name of the Christian cause. There are two definitive violent events in *De Niro's Game*, one which involves Bassam's torture by Abou-Nahra's men, and another which depicts George's participation in the Sabra and Shatila massacres. In the first example Bassam is taken into the *Majalis*, the militia headquarters, and is accused of murdering Abou-Nahra's most important financier, Monsieur Laurent. Even though Bassam has no information regarding Laurent's death, Abou-Nahra and his most trusted protégé, Rambo, subject Bassam to hours of torture. In the few days that he spends in the underground *Majalis* he is deprived of food, denied sleep, constantly beaten and water-boarded. These horrific acts are not explicitly reported by the protagonist, nor is the degree of his suffering. This is evident in the following scene where Rambo attempts to extract information from Bassam by plunging him under water for extended periods:

> Fuck him, I thought, I will hold my breath and dive under the sea [...] I will stay there and watch the tourists passing in that cruise ship again. This time I will wear my best tuxedo and show those foreigners that I can swing, and wave my dancing stick in the air to those mambo tunes with a belly dancer on each side of my hips, with sexless angels who watch me with envy [...] with a few underground Playboy Bunnies with soft white cotton tails. Fuck him; I will sleep in a cabin with two beds and room service. Fuck that brute [...][67]

What Bassam's stream of consciousness records is not the pain or terror he is actually suffering but the capacity to escape and resist that terror by imagining an alternate discursive reality. Through his expression of resistance, imagining himself on a cruise ship in his best suit and sleeping in a spacious cabin, Bassam is able to distance himself from the brutality of his torturer. Phrases like "fuck him" and "fuck that brute" are a register of the protagonist's ability, however ineffective, to resist Rambo at a level removed from the reality of his torture. This form of resistance intensifies the horror of the militia's actions because, as Theodor Adorno explains in his essay "Commitment", to depict violence is to diminish some of the horror involved:

> [the] artistic representation of the sheer physical pain of people beaten to the ground by [for example] rifle-butts contains, however remotely, the power to elicit enjoyment out of it. The moral of this art, not to forget for a single instant, slithers into the abyss of its opposite.[68]

What Adorno advocates here is the need to find ways to represent the pain of violence without transforming that representation into some form of pleasurable obscenity. Bassam's scenes of torture maintain the intensity of the horror that the militia exercises precisely because the language distances itself from the pain and suffering of violence.

The brutality of the city's local army is heightened in the novel's second violent instalment, the massacres at Sabra and Shatila, despite the fact that in this example the actual torture that is committed against the Palestinians is fully narrated by George. George does not conceal the acts of carnage in the language of disassociation and, as a result, actually engages in what Adorno reprimands: the representation of acts of violence for enjoyment. George begins by explaining to Bassam how the militiamen, whom he likens to a pack of "Fifteen hundred lions", were intent on avenging the death of their leader, Al-Rayess, the novel's representative of Bashir Gemayel.[69] George laughs as he tells Bassam "We must have killed ten thousand of them".[70] As George's story escalates in its brutality, he struggles to record the quantity of the killings that took place at the camps. His sentences become clipped, broken and hurried – "People were shot at random. Entire families killed at dinner tables. Cadavers in their night-clothes, throats slit; axes used, hands separated from bodies, women cut in half."[71] There is no trace of mercy in his reconstruction of the massacre, even when he depicts the one woman he finds still alive "on the floor [of her home] surrounded by her dead daughters". He tauntingly asks her "You want to join your family, don't you?" and she replies, "You might as well finish what you started, my son". He proceeds to hit "her with the butt of my rifle, many times, many times, like this (and he [George] punched the air with his gun). Blood sprang from her head like a hose."[72]

What is not clear in George's seven-page rendition of the militia's actions is how he and the militia are serving the Christian community by killing so many unarmed refugees. Even though the army is told by an Israeli officer that "there were still a few armed pockets in the Palestinian camps" and Abou-Nahra orders his men to "purify the camps", not one person that George reports to have killed is anything other than a civilian.[73] If these men are not protecting the

Christians from the Palestinian, Arab and Muslim threat, what then are they so eager to kill for? According to reports from actual militiamen who participated in the 1982 camp massacres, the act of killing often elicited a form of erotic sensation. This is especially the case when the murders took place in full view of religious icons. One Maronite militiaman explains that during the massacres he "wore the crucifix [. . .] while butchering in a deliberate desecration of the cross, a transgression that gave me [. . .] an erotic thrill [. . .] Since participating in the [. . .] massacres [. . .] I am waiting for a human who would make me engage in a sexual relationship" with the same level of satisfaction.[74] In several instances in *De Niro's Game*, Bassam observes the marked presence of Christian icons around soldiers' necks and on their weapons. Abou-Nahra, for instance, always wore a "long thick chain around his neck [with] a collection of icons and crosses" and Joseph Chaiben, a Maronite soldier, held a "Kalashnikov [that] had the Virgin Mary on its wooden butt".[75]

Clearly, as Jalal Toufic explains, the "massacre [. . .] could not have been only a revengeful retaliation by Lebanese Maronite Christian militiamen for the assassination [. . .] of [. . .] Gemayel [. . .] but must have been [. . .] an orgy of *jouissance*" and "an erotization of horror".[76] In order to relive that *jouissance*, the militiamen must narrate and re-narrate the violence of the massacres. What this reveals is that the Maronite soldiers were not actually fighting to defend or protect the Christian cause in Lebanon but were actively engaged in desecrating it through their sexual prowess. By allowing George to narrate the brutality of the murders, thereby refusing "to forget [or conceal them] for a single instant", what Hage's most closely examined Christian solider exposes is the degree to which the militia organisation's actions violate the very Christianity they claim to protect.[77] To that end, Hage's novel actively undermines the Maronite disposition prevalent in 1980s East Beirut by portraying the threat to the Christians as stemming from their own internal degradation.

Another important way that *De Niro's Game* attempts to undermine the Christian view is through the novel's intertextual engagement with Albert Camus' *L'Étranger*, translated as *The Outsider* or *The Stranger*. Camus' seminal novel, published in 1942, was originally seen "as a statement about the absurdity of mortal life".[78] Camus thought of himself as a philosopher of the "absurd" which, according to English Showalter, Jr., is closely linked to an existentialist tradition engaged in exploring the "meaninglessness of existence".[79] The novel's protagonist, Meursault, a Frenchman in colonial Algeria, became the vehicle through which Camus was able to "formulate a way of living within the absurd".[80] This is why Meursault has been characterised as an "anti-hero [. . .] [who] has no faith in any cause",[81] as someone who "refuses to play the social game" by, for example, openly grieving at his mother's funeral and as not belonging to Catholic France because of his rejection of Christianity.[82] It is in Paris, having finally fled Beirut, that Bassam, now an illegal migrant and an "outsider", reads Camus' renowned novel. Certainly there are many characterological affinities between Camus and Hage's protagonists. Bassam, Gana suggests, "is a Meursault in reverse – an 'undocumented' Arab with a gun [. . .] ready [. . .] to kill a French man".[83] Both characters refuse to openly mourn the loss of their mothers (Bassam's mother dies when a bomb falls on her apartment) and both reject or question Christianity. However, to simply perceive Hage's incorporation of Camus as a way to underscore Bassam's alienation or outsider status in Paris would be to overlook the colonial context of L'Étranger.

In the first two decades of its reception, L'Étranger was critically lauded and Camus was seen, more so than any other European writer, to represent "the Western consciousness".[84] Camus' success rests on his creation of a fictional image of dwelling in the meaninglessness of life. In the first wave of criticism that dealt with the novel, very little attention was given to the representation of Arab characters and the text's Algerian setting. This is alarming because what lies at the centre of Camus' novel is the murder of a nameless Arab by Meursault. Meursault is subsequently arrested and tried in court. During the legal proceedings the prosecutors mount a case against him based not on evidence for his inexplicable homicide but on the fact that he did not grieve for his mother's death in a sufficiently acceptable manner. Consequently, the murdered Arab or the colonial Algerian setting of this "French" text are depicted as having next to no significance. What is even more subversive is that the novel does not openly argue that Arabs are inferior to Europeans. As Philip Thody points out, "the way in which the events of the story are presented" assumes that it is only "European concerns which are sufficiently important to deserve [. . .] detailed consideration".[85] Due to its intensely European focus, it took the passage of 20 years before any critic realised that Camus' book could be read in a "racialist" or "colonialist" manner. Henri Kréa and Pierre Nora were the first to put forward this idea in 1961, and since then other scholars like Conor Cruise O'Brien, Philip Thody and Edward Said have extended the colonial and post-colonial reading. For Said, Camus' novel is "not merely representative of so relatively a weightless thing as 'Western consciousness' but rather of Western *dominance* in the non-European world".[86]

France's involvement in Lebanon, while by no means identical to the Algerian experience, left its colonial imprint on the Maronite community. The European power was perceived as patron and ally of the Maronites against the surrounding Muslims and Arabs. Hage's intertextual incorporation of Camus' novel activates a colonialist reading, where France's imperial interference in Lebanon becomes apparent. Through Bassam's narration, *De Niro's Game* questions the Maronite affiliation with the French and exposes the relationship as highly imbalanced. This relationship, strengthened during the decline of the Ottoman Caliphate in the eighteenth century, saw the French "safeguard [. . .] the interests of the Maronite community and protect [Lebanon's] physical existence".[87] The creation of modern Lebanon in the 1920s came about as a result of French intervention. In the post-World War I era, with the disintegration of the Ottoman Empire, France was appointed as the mandate/colonial power that would guide Lebanon to independence. The Maronites, driven by the long-standing desire for a sovereign existence, had a vested interest in creating a Christian homeland in the Middle East and worked with the French political powers in order to ensure that this took place. According to Sami Ofeish and Sabah Ghandour, "Lebanon within its current borders is the offspring of the common interests of the French colonials and the influential Maronite comprador".[88] Despite Lebanon's independence in 1943, French influence has been maintained in Lebanon largely in the educational system, where it is the main language of instruction.[89] This, for Yasir Suleiman, has a clear impact on Lebanese national identity: "Support for French on the Lebanese cultural scene is generally linked to conceptualizations of Lebanese national identity which propel it outside the Arab orbit and lodge it in the sphere of a Western or non-Islamic Mediterranean culture."[90] In that regard, as Ofeish and Ghandour argue, Lebanon's post-colonial Christian generation is heavily socialised by and identifies with the West in general and France in particular.[91]

During his short stay in Paris, Bassam's status as an "outsider" is complicated by this education and social identification with France. It is noted that he possess an excellent command of the French language and that he was taught in secondary school an idealised and heroic version French history.[92] His fluency in French and his knowledge of French history are, however, of little significance when he is targeted by a group of nationalist vigilantes the night he arrives in France and is even shunned by a French-Algerian when he makes a request in Arabic for *khall* (vinegar) to remedy his mounting fever.[93] It is these incidents that spark Bassam's interest in France's dark and unacknowledged colonial legacy. At this point, Bassam recalls his own family's contribution in assisting France against Nazi fascism:

> I remembered the story of my grandmother [...] who in her womanhood ironed French soldiers' shirts for a few tin coins – and the story of her brother, who during the Second World War joined the six thousand Lebanese who fought [...] under the command of the Force Française de la Libération.[94]

When Bassam walks "the Parisian streets looking for [his] ancestors' names on marble plaques, on arches of triumph" he fails to find a commemorative plaque that honours the Maronite contribution to the French resistance.[95] In other words, he finds no trace of the Maronite assistance to the French in the architecture of this European metropolis. Clearly, then, the notion that the Maronites are culturally part of the French sphere rather than the Arab one is undermined by Bassam's observations of Paris and his experiences in that city.

What Bassam's interlude in Paris also reveals is the flawed nature of Maronite claims to their non-Arab origins. This claim underpins Phares' discussion of the link between Lebanon's Christians and Israel. In an interview with an online Israeli journal, Phares begins by stating that the Maronites and Israeli-Jews are the region's only non-Arab and non-Muslim communities. He then goes on to describe the historically rooted alliance between the two, despite drawing on evidence that pre-dates the advent of Christianity. Phares argues that the Maronites are the

> descendants of the Phoenicians, who lived on Lebanese territories at the same time as King David and Solomon. The very first [trade] agreement between [. . .] the ancient Israelite State and any nation was with the King of Tyre [a city in South Lebanon] [. . .] So we are talking about the oldest [. . .] alliance between the Hebrew Nation and the Phoenicians [. . .] [Today's] Lebanese Christians are naturally on the side of the Israelis [rather than the Arabs] because of this long history.[96]

What Phares describes as the Christian's "natural" bond with the Israelis was fortified in the 1980s when Bashir Gemayel became the leading figure in East Beirut. His domination of the Christian political scene gave rise to the development of what Ghassan Hage refers as the "Israeli-LF project", where these two groups formed an alliance against common enemies like the Palestinians and their Muslim sympathisers.[97]

The partnership between Israel and the Christian militia is reflected in De Niro's Game when Joseph Chaiben tells Bassam of the increasing Israeli presence in Lebanon: "Joseph mentioned that he has seen a few Israelis on the street recently. They are coming he said [. . .] you will see them here, chasing out the Syrians and the Palestinians."[98] When the Israelis finally do arrive in Lebanon they are not greeted in Bassam's first person narration with euphoria: "Israeli soldiers entered our land, splitting rivers and olive trees."[99] Unlike his fellow Maronites in the city, Bassam does not perceive the Israelis as saviours or allies of the Christian cause but as invaders.

When he reads the newspaper headlines of the siege in West Beirut, which refer to "*Christian forces* [. . .] *allying themselves with the invaders*", he positions readers to also view the entry of Israel's army as an invasion.[100] In that sense, as Salah Hassan argues, "for Bassam the [Lebanese] state is undermined by the Israeli assault".[101]

Not only is Lebanon's sovereignty compromised by the Christian alliance with Israel, but also the actual militia's autonomy is called into question. While not recognising this himself, George's details of the massacre suggest that Israel is not marginally involved in the camp deaths but is at the forefront of the action. George reports how, at nightfall when the soldiers' visibility is impaired, Israeli aircraft assisted by "drop[ping] 81-millimeter illumination flares. The whole area was lit up; *it was like being in a Hollywood movie.*"[102] The reference to Israel's participation in the making of this "movie" by providing the necessary lighting and assistance reflects their role as directors who stage events in Lebanon and manoeuvre the Christians for their own self-interest. This suggestion made, albeit unwittingly, by George is confirmed when Bassam reaches Paris and connects with George's half-sister Rhea Mani. Rhea tells Bassam about George's deceased father, Claude Mani, a former French diplomat stationed in the Middle East prior to the civil war, who courted George's mother briefly and left Beirut before he knew of her pregnancy. When he learns years later that he had fathered a son, Claude does not return to Beirut because, as Rhea explains, "Beirut became dangerous for people like him".[103] In her reference to "people like him" Rhea infers that as a Jew, Claude could not safely return to the region to locate his son.

Claude, however, was not simply a diplomat but was also, as his colleague Roland Meusiklié reports, an agent of the Israeli intelligence organisation, Mossad. Roland explains to Bassam how Mossad "recruited [George] on his trip to Israel. George knows all about his father".[104] To that end, George is shown to be an agent of Israel, but he is not alone. As Roland explains: "We [Mossad] have [many] agents with those Christians."[105] In this clever turn of events Hage links the French and the Israelis and illustrates that they are engaged in a treacherous game to undermine the sovereignty of Lebanon and exploit the lives of the Christian militiamen. By sending his protagonist to Paris, Hage exposes how the Maronite belief in its non-Arab identity and its "natural" alliance with the French as well as the Israelis has not serviced the community but held it hostage to powerful forces that have been able to violently penetrate the small domain of East Beirut.

Conclusion

The representation of the city as a space that undermines its own integrity and sovereignty is, as outlined in this chapter, a key feature of *De Niro's Game*. George, like many of his fellow residents, subscribes to the historically-dominant Maronite ideology that positions Muslims as a threat to his community's existence and asserts that Israeli-Jews are the natural allies of Lebanon's Christians. In Hage's wartime narrative East Beirut is, as a result of this Maronite disposition, an insular place that fortifies itself against the projected Muslim and Palestinian threat. It is not marked by the cosmopolitanism that Weber identifies as a defining aspect of urban spaces but instead is an arena that attempts to isolate itself from diversity and difference. George and his militia colleagues are implicated in the insulation of East Beirut, while Bassam's character helps to uncover that the most potent danger to the Maronite community lies within. The characters of Bassam and George reflect what the sociologist Robert Park has identified about urban culture – that a city's character is shaped not simply by its physical organisation or its architectural structures but by the habits, customs and traditions of its human inhabitants.

These customs and traditions have, despite the removal of the East/West divide in post-war Beirut, filtered through to the contemporary era. This is due to the country's profound failure to engage with its conflict in an effective manner and, as explained, the Maronite community's unwillingness to critically reflect on its role in the war. Hage attributes his ability to write such a difficult and confrontational narrative regarding the sectarian community he grew up in to his migration. In his acceptance speech for the IMPAC award Hage connects his ability to portray the "truth" of the war and discard "tribal self-righteousness" with his expatriation: "Little did I know then that my departure [from Lebanon] would transform me into a creature who loathed borders and their violent winds that give importance to the flags of warriors marching to the battlefield."[106] In effect Hage had to leave Beirut and reflect upon its war with both the geographical and temporal distance that being in a state of diaspora provides.

The critical distance that is afforded by dispersal is also a feature of Part II's examination of home and domesticity. In Chapters 5 and 6 the focus shifts from the urban environment of Beirut to the social and familial relations that prevail in the domestic sphere. Home is a deeply intimate space and one that is, like Park's metropolis, shaped by its inhabitants. Diaspora scholarship, and in particular the work concerned with Lebanese dispersal, tends to focus on the concept of homeland rather than home. In that sense, Lebanon is often the generalised "home" of displaced Lebanese, rather than the local village, town, suburb or the domestic residence. The next chapter openly complicates this construction and contends that home in diaspora fiction can indeed be represented as the small-scale household and the intimate domestic dwelling.

PART II

HOME, MOBILITY, IMMOBILITY

CHAPTER 4

DOMICILE AND DIASPORA: WOMEN WRITE THE HOME

This part examines the concept of home in relation to diaspora and does so by focusing on two novels, *Somewhere, Home* by Nada Awar Jarrar and *The Night Counter* by Alia Yunis. Both these texts display a central concern with the domestic but, as will be illustrated, do not entirely complement the way that home is constructed by scholars of diaspora. In fact, while Jarrar and Yunis engage with the grand narrative of the value of home, they do so by actively resisting conventional conceptualisations of it in the context of dispersal. This chapter outlines these portrayals of home both within the field of diaspora scholarship and in theorisations of domesticity. In both these contexts home is a multi-faceted concept. It is classified as either a challenge to mobility or its necessary partner, and is also seen as integral to feminist constructions of belonging. These issues of mobility, stasis and feminism are outlined in this chapter and frame the analysis of Jarrar and Yunis' novels in Chapters 5 and 6.

Home is a central issue in the convergence of diasporic and domestic discourse. Indeed, diaspora generally entails a subtext of home. At the level of etymology, diaspora is derived from the Greek verb "to scatter" and, as Avtar Brah notes, it refers to "a 'home' from where the dispersion occurs".[1] William Safran also insists upon this idea of an authentic and original home base. He argues that members of a diaspora deem "their ancestral homeland [...] [as] their true, ideal home".[2] In that regard, Israel and Greece are referred to as the "true" homelands of the dispersed Jewish and Greek communities. This tendency among scholars like Brah and Safran to strongly accentuate the idea of home when discussing dispersal is echoed in the various books and articles concerned with Lebanese migration. Paul Tabar, for instance, suggests that "the key feature in defining [. . .] [diaspora] is the presence of an orientation to a symbolic homeland".[3] He goes on to argue that the essence of possessing a diasporic identity is rooted in "longing for an imaginary and deferred homeland".[4] Similarly, Dalia Abdelhady states that "Homelands and the ongoing relationships that immigrants possess towards them are central to the study of immigration processes".[5] In doing so she grounds her discussion of Lebanese diasporans in relation to the homeland they left behind. In fact a major concern in Abdelhady's work is to articulate how Lebanese diasporic subjects represent and relate to their previous homeland of Lebanon.[6] What these examples from Brah, Safran, Abdelhady and Tabar reflect is that home in a diaspora-specific context generally represents the homeland.

Of course the term "home" is much more complex than these diaspora theorists suggest and, as Angelika Bammer acknowledges, it is a "particularly indeterminate" concept.[7] Not only does home refer to "the mythic homeland of your parents or ancestors", but also in an intensely intimate sense, "to the place you grew up in".[8] Bammer claims that the terms "home", "homeland" and "nation" are "quasi-synonymous". "Nation", for example, is "naturalized in domestic, familial terms [such as] 'homeland' [. . .] or 'fatherland'". To that end, these terms "operate within the same mythic metaphorical field" that privileges domestic terminology.[9] As Bammer explains:

> Both [nation and home] are fictional constructs [. . .] stories [that have] the power to create the "we" who are [. . .] telling them. This power to construct not only an identity for ourselves as members of a community ("nation", say, or "family"), but also the discursive right to a space (a country, a neighbourhood, a place to live) [. . .] is [. . .] at the heart of what [Benedict] Anderson describes as the "profound emotional legitimacy" of such concepts

as "nation" or "home". In this light, the [. . .] ideological slippage between these two concepts is not at all surprising.[10]

Eric Hobsbawm complicates Bammer's view that home and nation are ideologically comparable categories. Hobsbawm focuses on differing meanings of the term based on the lived experiences of the homeless and the migrant. From the perspective of the destitute, home acquires its "simplest definition [as] 'a roof over one's head'".[11] This explanation from Hobsbawm signifies the importance of a dwelling space, indeed a house, when one thinks of home. According to Peter Somerville, home has at least six dimensions or "key signifiers".[12] Some of these dimensions connote the material form of home, such as "home as shelter", "home as abode" and "home as privacy".[13] In addition, there are the emotional attachments or what Hobsbawm refers to as the "nostalgia" that one develops for a past home.[14] In Somerville's terms the key signifiers in this instance involve "home as hearth", "home as heart" and "home as paradise".[15]

From a migrant's perspective, however, home is very often "linked to the old country".[16] So when "expatriate Englishmen – colonial administrators in the past, or businessmen today – talk of going home or taking leave, they do not mean to their domicile [. . .] but [to] England". Similarly, "when adults in exile remember where they came from, they remember *Heimat* [homeland] and not the domestic hearth which defined their family home".[17] These observations from Hobsbawm regarding expatriates, migrants and exiles are reminiscent of the claims made by several diaspora theorists which privilege "the homeland" as the single expression of home and downgrade, or simply overlook, the importance of the domestic hearth and the family dwelling.

While initially it seems that Hobsbawm supports this view of the homeland, he soon undermines this very construction when he describes his childhood home in Vienna. He begins by acknowledging his own migrant status as "someone who has [. . .] moved from country to country".[18] But when he describes the Austrian city he does so in terms of domesticity. As the following extract illustrates, the metropolis is mapped through Hobsbawm's idea of home as "household, family [and] face-to-face [intimate] relations":

When I returned to the Vienna I had left at the age of 14 [...] I found myself looking for [...] the houses [...] where I had lived, the street down which I had walked to school, the station one got off to visit grandmother [...] the café where grandfather used to go in the evening [...] and which bore the Homeric name Café Ilion. And I felt a sort of childhood joy when I discovered that nothing had changed [...] and a childhood disappointment when it turned out that Café Ilion was no longer where it had been and where it should have stayed [...] As I pass [through the city now] I look up at the window behind which I slept [...] [and] look down at the park by the Danube canal, where I was taken to play.[19]

Here Vienna is depicted in personal and intimate rather than detached terms. The city is not constituted as a bustling space of industry and economy but by the coffee house Hobsbawm's grandfather frequented, the street his grandmother lived on, the window under which he slept and where he "was woken one morning with the news that [his] father had died" and the local park where he played.[20] When Hobsbawm finally concludes that "Vienna still evokes home in this literal sense: *Heim* [home], not *Heimat*" he reveals, contrary to his original presentation, that for migrants *heim* – that which implies a house, an abode, hearth and paradise – is highly significant and not secondary to *heimat*.[21]

This observation from Hobsbawm is reflected in Alison Blunt's *Domicile and Diaspora* which, as the title of her book suggests, focuses on the concept of home from a diasporic perspective. Blunt explores the spatial politics of home via three scales – "the household", "the national" and "the transnational" – and centres her discussion on Anglo-Indian women. These women, the products of empire and British colonial expansion, are the descendants of "the children of European men and Indian women, usually born in the eighteenth and early nineteenth centuries".[22] Generally they are "English-speaking, Christian and culturally more European than Indian".[23] Today they reside "across a wide diaspora, particularly in Britain, Australia, New Zealand, Canada and the United States".[24] Through her examination of these women, Blunt illustrates that of the three scales that define home the household category is the most crucial for this dispersed community. This is due to the inherently personal nature of the household, which is seen as a register of everyday events that take place at the level of the family and the local community.[25] Unlike the latter two scales, which reflect an interest in home when it intersects with identity, nationality and transnationality, the household is most concerned with "social reproduction, material culture, domesticity and everyday life".[26] It is also the place that accommodates the national and the transnational elements of home through, as Blunt suggests, the quotidian acts of women in the domestic space. In fact, for Anglo-Indian women "an identification with Britain and/or India as home was reproduced on a domestic scale" and through their roles "as wives and mothers [. . .] a distinctively Anglo-Indian domesticity" was fashioned.[27]

It is these "everyday" elements of home that are at the forefront of the two diasporic novels by Jarrar and Yunis. As suggested earlier, both *Somewhere, Home* and *The Night Counter* complicate the established orthodoxy within diaspora scholarship by focusing, like Blunt, on the minutiae of domesticity. By concentrating on domesticity in this way, these novels engage with a topic that has come increasingly under examination. Indeed, as a category of scholarship, the "magnitude of research on home is growing exponentially".[28] This is true not only in the social sciences, in disciplines like geography or sociology, but also in the humanities, in literature and history, for example.[29] Across these disciplines home is generally defined in two ways: "home versus movement" and "home as movement". These two constructions have a particular resonance with the way home is conceived of in a transnational context. Quite appropriately, Jarrar and Yunis' texts reflect these different understandings of home.

Home's Fixity and Mobility

According to Nigel Rapport and Andrew Dawson two features, "fixity" and "centrality", define the way home is most readily received and understood. They argue that "Salient among traditional conceptualizations of home was the stable physical centre of one's universe – a safe and still place to leave and return to".[30] In this formation home is conflated with the imagery of a house, and is even perceived as a synonym of house.[31] Of course, home and house are not interchangeable concepts simply because, as Joseph Rykwert's outlines, the latter is defined by "brick and timber, mortar and trowels, carpentry and masonry", while the former "does not require any building".[32] Similarly, Mary Douglas argues that "Home [. . .] does not need bricks and mortar, it can be a wagon, a caravan, a boat, or a tent".[33] What differentiates home from house, then, is that home is not grounded or fixed in any one place. The examples that Douglas lists as possible domestic spaces, like the wagon or the tent, reinforce the idea of home's mobility. However, while these theorists are happy to undermine "fixity", the first defining feature of home, they are not so liberal with the second feature of "centrality". In fact they retain a sense of home's inherent centrality by arguing, in Douglas' words, that the "minimum home has orientation" and offers "directions of existence" from which to proceed.[34] Likewise, for Rykwert, home is always "the centrifugal hearth, the fire burning at the center of my awareness".[35] Thus, as Rapport and Dawson claim, "being at home in an environment mean[s] being, if not stationary, then at least centred".[36]

The traditional construction of home that Rykwert, Douglas, Rapport and Dawson present here is not concerned with dispersal *per se*. Despite this, the argument they put forward mirrors how diaspora engages with home, especially considering the stress that certain diaspora scholars place on home's centrality. Safran is a strong advocate of the centrality of home in his essay on diaspora. In fact his primary characteristic of diaspora communities states that its members "have been dispersed from a specific original '*center*' to two or more *peripheral* or foreign regions".[37] The "centre" in Safran's words constitutes the "original homeland", the "ancestral homeland" and the "ideal home".[38] Similarly, the literary scholar Diana Brydon advances the same view of home, but only when she pairs it with or positions it against diaspora.[39] Basing her argument on a reading of

Lily Cho's article "The Turn to Diaspora", Brydon writes that it is "unitary, rather than dilemmatic notions of home [that] tend to anchor diaspora studies in ways that focus on singularities [...] [and] essentializ[e] home as a given".[40] Despite advocating a "re-turn to home" as an avenue to rethink the valency of the concept, Brydon ultimately conflates home with homeland when she mentions dispersal. In the short paragraph she dedicates to discussing diaspora, home immediately becomes a register of "national or ethnic homes".[41]

For Rapport and Dawson, the concept of home as a stable centre is "anachronistic" because it "provides little conceptual purchase on a world of contemporary movement".[42] This view of home is related to the second way it is categorised – "home as movement" – and seeks to unseat centrality as a defining feature. Ironically, despite Safran and Brydon's assertions, it is from within diaspora scholarship that the most strident arguments have been made in favour of home's inherent mobility. The anthropologist James Clifford was one of the first to highlight this. He specifically targets Safran's "Diasporas in Modern Societies" and argues that rather than focus, as Safran does, on a fixed national territory, home should be oriented towards "a reinvented 'tradition', a 'book', a portable eschatology".[43] In place of a centralised home, Clifford asserts "decentred" and "lateral" connections that promote "overlapping networks of communication, travel, trade, and kinship" among transnational peoples. In short he claims there is a risk that "specific local interactions" may be overridden if the "centering of diasporas around an axis of origin and return" is maintained.[44]

Clifford's intervention here, which exposes home's decentred reality in relation to the diasporic context, is further refined by Roger Rouse. In the inaugural issue of the *Diaspora* journal, Rouse writes about the migration of people from Aguililla, a rural township in Mexico, to America. He drills down into the daily lives of these migrants and concentrates on their domestic practices and kinship relations in order to illustrate how their experiences in the US have "forged [new] socio-spatial arrangements" that challenge the dominant ways of reading home in a diaspora context.[45] Rather than simply associate home with a singular place, in this case the

Mexican homeland, what these migrants' stories reveal is that the maintenance of home is actually dependent upon kinship ties. "Today" writes Rouse, "Aguilillans find that their most important kin and friends [. . .] live hundreds or thousands of miles away". Most importantly, these migrants "are [. . .] able to maintain these spatially extended relationships [. . .] actively [. . .] [through] telephone [conversations] [. . .] allowing people not to just keep in touch periodically but to contribute to decision-making and participate in familial events from a considerable distance".[46] For diasporic Mexicans, then, home is not attained by return visits to the homeland but through ongoing personal or familial relationships, facilitated by technology, like telephone and email, that transcend distance and enable mobility.

Rouse also highlights that such family-oriented relationships work towards the creation of "home" in the new host country. He explains that "Aguilillans have [. . .] sustained an attachment to the creation of small-scale, family based operations" in the US in order to build a supportive network in both social and economic terms.[47] This and the capacity to maintain homely connections despite distance suggests that it is highly inadequate to characterise the migration of Aguilillans "as a movement between two distinct [Mexican and American] communities [. . .] [with] distinct sets of social relationships".[48] Rather, what these relations of kin make clear is that home can no longer be so discreetly and singularly represented as "the homeland". As this example of the Mexican diaspora shows, home cannot be defined as the rural township left behind nor the new home established in America but is a communal space that is created in the changing links between home and host countries. Home is, therefore, multiple and mobile; it is "a single community spread across a variety of sites".[49]

In addition to Rouse and Clifford's influential work, where the relationship between diaspora and home has been recast so that a mobile form of domesticity is a key feature, the work of Avtar Brah and Svetlana Boym illustrates diaspora's capacity to undermine the traditional and anachronistic ideas regarding home's singularity. Brah indicates that while desire for home, what she specifically terms a "homing desire", affects diasporic subjects, such yearning "is not the same thing as desire for a 'homeland'".[50] Rather, "Diaspora places the discourse of 'home' and 'dispersion' in creative tension, *inscribing a homing desire while simultaneously critiquing discourses of fixed origins*".[51] In a complementary manner, Boym's notion of "diasporic intimacy [. . .] is rooted in the suspicion of a single home" and stands in stark contrast to "utopian images of intimacy [that stress] [. . .] authenticity [of home] and ultimate belonging".[52] In Boym and Brah's exploration of diaspora and domesticity, the terms "desire" and "intimacy" suggest that these scholars are interested not in what it simply means "to be at home" but in the emotive and aesthetic constitution of home; that is, how one "feels at home".

A corollary of this sensory experience is how one comes to develop a sense of belonging in a new home. For transnational people, who traverse routes and are not rooted in any one place, this is a particularly potent question. This concept of belonging has shaped the debate among feminist theorists in their discussions of home. On the one hand, there is the argument that women naturally belong in the home. In this construction, as the geographer Gillian Rose outlines, home is viewed as a place of repression for women. Rose suggests that domesticity has been largely framed in patriarchal terms so that women and homes are understood as having the same functions – to provide nourishment, comfort and security.[53] On the other hand, there is the argument that the domestic space acts as a safe haven for women who are marginalised and poorly treated in the external social environment. African-American feminists have been especially prolific in advancing this case. bell hooks, for example, has shown that in response to the devastations wrought by slavery and racism the "construction of a safe place", what hooks terms a "homeplace", was necessary for "black people [to] affirm one another and [. . .] [to] heal many of the wounds inflicted by racist domination". For women who suffer under these conditions, a sense of belonging to a "community of resistance" within a "homeplace" is closely aligned with freedom and liberation.[54] Clearly, what these converse assessments of home mean is that in "different contexts, the idea of 'home' serves different functions, sometimes resistant, sometimes reactionary, and sometimes a combination of both".[55]

It is this combination that is exhibited within the two diaspora novels examined in the following chapters. Written by women and containing various female protagonists, Jarrar and Yunis weave their narratives around the contrasting elements of home. Yunis' *The Night Counter* concentrates on the mobility of home. This is despite the female protagonist's obsession with the family house she has inherited in rural Lebanon. The protagonist, Fatima Abdullah, is Lebanese-born but has lived in America for almost 70 years. In that period she has not seen the house she is so keen to pass on to one of her ten American-born children and several grandchildren, all of whom are scattered across the US. Similarly *Somewhere, Home*, Jarrar's tripartite novel, also contains a house in rural Lebanon that captures the imagination of three female protagonists. This house, which functions as a symbol of the domestic space in multiple ways, stresses a vision of home that is fixed and anchored in a specific place and on a particular piece of land.

CHAPTER 5

STASIS AND DOMESTICITY IN NADA AWAR JARRAR'S *SOMEWHERE, HOME*

In 2004 Jarrar's *Somewhere, Home* was awarded the Commonwealth Writers Prize in the category of Best First Book for the Southeast Asia and South Pacific Region. Even before receipt of the prize, between its 2003 release and its 2004 award, reviewers critically lauded the novel. Their praise is centred on the "tender and moving" stories of the text's three female characters and the "delicate" portrayal of difficult issues like war and exile.[1] Although violence and displacement are not limited to the Lebanese experience, Jarrar's ability to depict the hardships of dislocation and civil violence in such a poignant manner have been essentialised by reviewers as a feature of the modern Lebanese condition. Rayyan al-Shawaf claims that there is no better placed writer "than a Lebanese [one] to convey the melancholic drama of exile [. . .] the insistent pang of homelessness [. . .] [and] the recurring theme of departure".[2] It helps, of course, that Jarrar has dealt with these issues firsthand. At the age of 17, on holiday with her family in England in 1975, the civil war deferred their return. According to the writer "We thought the war would last a couple of weeks, a couple of months, but it lasted years".[3] Ultimately, Jarrar's expatriation continued throughout the war period for approximately two decades. During her absence she lived in Washington, London, Paris and Sydney.

The war's impact on Jarrar and the resulting migrations it compelled the author to undertake cannot be underestimated. Indeed, these constant upheavals have greatly shaped Jarrar's perception of her life, which she divides into two distinct parts: before the civil war, a period she associates with a sense of permanence and stability; and after the war, a period shaped by personal exile and return.[4] These two phases also capture the author's competing representations of home. A survey of statements made by Jarrar in various articles and interviews show that she possesses no fixed view of the domestic. On the one hand, she claims that she has learnt to develop "a more accommodating notion of home" as a consequence of her 20-year exile.[5] Upon her return in 1995, she "imagined Lebanon to be the place [she] had left" but soon realised that "it wasn't". In order to remain Jarrar decided that she had to "accept" Lebanon as it currently was, even if that included the "many things [...] that [she is] not happy with" and a growing sensation of her lack of fitness there. Perhaps as a result of these confronting changes Jarrar insists "you can make a home for yourself wherever you go", thereby diminishing the connection between home and place.[6] In an extremely contradictory manner, Jarrar has also been recorded as saying "I have always thought of home as place [...] People are extremely important but the place has to be the foundation".[7] While this reflects the stability she associates with her pre-war existence, this statement was made during the second phase of her life where home apparently became more open in its definition and location.

In his review of the novel, Chris Brice attempts to reconcile these two contradictory positions. He includes a quote from Jarrar where, after dismissing the importance of national identity and place-based homes, she insists that even if all these things do change "the culture remains. The culture is very important."[8] This statement inspires the title of Brice's article "Home is where the culture is" and suggests that culture resolves the fundamentally conflicted views Jarrar articulates about home. Brice's attempt, however, at accounting for Jarrar's inconsistency by resorting to her comments on culture is not entirely successful. This is because Jarrar's seemingly neutral idea that "the culture remains" infers that culture does not undergo change and that a certain essence of Lebanese culture can still be found despite the the "horrendous civil war" and the changes that would have taken place "anyway whether or not the civil war had occurred".[9] In other words, this idea of the permanency of culture is, ultimately, in accord with the limited view Jarrar holds of home, because if culture does not change, then the home-place of that culture also remains fixed.

This sense of permanency is what is strongly asserted in Jarrar's debut novel, despite the upheavals of war and migration that her characters face. This is most clearly conveyed by the inclusion of a single domestic dwelling that recurs throughout the text and has a marked impact on the three female protagonists. The text, however, simultaneously manages to represent home as a changing and evolving category, as a concept that is not reducible to a single entity and one that can only be defined in a pluralistic manner. In fact, throughout the novel domesticity is sometimes connected to family, at other times it is conflated with homeland and, in some instances, it is even suggested that home can be a geographically shifting site. Without resorting to Jarrar's own personally mixed views of home, how can one account for the capacity of this novel to convey such plurality while also maintaining a sense of permanency and fixity about home? This is an especially important question given that the stasis of home is not clearly identified by the several critics of this novel. Most reviewers, such as Chris Brice, May Farah and Rayyan al-Shawaf, applaud the novel's engagement with the issue of domesticity, its female-centred perspectives and its stress on the personal and intimate traits of home. In her study of *Somewhere, Home*, Syrine Hout does note the "regressive pull towards home" but does not seem to fully explore the political import of such regression.[10] Despite arguing that the novel "illustrates an evolution in [a] process" that attempts to "traverse the gap between longing [for home] and belonging [to home]", Hout does not explain how the text achieves this.[11] By overlooking how the novel is structured, assessments of *Somewhere, Home* also disregard the underlying conservatism and essentialism that drives the evocation of home in this novel. Yet, despite this collective oversight, it is the actual structure or form of this novel that explains the inconstant representation of home.

The Form of the Novel

In terms of its structure, *Somewhere, Home* is divided into three parts, each with a discrete storyline that focuses on one of three female protagonists – Maysa, Aida or Salwa. These characters function independently of one another and the circumstances that inform their search for home are varied. For these reasons Hout treats this novel as a collection of short stories rather than a single text. What this short story format facilitates is the pluralistic representation of home across the text's multiple parts. In order to structurally bind her novel, however, Jarrar incorporates one unifying feature, the abandoned rural house, and inserts it into each narrative. This stylistic feature of the house and the fact that it recurs prompts al-Shawaf to argue that while Jarrar's text might "lack a single, coherent storyline" it is not a simple "patchwork of unrelated sketches" and therefore should be classified as a novel.[12] The presence of this house fixes the idea of home in place and as a result undermines the plurality the writer develops. The novel's oscillating form, then, is integral to its depiction of home as both stationary and multiple.

With regard to the novel's exploration of the plurality of the domestic, Jarrar draws on several conventional understandings of home, outlined in the previous chapter, by scholars of diaspora, such as Clifford, Tabar, Abdelhady and Cho, as well as researchers of home, like Bammer, Hobsbawm, Blunt and Brydon. The novel's representation of home in "Part I: Maysa", "Part II: Aida" and "Part III: Salwa" also resonates with these scholars' rethinking of home in a diasporic context. In Maysa's story, domesticity retains its most predictable attributes and is closely aligned with house and family. These associations are, of course, not new and, as Rykwert demonstrates, can be traced to antiquity: "The Romans got their *domus* [house] from the Old Indo-European root *dem* [meaning] family."[13] It is with this explicit connection between house and family that the novel begins. The opening lines, written from

Maysa's perspective, state: "This house, my house, saw its beginnings with the marriage of my grandfather. Built to hold the family in its overflowing numbers, the house became a meeting place for grandparents, aunts, uncles, children and numerous cousins."[14] Clearly, as Maysa explains, the construction of the house is contingent upon the family. Even the rooms are said to have "expand[ed] around [the family], like sunlight in winter" in order to accommodate their growing numbers.[15] The strength of this association between house and family is further attested to in Maysa's imaginative recollections of the past. Standing outside a bedroom, Maysa pictures "Salam, Rasheed, Fouad and Adel", her three uncles and father, "lying one against the other for warmth on mattresses placed together".[16] What these examples demonstrate is that references to the house in Maysa's section are inseparable from the family members that inhabit it.

This close relationship between home and family is further illuminated in the writing project Maysa undertakes. Similar to the macrostructure of the whole novel, which tells the story of three women, the microstructure of Maysa's narrative records the stories of three other women – Alia, Maysa's paternal grandmother, Saeeda, her paternal aunt, and Leila, her mother. Writing about her family is a long-standing desire of Maysa's. She tells her husband Wadih of her intention "to spend time on [her] own on the mountain to gather stories about [her] grandmother [and other female kin] and [. . .] put them in a book".[17] At the time the novel begins Maysa is pregnant and has relocated to the rural house to commence writing, using the war that has engulfed Beirut as a pretext to escape. Evidently, Maysa's project is motivated by a need to preserve the lives of past female family members by probing the memories that haunt her ancestral home. This domicile and the objects contained within it function, in Hout's assessment, as a "storehouse" of unwritten family memories that the protagonist transforms into permanent records by, literally, "etching [them] on paper".[18] It is for this reason that various household objects are explained by Maysa in terms of a connection to particular family members. The "wooden-backed chair", for instance, located near "the southern window" conjures a vision of Maysa's grandmother, Alia, sitting by the window "watching [. . .] her children running home from school".[19] Likewise, the garden at the front of the house reminds Maysa of her aunt Saeeda's successful efforts to create a herb patch. It is reported by the protagonist that her aunt "spent so much time tending to [it] [...] that the heady scents [of basil, thyme, parsley and mint] seeped into [Saeeda's] clothes and skin".[20]

In "Part II: Aida", the representation of domesticity moves away from the conventional notion of family and is depicted in relation to two other features. First, a relationship between home and homeland is asserted. Rosemary George, writing from the perspective of domesticity rather than diaspora, argues that the association between home and homeland might not reflect the primary connotation of home but is just as relevant. This is because a reference to "homeland" in discussions of "home" points to the latter "word's wider signification as the larger geographic place where one belongs: country, city, village, community".[21] This is not unlike Eric Hobsbawm's previously noted impressions of Vienna-as-*heim*. The same is said about Aida's perceptions of home in Dawn Mirapuri's assessment of Jarrar's novel. Mirapuri argues that "Jarrar connects Aida's personal nostalgia for aspects of her childhood with nostalgia for Beirut itself, thereby linking the personal past with a broader communal and social history".[22] Residing, when her story begins, in a European city that is never clearly identified, Aida's "near perfect memory for the minutiae of her past" is swiftly connected to her "recollections of home".[23] Despite the war that rages there and her family's need to flee the city because of it, Aida's perception of the metropolis remains unaltered – it has, as she says, "a flavor of endlessness".[24] This is why, in Aida's mind, the city-home is glorified in the present through idyllic memories of her childhood past:

In her mind's eye she saw the sea, a soft, blue Mediterranean, and smelled the air that floated above it, a mixture of hope and God's breezes. She recalled the sounds that had once greeted her mornings, voices and places and the unrelenting hum of activity, so that even now, whenever silence came after her, echoes of a home long gone would rush into Aida's ears and fill her heart.[25]

Unlike the Maysa story that fixates on the domestic space and various household objects, in this part home is depicted in reference to Aida's childhood city.

In addition to this, home is also explained in terms of the security it imparts. As Peter Somerville observes, emotional attachments to home are centred on the notion of security, of feeling safe within a warm and stable environment.[26] But this environment need not be defined by a house. Hout suggests that for Aida her sense of security "is not [...] attached to a domicile [...] [but] is concentrated into one person, Amou Mohammed, a poor Palestinian Muslim refugee who looked after [Aida] and her sisters and thus became [Aida's] emotional reference point".[27] The importance of Amou Mohammed's role as Aida's "safety-net" is conveyed when Aida reflects upon her childhood decision to climb a high concrete wall with her older sister, Sara. When she "realized how far away the ground was she began to panic" but Amou Mohammed soon arrives to rescue her.[28] He soothes her fears by telling her "I'm standing right underneath you. All you have to do is swing your leg over and jump".[29] These words restore Aida's sense of security and she throws "herself into his tight grasp".[30]

The final instalment, "Part III: Salwa", presents the most complex view of home. This is because Salwa's text extends the ideas of home initiated in the first two parts. Salwa, renamed Sally after migrating first to Louisiana in the US and then to Kingston in South Australia, tells her story as an aged woman living in a nursing home. Starting life as a poor child in a Druze village, Salwa becomes preoccupied by her father's ongoing absence in Brazil. Even though his obituary appears in a newspaper many years later confirming his death, Salwa remains hopeful that they will one day reunite. The poverty that she, her mother and sister are subject to compels Salwa to accept a marriage proposal from a much older and wealthy man. When she is 15, after having given birth to her first child, Salwa's husband, Adnan, secretly plans their voyage to the US and it is 27 years before Salwa returns to her native village. By this stage she, Adnan and their four children have long settled in Kingston where Adnan works alongside his brother in their small business. The family that she creates with Adnan in faraway Australia orients her sense of happiness and belonging, despite a relentless desire to "go back home [...] [where] we'll be well taken care of".[31] Settling in the rural South Australian town presents a turning point in Salwa's life where she finally acknowledges her surprise at "the unencumbered pleasures that fill [her] new life". The "certainty of [her] children's love and the growing affection [she has] for [her] husband" help Salwa foster a "cheerful and content" demeanour.[32]

Given Salwa's peripatetic life, the depiction of home in her story is reflected in terms of a diasporic reality, where home tends to manifest itself in several places. Hout argues that Salwa's memories are not situated in any one place "but unfold through the superimposition of native and foreign lands".[33] As Salwa's story progresses home is not simply equated with one homeland but shifts across geographical sites. A striking example of this takes place during Salwa's laborious sea voyage back to Lebanon. She rejects Adnan's wishes that their daughters "find good husbands" during their stay there because "there are plenty of boys back home [in Australia]. We don't have to go all the way to Lebanon to find them."[34] In the same scene, however, as the ship approaches Beirut's port and the city comes into full view, Salwa excitedly proclaims to her daughters "We're home, we're finally home".[35] Indeed, having lived in Australia for over 20 years Salwa has fashioned for herself a sense of home, but this does not mean that she disregards the nostalgic pull of her native Lebanon as another home. As her speech registers, Salwa's sense of home remains divided between two places. Her simultaneous referral to both Australia and Lebanon as home points to the fractured and unanchored nature of domesticity for a displaced character like Salwa.

In light of this, Salwa's story adds another layer to the varied and pluralistic view of domesticity that is established in Maysa and Aida's narratives. The novel begins with Maysa's story and suggests that home is synonymous with house and family; it then moves on to Aida's instalment and illustrates how home can be confused or conflated with homeland; and finally it uses Salwa's narrative to posit a representation that positions home as a geographically shifting site. Such pluralism is facilitated by the novel's unconventional structure and certainly points to an increasingly "accommodating" notion of home – one in which the author claims to invest a great degree of faith. This argument, however, is only sustainable if one neglects the important feature of the house, which persists throughout the text. Making the house the focus of one's reading of the novel exposes the intrinsically fragile and precarious existence of home in both abstract and material senses. In other words, while the narrative attempts to forward a vision of domesticity that is open and accommodating and that recognises that home can exist anywhere, the house's very inclusion destabilises this. This is because the domestic dwelling is, as Gillian Dooley explains, not merely a narrative device that provides the text's unifying thread but is also invested with symbolic authority. The house provides "an unattainable symbol of home to [the] characters in each of the stories".[36] This is a profoundly conservative representation of domesticity that not only grounds home in a single place but suggests that only one essential home is ever attainable.

The novel explores this narrow perception of home via three modes. First, the fact that the house is located in a rural setting is of particular significance to the Lebanese pastoral idyll that developed during the state's founding years, especially after independence in 1943. The rural regions, chiefly the mountain districts, represent in various cultural and artistic works the Lebanese heartland, while the cities are seen as inauthentic sites of Lebanese culture. Second, the novel maintains certain patriarchal structures that are related to domesticity and family. This is ironic given that the text is credited for leaving such structures behind in favour of affirming female-centred narratives. Third, and most controversially, the novel's representation of displacement in "Part II: Aida" is reductive because it equates the protagonist's need to abandon Lebanon's war situation with Amou Mohammed's exile from Palestine. In this context it is no surprise that the Aida instalment sustains the need for a central or fixed home.

Lebanese Pastoral

The pastoral in *Somewhere, Home* is explored as a counterpoint to city-life. In fact, it is argued by Rayyan al-Shawaf that Jarrar's text juxtaposes "the sturdy, dependable village house" with the "uncertainties of the Lebanese civil war".[37] This comparison captures the attraction many city and suburban residents in Lebanon harboured towards the mountain during the war period, where some fled to rural homes in order to escape the violence.[38] The Maysa instalment emphasises this kind of urban-to-rural migration and to a certain extent attributes the protagonist's movement to the danger and instability of the civil unrest.[39] This, however, does not explain Maysa's continued presence in her ancestral home for several years after the termination of hostilities. She even remains after her daughter elects to leave the countryside and return to the city. At this point Maysa's use of the war to justify her withdrawal is no longer valid. Furthermore, the absence of any vivid description regarding the "uncertainties" that the civil war produces means that the juxtapositions al-Shawaf alludes to are not entirely traceable within the text.[40] Similarly, in Aida and Salwa's narratives the war escapes concentrated depiction. Aida's recollections of Lebanon are located in the pre-war era and even though Amou Mohammed is brutally murdered by a Lebanese militiaman, the reader is spared the minute details that are legion in other war novels like *De Niro's Game*.[41] For Salwa, the war is something that takes place after her migration, and she witnesses no part of it. Thus, the appeal of the mountain house, to Maysa especially, cannot be explained entirely in terms of the war threat. Rather, the fixation with the mountain points both to an engagement with a literary history that emphasises a particular idealisation of the country and to a specific Lebanese cultural tradition that valorises the rural districts.

In his seminal text *The Country and the City* Raymond Williams outlines the appeal of rural areas within the canon of British literature and exposes the conventional logic that underpins representations of the country. Despite arguing that the city and country are changing historical realities that do not embody one tradition or meaning, Williams nevertheless concludes "that the common image of the country is [...] an image of the past" and that the "pull of the idea of the country [remains oriented] towards old ways, human ways, natural ways".[42] Similarly, in the tradition of Arabic literature,

Shmuel Moreh shows that while Arabic poetry's representation of the country is indeed complex, an essential reductiveness persists. Writing specifically about post-Islamic Arabic poetry, Moreh explains that "the conflict between [the] city and country" is expressed in terms of sedentary practices versus nomadic, or Bedouin, customs.[43] In "pro-Bedouin literature" of the nineteenth and twentieth centuries, not unlike the pastoral literature Williams examines, poets tend to "praise the simple, healthy, traditional way of life of the Arab Bedouins, exalting their natural wisdom and intelligence and their superiority to the learned and sophisticated sedentaries".[44]

In terms of the Lebanese literature that emerged in this period, the praise extended to rural districts was shaped by the state's historical particularities. Migration, for instance, deeply affected Khalil Gibran (1883–1931), one of the most prominent writers to emerge from the Arab world in the twentieth century. Unlike his nineteenth century counterparts, who stress a specific affiliation to nomadic customs, Gibran's focus shifts to the country and as a migrant from a village located in North Lebanon his rural idyll can be traced to the Lebanese mountains. One poem that conveys his passion for the mountain is "The Procession" (1918), published two decades after his settlement in Boston. In this poem Gibran depicts the city as a site of corruption and dualism, while the country, symbolised as "wood", is ascribed the converse qualities of "unity, innocence, harmony and equality".[45] Moreh describes Gibran's poetics as "romantic" and shows that his depictions of the country are framed by a conservative agenda that emphasises a "return to a simple, primal state of nature".[46]

This intense concentration on the Lebanese mountain in Gibran's poems, which emerged in the early to mid-1900s, is not without historical coincidence. It corresponds with the mass movement of rural dwellers to Beirut. As Samir Khalaf documents, between 1932 and 1964 "the capital trebled its residential population" as a result of a relentless rural exodus.[47] This movement, Christopher Stone notes, "heightened the sense that the true nature of Lebanon lay in the folk of the villages or farms — or in one's own childhood or past — left behind".[48] Just as Gibran developed a deep sense of longing for his mountain home from the vantage point of America, so too did these rural migrants. Their nostalgia was also marked by a concentrated level of anxiety which stemmed from the fear that mountain culture would be completely lost as rural residents abandoned the landscape. One response to this fear was the composition of several texts by a professor of Arabic, Anis Frayha. Stone contends that Frayha's most important contribution was *The Lebanese Village: A Civilization on its Way to Disappearing* (1957) because it made a clear and "conscious attempt to record [. . .] a mountain culture [. . .] [that Frayha] saw as being in danger of extinction".[49] Frayha's book not only relies almost entirely on his own recollections for its content but in particular on his childhood memories to reconstruct the village life that he experienced before his departure to Beirut.

Frayha's testimonial account of everyday mountain life focuses on, as Stone reports, "the lullabies sung to a child by his mother, the games children play in the village square, the stories of spirits and ghouls told to children sitting around the fire in the winter".[50] This record, with its emphasis on the experiences of the child, can be described as folklore because, as argued by Robert Georges and Michael Owen Jones, writers "usually draw upon [. . .] childhood memories when [. . .] incorporating folklore into" their texts.[51] The word folklore denotes certain expressive forms or behaviours "that we judge to be traditional [. . .] because they are based on known precedents [. . .] and [. . .] because they serve as evidence of continuities and consistencies through time and space".[52] Speaking of the processes of folklorisation in 1950s and 1960s Lebanon, Samir Khalaf argues that it was Lebanese identity that was being vigorously reimagined and reattached to its mountain heritage: "this reimagining began to assume a 'folklarized' character, particular to popular music, folk dance, musicals, and dramatic performances that re-enacted village squabbles [and] heroic affrays [. . .] [by] employing [Lebanese] vernacular and colloquial expressions" and dispensing with formal Arabic.[53] Of course all of these forms of folklore, including Frayha's text, are selective. Frayha writes about his own rural village, Ra's al-Matn, which contains a mixture of Greek Orthodox and Druze Muslims. He is explicit about excluding the coastal cities from his conception of Lebanese folklore because such areas "were never part of old Lebanon, Lebanon of the mountain and village".[54] What is more alarming is that he rules out incorporating Islamic customs because their folklore is not the folklore of the "original inhabitants of old Lebanon".[55] Thus, from its inception, the domain of Lebanese folklore is the village, and even more specifically the Christian mountain village.

Frayha's selectivity is, of course, not unique and mirrors the artistic production of various folklorists like Said Akl, a Lebanese poet, and Wadih al-Safi, a singer and composer. In terms of this artistic production, Rahbani musical theatre had the greatest impact in solidifying the centrality of the mountain in the post-republic period, after 1943 and through to the 1970s. The Rahbanis were comprised of Assi and Mansour, collectively known as the Rahbani Brothers, and Fairouz, Assi's wife. These three, the men as playwrights and composers and Fairouz as lead heroine and singer, overwhelmingly dominated the Lebanese performing arts scene and, according to Khalaf, "emerged as mentors and role models to a nascent but talented coterie of popular artists".[56] While their musicals were not the only forms of artistic output in this period, their plays nonetheless shaped and exemplified the cultural milieu of the era and, therefore, warrant special attention here. Most notably, like Frayha, their vision of Lebanese culture is a particular and exclusive one.

In his comprehensive work of the Rahbani Brothers and Fairouz, Christopher Stone argues that in Rahbani "musical theatre [. . .] the stage is turned into an anthropological and folkloric museum of Lebanese village life".[57] One aspect that critics and admirers have used to classify the plays as a distinct form of Lebanese folklore is the Rahbani Brothers' adaptation of oral stories into their theatre. It is well known, for example, that productions like *The Holiday of Glory* (1960) and *The Night and the Lantern* (1963), both set in mountain villages, drew inspiration from the tales the Rahbani men's illiterate grandmother told them when they were children.[58] Such plays illuminate how the mountain regions preserve the simplicity and honesty of village life. One play in particular, *Hala and the King* (1967), although classified as the first of the Rahbani "urban" plays, conveys most clearly the qualities of the Lebanese village that the Rahbani trio promoted. Set in the city kingdom of Selina, *Hala* retains its connection to the mountain by transporting two rurally-based characters, Hala and her father, to Selina. As a result the play emphasises a great degree of urban-for-village nostalgia beginning from the moment Hala enters the city square. Here the protagonist registers an intense desire to return to her village. In the modernised space of the city, the play's heroine can only register feelings of estrangement and a heightened sense of anxiety for the simplicity and stability she associates with her mountain home: "This is the first time I have been in the square of a city and as soon as I got here I missed the talk of my mother, my siblings, my village and the shade of the trees."[59] The play's plot is complicated by the belief, of the king and his people, that Hala is a princess awaiting the king's marriage proposal. Hala, exposed to the king's riches and the comforts of the palace, repudiates the king's advances. Her refusal to marry is couched in evocative, pastoral language that conveys a bias towards the rusticity of the mountain and the certainty of knowing that what is contained there remains unaltered: "Our house is run-down, my bed is old, but I won't sleep until I put my head on my pillow there."[60]

Hala and the King expresses, mainly through its heroine, a desire for the rustic and stable life of the village from the vantage point of the city. Hala's nostalgically worded impressions of the village are set against her rejection of the modernity that shapes her life in the metropolitan kingdom. Such sentiments and impressions would have resonated with Beiruti audiences who, at the time of the *Hala* performances, could still be described as first- and second-generation city dwellers, given the migration patterns described above. The pastoral language invoked in this play provides seductive images of the simplicity associated with the Lebanese village. Such longing for the simplicity and certainty of the past bears, according to Richard Terdiman, an almost symbiotic relationship to modernity. In his text *Present Past*, Terdiman characterises modernity as an epoch of crisis and anxiety. He argues that as a result of the upheavals that defined nineteenth century Europe – the French political revolution and the

English industrial revolution – Europeans began to experience a "memory crisis", a disturbance or rupture of their links with the past, "a massive disruption to traditional forms of memory" and knowing.[61] This crisis was instigated by the social changes that were by-products of the political and economic revolutions. Lebanon did not embark upon intense industrialisation like Britain did, nor did it experience a single defining political revolution as took place in France in 1789. It did, however, experience in the 1950s and 1960s a period of rapid modernisation. Beirut in particular was transformed by this in terms of its population size and the diversity of its inhabitants. What this means is that the village life Hala yearns for would not have seemed alien to the 1960s Beiruti audiences who were experiencing the urban upheavals associated with modernisation in that period.[62]

In terms of Jarrar's novel, the pastoral is asserted through two protagonists' stories where the simplicity of mountain life is made obvious. In Part I bucolic language is deployed to explain Maysa's desire to remain on the mountain indefinitely. This coincides with the turn of the season where "Spring makes its way into my [Maysa's] heart and lifts my spirit [. . .] I breathe in long and deep and imagine living on the mountain for ever, my child and I self-contained in our splendid, crumbling house".[63] As Maysa anticipates, her life on the mountain is one of romanticised self-containment and domestic ritual. She calls on few people to assist her while in the house and tends to its maintenance herself. There is a marked simplicity in her "Painting [of] a rickety shelf [. . .] mending a curtain hem [or] kneeling on the kitchen floor and scrubbing the beautiful arabesque tiles" as she "dwells on the details of daily life [. . .] [her] soul's longings [. . .] [and her] joy of [domestic] labour".[64] Her quest for a simplified life also sees her alter the house so that she utilises only one room. In the first few weeks of her arrival Maysa relocates her belongings to "the large room adjoining the kitchen".[65] This includes her bed, which is "tucked into one corner with a large sofa across from it [. . .] a Persian carpet woven in red geometric patterns [and] [. . .] lined up against one of the walls is [. . .] [an] oak dressing table [. . .] stained with age".[66] She installs an all-purpose wood-burning stove that will "boil water for bathing [. . .] do most of [the] cooking throughout the winter" and keep the room sufficiently heated.[67] The kitchen is stacked with preserved fruits, pickled cheeses and olives, and sacks are filled with grain and pulses.

Such acts of storing dry goods and segregating parts of the house suggest that Maysa relishes the frugal and simple lifestyle she finds in her ancestral home. In fact she rejects Wadih's attempts to renovate the house so that they can live there comfortably as a family. His suggestions to "add on another bathroom, especially now that the baby is coming" or build a "bright kitchen that opens onto a large dining room" are all met with suspicion and indignation by Maysa.[68] Rather than thank Wadih for his thoughtfulness, she simply "shakes [her] head and looks down at the [architectural] drawings" in silence.[69] Her unsuccessful efforts to circumvent her husband's desire to modernise the domestic dwelling mirror her inability to completely avoid the traces of modernity that creep into the village. She is forced, for example, to cut short her ritual of having breakfast on the terrace by the noise that invades the village. First, a school "commuter bus inches its way up a steep hill" and then "cars appear, dozens of them [. . .] whiz[ing] up and down the main road".[70] Maysa does not welcome the "frenetic" movement of these "machines" and returns "back into the quiet of [her] house lest the anxiety invade [her] too".[71] Her retreat into her ancestral home, as well as her inability to accept Wadih's attempts to modernise the living space, exemplify Terdiman's argument regarding the anxiety that modernity produces. For Maysa the house both facilitates and allows her to recreate the simplicity that marks the pre-modern era.

While the house is featured only minimally in the second instalment of the novel, its presence still conveys a sense of bucolic simplicity.[72] Aida's contact with the house, only recently abandoned by Maysa, takes place after her return to Beirut in the post-war era. The new Beirut disappoints Aida. It reflects none of the "Once elegant areas with luxuriant trees and wide, clean streets" she knew before her family's evacuation.[73] The present city with its "shabby streets [. . .] shocked her [. . .] [and] filled Aida's mind with doubt".[74] It is not until her day-trip to the village and her encounter with the house that Aida registers a sense of gratification with regard to her return. Sitting on the house's front porch and surveying the view of "the village and the valley [...] and [...] [the] mountains" Aida feels "an instant sense of calm".[75] After this moment and back in the city Aida continually "imagines walking through [the house's] front door [...] and feeling once again the peace that she had found there".[76] Her time at the house is transformative because, despite spending years abroad and dreaming nostalgically only of Amou Mohammed and Beirut, Aida suddenly states that "Beirut had [...] lost its charm, seemed tired and indifferent to her passions".[77] As a child of the city, with no explicit ties to rural Lebanon, her attraction to the house and village can only be explained by taking into account the historical significance of the mountain in Lebanese folklore. The uncertainty Aida conveys with regard to changes in post-war Beirut is remedied by her encounter with the pastoral setting. Her intentions to establish a nursery school there, even though quickly aborted, represent the one effort Aida makes to anchor herself and establish some form of stability in her life.

Home as Archive

The potential for stabilisation that the house symbolises in Aida's narrative is more concretely asserted in Maysa's text in Part I of the novel. This is largely bound up with the fact that the house acts as an archive for the memories Maysa uses to complete her writing project. In his extended essay *Archive Fever*, Jacques Derrida reflects on the transformation of Sigmund Freud's former residence into its current state as the Freud Museum. Given that the house is depicted by Maysa as a storehouse of family memories, Derrida's text is particularly instructive for understanding how the domestic archive operates in Jarrar's novel. Derrida makes the crucial point that archives are politically unstable: "every archive is at once institutive and conservative. Revolutionary and traditional."[78] Several reviewers of Jarrar's novel suggest that its institutive potential lies in the archive Maysa utilises to construct the accounts of her three female kin – her grandmother Alia, her aunt Saeeda and her mother Leila. Rayyan al-Shawaf, for instance, argues that the novel "adopts a [new and] refreshing approach" precisely because of its "female-centred narratives".[79] In that sense, al-Shawaf regards *Somewhere, Home* as not just a text dominated by women's stories but also a kind of feminist treatise. While other novels "by Arab and Lebanese writers" tackle "in a heavy-handed [...] manner" various political issues, Jarrar's narrative is set apart from these because it "emphasis[es] home as a personal, filial and maternal concern". Unlike novels that are constructed in a "typically" masculine manner, Jarrar's does not use home to advance "a political or national ideology".[80] And yet, despite al-Shawaf's argument, the "revolutionary" promise of Maysa's archive is eclipsed by the exposition of two interrelated archival principles Derrida identifies in his essay – consignation and repetition. These two elements when applied to Part I of the novel illuminate the underlying domestic conservatism in *Somewhere, Home*.

Derrida's analysis of the archive begins with the root word "*arkhē*" and its dual meanings of "commencement", "*there* where things *commence*", and "commandment", where law and order are exercised.[81] In *Somewhere, Home* the house is the undisputed place of commencement: "That house" states Maysa, "is where everything began."[82] However, with reference to commandment things are much more complicated, especially because authority and gender are introduced: the commandment is "the principle according to the law, *there* where men and gods *command*, there where authority [...] [is] exercised, *in this place* from which *order* is given – nomological principle".[83] Derrida refers to the commanders of the archive as male, but in Jarrar's text it is the women who are its custodians. Consequently, as Maysa's meditations reveal, the female characters in Part I are endowed with absolute authority and knowledge. This is especially true of Alia who, when asked by Maysa if "she [Alia] had ever wondered what her children's future would be", simply replies "I knew".[84] In another scene Maysa's midwife, Selma, explains that Alia knew to "accept [...] her fate like most women did in those days" to "just get on with it" despite the absence of her husband and the hardships of raising her children alone.[85] By simply "getting on with it" Alia, as well as Saeeda and Leila, are perceived by Gillian Dooley as "always right" about everything like "the sex of their unborn children" or how to "suffer patiently" as they wait for husbands to return from abroad, as Alia and Leila do, or for a life free of servitude to ageing parents and parents-in-law, as is the widower Saeeda's fate.[86] These examples reference what Doris Lessing expresses as "a kind of womanly certitude" where what is "known" is assumed and requires no logical explanation.[87] Although this is not precisely what Derrida had in mind when he referred to the "nomological principle" that underpins archives, his phrase nonetheless captures the certainty and authority these female characters project in Maysa's stories.[88]

In light of these examples one could argue, as Mathu Banerji, Chris Brice and Rayyan al-Shawaf do, that *Somewhere, Home* is revolutionary because it not only exposes the private lives of women but it also allows the marginalised voices of women to tell their own stories. Such a position resonates with Antoinette Burton's *Dwelling in the Archive*, a text that examines the domestically-driven memories of three Indian women. In her epilogue Burton argues that "one of the major premises of women's and feminist history has been that the inclusion of heretofore excluded subjects makes for a more true, more just, more 'historical' history".[89] However, such "triumphalism" about feminist texts and their "capacity to see [or make visible] all [. . .] subjects" should be "strenuously resisted" because "following that line of argument would require us to submit to a redemptive view of history that [. . .] does not do much to get us beyond the [. . .] presumptions [. . .] of total vision".[90] Just because Jarrar, through Maysa, utilises the mountain house as an archive to construct a female-focused narrative, this does not automatically mean that the genealogical history Maysa writes subverts the patriarchal structures it seeks to displace. It also does not mean that the novel succeeds in presenting a narrative that diverts from a typically narrow view of home. In fact these two elements are strengthened in Maysa's narrative not in spite of the female-biased archive but, rather ironically, because of it.

In *Archive Fever* Derrida labels archives as deeply and inherently patriarchal. He argues that the archic function is gendered – it is "in truth patriarchic".[91] Also, as quoted above, the archive is "where men and gods *command*" so that these history-laden storehouses have masculine guardians.[92] While it is true that Jarrar inverts this structure in Part I, positioning women and their memories as architects of their own history, upon closer examination it becomes clear that certain marginalised male characters retain a commanding role. The first memory of the house Maysa records is acquired from her father, rather than one of the three women who are the subject of her writing project. This memory, a fall that leaves a permanent dent on her father's forehead, is so important to Maysa that she attempts to possess it by "holding [her] hand against the hollow in [her] father's scalp and imagining [. . .] [she] could feel the memory of the fall".[93] Like this recollection, most of her childhood impressions of the house are a product of her father's stories. During her childhood, her father "would call to [her] [. . .] and speak to [her] of his life in this house in fragments, in snatches of colour and longing".[94] So, not only is Maysa's father a pivotal starting point for her writing task, his presence actually defines or frames the parametres of her narrative arc. It is he who provides the connecting line between the three women, Alia as his mother, Saeeda his sister and Leila his wife, and he who inspires Maysa to write their stories.

This, however, is not the only way the archive maintains patriarchal power. When Derrida describes the "men and gods" who command, he does not simply mean that they are male but that they act as *archons*, or superior magistrates, with "recognized authority".[95] Derrida draws on the Greek word *arkheion*, "a domicile, an address, the residence of the superior magistrate", to show that it is in these private quarters that "official documents are filed". Not only are the "archons [. . .] the documents guardians" they also "have the power to interpret the archives. Entrusted to such archons, these documents in effect speak the law" and, of course, the history.[96] As the author of her family's history, Maysa can be described as the *archon* of her ancestral home. It is she who exercises interpretative power and selects what to include in her history. This is especially true when she admits to the reader, just before she begins her first narrative, that she is forced to rely on her own imagination to fill in indefinite gaps:

"Memories and imaginings mix together in my mind so that I can no longer tell which is which."[97]

In Alia's story, the unknown aspects of her relationship with her absent husband, Ameen, organise Maysa's narrative of her. Maysa seeks to understand why Alia, alone in the mountain and facing various hardships, resists asking her husband to remain in Lebanon rather than work abroad. Questions like "What did Alia really feel [about Ameen's absences]? [. . .] Did she love Ameen or had she merely been part of a destiny she could not avoid? Did she long to go with him to Africa and did she miss him when he left?" weigh heavily on the protagonist.[98] When these questions yield no answers, Maysa confesses the "truth is I don't know. I strain to remember the look in [Alia's] eyes and come up with little more than [. . .] distance [and] [. . .] secrets that [Alia] will not disclose".[99] Despite admitting to not knowing, Maysa resolves some of these questions in the narrative she constructs by inserting a letter addressed to Ameen from Alia. The contents of this correspondence, never actually mailed to the recipient, express the adversity Alia faces, the loneliness she feels, and infer that Ameen should return home.[100] There is no suggestion in the novel that Maysa actually unearths this piece of documentary evidence. As *archon*, however, she is able to exercise her authority and interpret her grandmother's history as one of emotional deprivation, even if that means constructing memories to suit narrative outcomes. This kind of interpretation continues into the final two stories Maysa constructs. At their culmination, Maysa's role as the archive's ruling authority is absolute: "I make a fist with my hand and press hard. Here, I suddenly think [. . .] is where I will carry all the wandering recollections, all the thoughts that have been [. . .] here in a tight ball that only I can release."[101]

Maysa's capacity to select, interpret and construct the memories she metaphorically holds in her palm casts further doubt upon the veracity of her project. Her act of gathering together all the "wandering recollections" mirrors an important point Derrida raises about the archival principle of consignation. Derrida states that "*Consignation* aims to coordinate a single corpus [. . .] a synchrony in which all the elements articulate the unity of an ideal configuration".[102] While there "should not be any" hint of "heterogeneity or secret which could [...] partition, in an absolute manner" this corpus of material, when variation does occur it is suppressed.[103] Such suppression is evident in all three of Maysa's narratives, with the most striking example conveyed toward the end of Saeeda's story. Sitting on the terrace, Saeeda registers a "deep, wide anger" towards her mother and the house and questions her devotion to both. She feels a "sudden urge to get up and run, anywhere, away from her mother [...] beyond the house and the village and everything she had known".[104] While this moment threatens the consistent image that Maysa has constructed of the house as a sanctuary for all its inhabitants, Saeeda's temporary desire to secede is corrected only a few paragraphs later: "No, Mother [...] I don't want to leave our home. I never have."[105] Such narrative completeness illustrates the capacity of archives to stabilise history and, in effect, to downplay any traces of ambiguity and complexity.

Just as the heterogeneity of the archive is maintained through the suppression of unassimilable material, it is further safeguarded by the reproduction of similar facts and evidence. This is what Derrida refers to as "the logic of repetition compulsion".[106] For Derrida *"There is no archive [...] without a technique of repetition"*.[107] In an analysis of Maysa's character, Mirapuri describes her as being locked into a form of "compulsive repetition" namely because she writes "each of the stories of the women to reflect aspects of what she sees in herself".[108] The adoration Maysa harbours towards her ancestral home is reflected not only in Saeeda's narrative but also in Alia and Leila's stories. Alia professes her undying love for her house despite the loneliness she feels there without her husband and Leila, who lives in Beirut with her two children and husband, only ever expresses a sense of satisfaction during her family's regular Sunday trips to the mountain house.[109] So, despite recording traces of discontent among the three women she writes about, Maysa coordinates their narratives so that each of them reinforces her own attachment to the mountain home.

If Maysa as narrator effectively coordinates or, perhaps more accurately, orchestrates a set of stories that are constant in terms of content, the impression she imparts of her broader home, the mountain village, is just as homogenous. This is because the village where the house is located is, as represented in the novel, almost entirely populated by Druze inhabitants. The Druze, found predominately in Syria, Lebanon, Jordan and Israel, emerged in the eleventh century as an offshoot of Islam. During the Ottoman period in Lebanon they enjoyed privileged status with various rulers, or Emirs, appointed to administer the governorate of Mount Lebanon. Notable Emirs of this region include Fakhr al-Din II (1590–1633) and Bashir Shihab II (1788–1840).[110] While the Druze were an important community in the lead up to Lebanon's foundation and independence in 1943 they do not, unlike the other two major Muslim sects, retain a political position that is constitutionally secure.[111] The Druze are geographically oriented in Mount Lebanon and, like the Maronites, they perceive themselves as a mountain people.

Mount Lebanon is also the location of Jarrar's ancestral home and, like various characters in her novel, she is of Druze descent. It is this region of Lebanon that she has in mind when she writes her novel: "At the centre of the book is an almost sepia image that the author gives us of her father's ancestral home tucked away in a village on the side of Mount Lebanon."[112] Although her father's village is never mentioned by name in the novel, its seminal influence on Jarrar is revealed in the following statement where the author links the mountain and the Druze: "We are Druze, our family has lived in this village [in Mount Lebanon] for hundreds of years and I think of myself as a native of the mountain."[113] It is, therefore, not surprising that Jarrar's debut novel should focus heavily on this rural community and provide commentary on their religiously inspired practices.

The passing references to the Druze faith, although prevalent throughout the novel, are most intense in the Maysa instalment when she is taken to the weekly prayer sessions by the midwife Selma. Even though she is at first sceptical, Maysa finds inner peace during the prayer assembly. Her traditional and distinctly Druze headdress, a white veil, becomes Maysa's "most prized article of clothing, diaphanous and woven with light".[114] Maysa's new-found religious attentiveness is the point at which the novel's depiction of the mountain as almost entirely and exclusively Druze is most acutely revealed. Speaking of reincarnation, Maysa states that "Mountain people have long believed in the undying spirit, in lives that are like sea waves, coming and then pulling back. As a child, I remember hearing of loved ones who had died being declared reborn in faraway places."[115] What Maysa suggests here is that all rural folk maintain a traditional and religious belief in reincarnation. However, this statement is not as politically neutral as it first seems. This is because reincarnation is manifestly part of Druze theology. It is certainly not supported by Christians and is an element of Druze faith that casts them as heretics in the eyes of mainstream Islam. Maysa's use of the seemingly innocuous phrase "mountain people" actually segregates and excludes by implicitly suggesting that only the Druze inhabit the highland regions of Lebanon. This rhetorically excises the presence of an array of sects, like the Maronite community and various other Christians and Muslims.[116]

This language of exclusion is not unlike Anis Frayha's Christian-specific testimony of the mountain discussed above. It also resembles or resonates with a more complex dimension of the Rahbani plays that extends their bias toward rural Lebanon to include a Christian vision of Lebanese culture. For Stone, "the Lebanon of the Rahbani Brothers is not only a mountain and village Lebanon, it is also a Christian Lebanon".[117] It is tempting to conclude that the reason behind Jarrar, the Rahbanis and Frayha's religious exclusivity stems from their own religious backgrounds. This, however, can only be a partial and superficial explanation because it does not explain, for instance, dissident voices like Rawi Hage who is deeply critical of Lebanese Christian culture. Similarly the Druze author Rabih Alameddine, who resides in America, stresses the diversity of the Lebanese and does not reduce Lebanon to an emblem of Druze culture. Alameddine's novels – *Koolaids* (1998), *I, the Divine* (2001) and *The Hakawati* (2008) – maintain the reality of Lebanon's cultural and religious multiplicity despite his declared interest in representing the Druze because, as he states, Druze culture "get[s] so little press".[118] While this may also reflect Jarrar's motivation for her intense focus on the Druze, she unlike Alameddine, does so at the expense of multi-cultural and multi-religious Lebanon. Ultimately, what this exclusivity reaffirms is an intensely regressive presentation of home that is constant, homogenous and stable in Jarrar's novel.

Appropriating Palestinian Exile

This regressive representation of home is further explored in the second part of the novel, although in this instance it is undertaken in relation to the Palestinians, specifically Amou Mohammed and his family. What takes place in the Aida narrative is an alignment between the protagonist's experience of displacement and the hardships of exile that the Palestinian family endure in Lebanon. In a rather dubious manner, Amou Mohammed's exile is appropriated as a way to explain the alienation Aida faces in Europe and during her failed repatriation in Beirut. Revealed chiefly in the novel's intertextual engagement with a poem by Mahmoud Darwish, this appropriation not only diminishes the specificity of each exilic experience but also diminishes and homogenises the degree of suffering many exiles endure. According to Edward Said, while literary and cultural theory may have harnessed exile as an aesthetic and beneficially humanistic category, it still describes "the unhealable rift forced between a human being and a native place, between the self and its true home".[119] It also constitutes the "uncountable masses for whom UN agencies have been created [...] [and] the refugee-peasants with no prospect of ever returning home, armed with only a ration card and an agency number".[120] As Said notes, the danger of marginalising these negative qualities of exile leads to a "banaliz [ation] [of] its mutilations [and] the losses it inflicts on those who suffer them".[121]

These mutilations are conveyed in the novel through the character of Amou Mohammed, whose settlement in Lebanon after his expulsion from Palestine is indeed harsh and deprived. Although he exhibits no personal shame about his circumstances, his extreme poverty is well noted in the narrative. In order to provide for his large family, he like "many other Palestinian refugees [...] spent most of his time at his place of work, visiting his wife and children at the

[Shatila] camp on the other side of town on the occasional Sunday".[122] He is aware of his poverty, especially when compared to the wealth of his employers. Aida's clear privilege prompts Amou Mohammed to take her and her sister into his family's home simply because "It's about time you found out how poor people lived".[123] Inside his one room residence the girls witness what it is like to live in "total squalor".[124] The house, sparsely furnished, contains "only one bare light bulb", no chairs, table or cutlery.[125] Amou Mohammed tells Aida "many stories about the home that he and his parents had left behind when they were forced out of Palestine many years before".[126] The details of this place are not explicitly listed in the text but the reader is left to assume that life in Palestine was not as depressed as in the camp. The tragedy of Amou Mohammed's exile is further compounded by the fact that he is neither able to leave Lebanon and seek a better life elsewhere nor return to his native land. He, therefore, remains a refugee. This status affords him no security and like so many other Palestinians during Lebanon's war he is later thought to be killed by a Lebanese militiaman.[127]

Aida, in contrast, exiled from Lebanon directly due to the circumstances of the civil war is not as economically desperate as her former carer. Her period abroad, as well as that of her two sisters, spans various European cities. While each of Aida's siblings admits to missing Lebanon, especially Sara who reveals that "Lebanon's the only place where I have ever really felt the earth beneath my feet", neither fails to establish themselves in the host state.[128] Sara becomes a doctor and Dina, who "earned a very good salary", works in a recruitment firm.[129] Both "married and wore an air of permanence that had so far eluded" their sister.[130] Aida is unable to settle into any of the places she migrates to simply because Beirut retains primary importance. She admits to acquiring "more friends than lovers in [her] adult life, although neither lasted very long for Beirut was always there [...] [and] she had no heart to waste on new beginnings".[131] The immediacy of her former home is retained in these European cities and takes the form of Amou Mohammed, who appears to Aida as a ghost. He not only reminds the protagonist of her past but also urges her to return home. However, while Aida

registers a profound sense of emotional loss by constantly yearning
for Amou Mohammed and home, her displacement is not precarious.
Unlike Amou Mohammed's impoverished and immobile circumstances, Aida achieves financial security as a nursery school teacher,
moves freely across Europe, is able to resettle in Lebanon and, most
importantly, is not subject to violent attacks. In other words she may
be classified as an exile who is forced to dwell outside her native
homeland but this status does not impact upon her economically or
in terms of her personal security.

Despite these pronounced differences between the two exilic
experiences, the narrative unwittingly appropriates Amou Mohammed's displacement in order to explore Aida's. This is overtly revealed
in the novel's epilogue, after Aida's failed attempt to resettle in
Lebanon. The protagonist's final words read *"Tomorrow I will pack my
bags and hope to run away again and find* [. . .] *that place where my soul's
secrets remain, somewhere from which there is no further to go, somewhere
home."*[132] According to Mirapuri, these lines echo the following
couplet from the poem "The Earth is Closing on Us" by Mahmoud
Darwish: "Where should we go after the last frontiers?/Where
should the birds fly after the last sky?"[133] Labelled Palestine's most
renowned national poet, Darwish's text refers to the suffering of a
people who, in the aftermath of several massacres and expulsions, ask
where their next place of residence might be. The Palestinians, as the
poem reveals, precariously inhabit multiple frontiers and are always
aware that they possess "no state of their own to shield them".[134] The
conclusion to Part II of Jarrar's novel might similarly register a
quest for home, for a final dwelling place beyond which there is no
need to look, but this does not mean that this particular pursuit of
home is borne of the same circumstances that a Palestinian refugee
might face.

Such intertextual engagement, while of course highlighting the
novel's key themes of displacement, home and belonging, reveals that
the plight of the Palestinians is moderated when it is appropriated
and universalised. The use of the Palestinian narrative in this way has
precedence in the kind of memory and mourning that has been
sanctioned by the Lebanese state in the post-war era, especially in

relation to the Palestinian commemorative sites that have been erected there. According to Laleh Khalili's examination of Palestinian commemoration in Lebanon's refugee camps, the appropriation of these sites by the Lebanese is politically charged. For instance the Shatila camp, the site of the 1982 massacre, only became a memorial site in 1999 when Hezbollah transformed it into one. They did so by "building a wall around the mass grave and planting white roses and trees on the edges".[135] There have been other massacres staged against the Palestinians in Lebanon, such as in Tal el-Zaatar in 1976, but unlike Shatila, Tal el-Zaatar has no memorial attached to it. What distinguishes the 1976 event from the 1982 one is that "only by being championed by Lebanese [...] groups could [such a] site have become [...] memorialized, especially given post-civil war Lebanon's open hostility towards the presence of Palestinians in the country".[136] Hezbollah's enthusiastic transformation of Shatila into a memory place, almost two decades after the event, stems from the Party's own political agenda: "The appropriation of the Palestinian massacre site has transformed it into a transnational memorial that serves Hezbollah's political purpose [...] in reaching a foreign audience" and using the site as a space to comment on the suffering that all Arabs have had to endure.[137] Clearly, the implications of this kind of appropriation have shown how a memorial that is intrinsically related to violence against the Palestinians can effectively erase the true significance of the oppressed group.

Independent figures, such as intellectuals and activists, have also attempted to commemorate Palestinian suffering in Lebanon, but the level of appropriation has not necessarily been tempered. In 1998 the Lebanese radical architect, Bernard Khoury, was asked to design a nightclub in Maslakh-Karatina, a shantytown until 18 January 1976 when it was razed by the Phalangists in their efforts to "cleanse" East Beirut of its Muslims. Khoury constructed what became the BO18 nightclub in macabre form. The club is located underground, is shaped like a bunker or coffin and contains along the walls cut-outs meant to simulate sniper windows. Inside the shape of the tables emulate tombstones and each is adorned with a vase of wilted flowers. Khoury, making deeply political design decisions, consciously "admits that he has appropriated the memory place of Palestinians in order to provoke a debate about the history that the amnesiac society of Lebanon has chosen to neglect".[138] While his design aesthetic is wilfully confrontational, one of its unanticipated consequences is that it obscures the political message it seeks to impart. This is particularly evident in the fact that the BO18 nightclub does not mention the Palestinians who perished on that site in 1976 nor contain images that would allow the nightclub's clientele to connect the Maslakh-Karatina area to its history. Again, as with the Shatila memory place, the actual victims are rendered invisible in the face of the political motivations set by Lebanese. As Khalili concludes, the "lack of specificity of commemoration, of names or nationalities of [. . .] the dead, allows for an event to become [. . .] generalized, enabling many audiences [. . .] to assume the [. . .] suffering as their own".[139]

It is this generalisation and its consequence of obscured and diluted suffering that takes place in the Aida instalment of Jarrar's novel, specifically in the author's oblique reference to the Darwish poem. While Mirapuri is the only reviewer of *Somewhere, Home* to claim that Jarrar's novel engages with the Palestinian poem, thereby highlighting a neglected dimension of the text, she nevertheless overlooks the political implications involved. She celebrates the appropriation created by the use of Darwish, simply arguing that his "poetry provides a language through which Jarrar expresses the plight of the Palestinians *as well as of all other people who suffer expulsion, occupation, and exile*".[140] One important way to remedy such suffering is to provide a space, a home in fact, where one can dwell within its safe and secure confines. Amou Mohammed's lack of home, of a state to "shield" him as Said identifies with regard to the Palestinians in general, leads to his precarious existence and horrific demise. Arguing in favour of this with reference to the Palestinians or, to return to the parametres of the novel, from the perspective of Amou Mohammed, is justifiable. However, to do so from Aida's experience of exile is misguided because, as stated, her displacement is not riddled by poverty and her ability to return to her homeland is not denied. Doing so highlights how the novel maintains its conservative view of home. The resolution to Aida's story does not represent her accepting the changes in her former home. Nor does the text provide evidence that the protagonist realises that home can be perceived as multiple, rather than singular, dispersed, rather than fixed. Her failure to relocate the sense of stability Beirut once granted her prompts her not only to leave but to continue to seek that "somewhere home" from which there is no need to run. It is this sentiment, unfortunately and erroneously justified by the appropriation of a homeless Palestinian, that strengthens the text's central representation of home as a singular and fixed place.

Conclusion

This chapter began by exploring how Jarrar attempts to investigate home's multi-layered meanings through the novel's tripartite structure. While there is no doubt that the novel attempts to provide a nuanced representation of domesticity, it ultimately conforms to a rather confined notion of it. Its conservative articulation of home is both subversive and easily overlooked in favour of celebrating the novel's supposedly feminist agenda and its ability to universalise the plight of all those who are homeless. The very element of the novel that unifies its three parts is the rural house that captivates the text's three central characters. Ironically, it is this house that determines the limited representation of domesticity. The presence of a fixed dwelling place, however, need not lead to such regression. Like *Somewhere, Home*, Alia Yunis' *The Night Counter* also contains a house that is situated in rural Lebanon. In Yunis' text the house is also venerated by its owner. And yet, despite this, *The Night Counter* pursues a view of domesticity that is profoundly fluid and mobile. The following chapter focuses on Yunis' novel and illustrates that home is not necessarily an adversary of motion but can function as movement.

CHAPTER 6

HOME AND MOVEMENT IN ALIA YUNIS' *THE NIGHT COUNTER*

In their assessment of Yunis' *The Night Counter*, reviewers have noted both the novel's serious nature and its jovial tone. As Kathryn Kysar opines, Yunis delivers "a searing yet humorous commentary about the difficulties confronting an Arab-American living in post-9/11 United States".[1] Clearly, for Kysar, the text's seriousness is related to its political context. Carolyn See concurs, arguing that because Yunis writes about the years after September 11 her prose focuses on "how that sorrowful event affected members of the ordinary, law-abiding Arab American community".[2] Such "ordinary, law-abiding" citizens are represented in Yunis' novel by four generations of the Abdullah family, namely the protagonist and matriarch Fatima Abdullah. Fatima's grandson, Amir, an unemployed actor, is a terror suspect and this subjects his extended family to telephone wiretaps and the scrutiny of their private lives by FBI agents. Despite these weighty issues it is also these very events that determine some of the novel's light hearted and often hilarious content. The insertion of "two bumbling FBI agents" provides ample opportunity for various episodes of misadventure.[3] The spying and phone taps yield mixed results because the agents display a unique capacity to misunderstand almost everything they see and hear. Apart from these incompetent spies, the curious cohabitation of Fatima and Amir ensures further amusement. When the novel begins it is made clear that Fatima, an 80-year-old grandmother who has spent the last 60 years as a housewife in Detroit, has recently divorced her husband, Ibrahim Abdullah, and now resides in West Hollywood with her openly gay and very camp grandson. Fatima reasons that she must remain with Amir because she "didn't want [. . .] [him] to be alone in such terrible [post-9/11] times".[4] She sets herself the task of "normalising" her grandson by introducing him to several potential brides. These scenes alone constitute some of the most comedic in the book.

Humour and its entangled relationship with the events of 9/11 are presented as important features of Yunis' novel. September 11 not only provides a historical setting but it also allows Yunis to register the political changes taking place in the US and the hardships faced by Arab-Americans in the aftermath of the attacks. The author herself is aware of the complicated racial and identity politics involved in her book. According to Rola Zaarour, "Yunis was inspired to write her debut novel after 9/11 since she felt that, like other Muslims and Arabs, she had become 'mysterious' in the eyes of Americans".[5] Alongside this interest in the novel's political context, reviewers provide other summary judgements that focus on the narrative devices Yunis utilises. Most are in favour of Yunis' incorporation of Scheherazade, a well-known character from the epic *Alf Layla wa Layla*, literally *The Thousand and One Nights*. Scheherazade, who is typically cast as the storyteller in the various editions and translations of the *Nights*, is in the hands of Yunis the supposed "listener". As a result of this inversion Fatima is deemed the teller of tales. This role redistribution provides insights into the complex lives of an Arab-American family within the well-known narrative frame of *The Thousand and One Nights*. As Emily Holman argues, the "concept of this novel is a clear one. Its inspiration is 'One Thousand and One Nights', the collection of tales [. . .] that see the heroine, Scheherazade, save her own life by each night weaving a magnificent story."[6] This intertextual engagement with the *Nights* creates a sense of familiarity and intimacy.

Having recognised Scheherazade from the *Nights*, reviewers become absorbed by other aspects in Yunis' novel that are related to the original text. In Marjorie Kehe and Rola Zaarour's assessment, Fatima not only has a finite number of evenings to tell her stories but also that she will certainly die at their culmination. As the countdown begins, readers experience the tales that are the centre of the narrative. These stories primarily concern Fatima's native Deir Zeitoon village in Lebanon but also, given that she is a mother of ten children, involve tales about these "complex children who include an alcoholic Harvard cabdriver [...] a Texan housewife struggling to erase her ethnicity and an Internet matchmaker".[7] Furthermore, the novel explores the world around Fatima. This includes Amir's predicament as a struggling actor who specialises in terrorist roles and a soap opera star neighbour who is also Amir's jilted ex-boyfriend. Angered by Amir's dispassionate ending of their relationship, the nameless ex-boyfriend conspires with the two FBI agents to monitor the Abdullah family's movements.

From the perspective of reviewers, then, Yunis' novel is deemed a necessary as well as a heart-warming and entertaining read because it incorporates elements that are related to literary technique, primarily in terms of narration and intertextuality, while addressing significant political issues, such as cultural identity, surveillance post-9/11 and migration. Yet, despite recognising this diversity of themes, reviewers do not accord much weight to the importance of home and tend to only reference it in association with two aspects. The first is related to Fatima's preoccupation with her childhood house. Holman insists that this house and the question of its inheritance remain Fatima's "central concern throughout the [...] nights we spend with her and Scheherazade".[8] In the second instance, the importance of home is noted in relation to the author's biographical details. Yunis was born in Chicago but has also lived in a range of places like Kuwait, Lebanon, Los Angeles and Abu Dhabi. She is the daughter of Lebanese and Palestinian parents, both of whom migrated from their respective homelands. Such life experiences mean that Yunis is intensely preoccupied with home but not necessarily by one that is easily defined or stable.

Yunis' unique and mixed views of home are conveyed in a number of interviews that the author has given. On the Lebanese book show *Kitab*, Yunis endorses a deeply nostalgic notion of home that aligns with her protagonist's view:

> This lady [Fatima], the story of her life, is that her whole life is in America. She went to America when she was seventeen years of age, and all her life she yearns for her home in Lebanon [...] When I [the author] saw Lebanon for the first time [yesterday], after a five-year absence, I felt that I was Fatima myself. Because I, too, always yearn for this country.[9]

This essentialist representation of home is, however, undermined by Yunis in a subsequent interview during the launch of the German edition of her book. Here she comments that

> everyone always asks me "where is home?" And [the answer is] I don't know. I'm okay anywhere I go. I feel a bit like an outsider everywhere and I feel a bit like an insider everywhere. I suspect the US is the easiest place for me to live [...] just [because] it is my strongest language and [...] it's just the easiest place to be.[10]

Evidently, as this latter quotation suggests, home for Yunis is not limited in its representation by a geographically-grounded and unchanging house but rather by an intrinsic mobility that is contingent on where she happens to be located at a given point in time. By ignoring the significance of such comments along with Yunis' personal experiences of dislocation and relocation, *The Night Counter*'s engagement with forms of domesticity that deviate from more typical depictions, such as home-as-house or home-as-homeland, are overlooked. The alternative representations that the novel puts forward include the inherent mobility of Yunis' concept of home, which is realised in technologically-based practises, and the manifestation of home through narrative and storytelling. Despite their absence from reviews, such atypical representations are key features of Yunis' novel. These will be examined in detail in the latter part of this chapter but first it is important to consider why Yunis' diverse representations of home are overlooked and why their significance is misjudged.

Part of the reason for this oversight stems from a reading that rather narrowly follows the protagonist's own perception of home, one that she clings to throughout the majority of the text. This definition is established in the novel's opening scene where Fatima, who has only nine days left to live, expresses that her most "vital" concern is the house she remembers back in Lebanon. The extent of her devotion to the house is measured by the fact that despite "not [having] seen it in seven decades" she remains haunted by thoughts about who should inherit it.[11] In this first scene Fatima determines that her eight surviving children are unsuitable heirs because they all had "somehow ended up with their own thoughts and ideas" none of which involved any interest in her past home.[12] Her hope rests on her homosexual grandson, Amir, but her insistence that he must marry before claiming ownership of her property complicates this proposal. The remainder of the novel traps the protagonist between these untenable options and she strives, with increasing intensity against the ticking clock, to introduce Amir to potential brides. What Fatima's anxiety regarding the fate of her house exposes is her limited perception of home as one that unquestioningly associates domesticity with an architectural structure.

Having established a definition of home that aligns with Fatima's childhood dwelling, the novel proceeds to undermine this view of domesticity by expunging the presence of the house from the narrative itself. Fatima's house is marginalised over the course of the novel in two ways. The first is reflected in the minimal exposure of the house's interior design and layout. For example, in the first storytelling scene it is claimed that Fatima recounts to Scheherazade a "story about the house in Deir Zeitoon".[13] While it reportedly takes the protagonist "until the middle of the night to finish" it, the entire story is conveyed in a single sentence: "the tale [...] was about the chicken farmer's wife who hid [...] until her hens forgave her for accidently feeding them leftover omelet and they were able to lay eggs again".[14] Curiously what is missing from this sentence is any reference to or description of Fatima's home even though it is suggested that the subject of this story will be the house. This is entirely unlike what takes place in Jarrar's *Somewhere, Home*, where, as explained in the previous chapter, the novel is replete with descriptions of the house's interior.[15] Not only are such descriptions omitted in Yunis' primary chapter, it is also not until the penultimate and last chapters that any such details are communicated. Even in these instances, however, where some gesture is made towards describing the architectural structure that preoccupies the protagonist, the details provided are inexplicably scant. Apart from listing a few materials that were used in the house's construction – "limestone brick and cedar and olive wood trim" – and describing the "terra-cotta roof [. . .] [and] the four marble steps" that adorn its entrance, nothing else is recorded in the novel regarding the house's design.[16] This omission in documenting the particulars of the Deir Zeitoon dwelling marginalises it and by association suggests that home is not a significant theme in the novel.

Alongside this lack of description, the second way that the text disregards the house is through its literal destruction. This takes place in the closing scenes where Fatima is informed that the house she deeply yearns for no longer exists because it was razed during the early stages of the civil war. A letter from her former Lebanese neighbour, dated April 1989 but uncovered almost 15 years after its composition, confirms that "Deir Zeitoon was one of the first villages ravaged during the war" and describes the intensity of the violence which either killed or forced everyone in Fatima's family to escape.[17] It is not only the house that is devastated but also, as Fatima eventually discovers, the entire village is irreversibly altered. Certain hallmarks that the protagonist considers permanent fixtures in Deir Zeitoon – like the water fountain in the centre of the village square, the blacksmith's workshop and members of the Abdel Aziz clan – are no longer present.[18] The village square is now "congested with Internet cafés and beeping cars", the blacksmith migrated to America and "closed his shop fifty years ago", and no one from the Abdel Aziz family remains in the village.[19] These changes highlight the disjuncture between Fatima's memories of Deir Zeitoon and its current state. In addition, leaving Fatima's perceptions aside and focusing on the broader narrative, the house's destruction suggests that home is not a significant theme in this novel.

Such a dismissal of home represents one way of interpreting the text's assault on the house, one which relies heavily on plot, on narrative content and on adopting a view of domesticity that approximates the protagonist's view. There is, however, another possible explanation behind the author's marginalisation of the house. In this interpretation the house's destruction actually undermines the "home-as-house" model established in the opening pages of the novel and encourages an examination of domesticity that is much less content biased and more attentive to the way literature and story construct rather than simply depict home. To that end home and story are interrelated in *The Night Counter* in ways that extend beyond the nostalgic house-bound fantasies of Fatima.

Home, Family, Story

One of the ways that home and story are linked is evident in home's association with family and how the novel utilises family to develop Fatima's story. The connection between family and domesticity was discussed in the previous chapter, in relation to Nada Awar Jarrar's novel. For Jarrar home and family are intrinsic to one another and are in some cases, as Bammer and Rouse argue, synonymous terms.[20] In *Somewhere, Home*, the featured house is amply depicted in relation to its inhabitants. Maysa explains that the addition of family members saw the house expand in size and undergo a process of modernisation in preparation for the birth of her daughter. Bedrooms and various household objects are also described in reference to Maysa's family members, such as her father, uncles, aunt and grandmother. Describing a dwelling space in familial terms is, according to Chiara Briganti and Kathy Mezei, not unexpected and is "central to the domestic novel genre".[21] This descriptive mode is probably the result of the historically concurrent development of both literature and family. As Briganti and Mezei explain, the "rise of the novel and the idea of the nuclear family home emerged simultaneously during the eighteenth century".[22]

The centrality of family displayed in *Somewhere, Home* is just as marked in *The Night Counter*. The lives of the ten Abdullah children, numerous grandchildren, Ibrahim and Fatima are extensively explored. Unlike Jarrar's text and in contrast to what is seen by Briganti and Mezei as characteristic of novels that deal with domesticity, however, family does not facilitate the depiction of the house in Yunis' novel. What family does enable is the exploration of domesticity in the absence of an architectural structure. In this case it is not so much the structure of the house that is at issue but the structure of the text itself. A close examination of the novel's chapters reveals that Fatima's family determines its structure. Each chapter appears to be organised both temporally – chapter headings like "The 1000th Night" or "The 1001st Night" indicate this – and around narrating the story of a particular Abdullah. As Yunis herself explains:

> I counted [Fatima's] children and she has ten. Two died young [...] and I wanted [...] every [remaining] child [...] to tell a story. So every one of her children had a chapter in the book. I counted them as eight and I wanted her husband [...] to have a chapter. I thought I would count back nine nights from 1,001.[23]

While the allocation of children to chapters is not as evenly spaced as the author suggests, the stories of the Abdullah clan are nevertheless incorporated into the novel. The 993rd night, for example, focuses on Zade, Fatima's grandson, who runs a successful dating agency for Arab- and Muslim-Americans. His mother, Nadia, is Fatima's fifth child and a "widely quoted [professor] on Middle Eastern languages".[24] On the 995th night the story of Laila, Fatima's eldest child, is recorded. Laila is the only offspring of Fatima's first husband, Marwan. In the chapter dedicated to her, readers learn of Laila's breast cancer and her frustration at her husband's newfound allegiance to Islam. Laila takes revenge against this excessive devotion to Allah by feeding her husband and his Muslim companions pork chops on the evening that the novel documents her story.[25] The 1,000th night concentrates predominately on Bassam, one of the younger Abdullahs. Bassam is a recovering alcoholic who works as a driver for rich Saudi and Kuwaiti tourists in Las Vegas. He explains that his alcoholism stems from the death of his two brothers, a tragedy that turned his parents' home into a quiet and unbearable place.[26] He drinks his father's *araq*, an alcoholic spirit imported from Lebanon, in order to escape the silence at home. Even though his mother insists this drink is reserved for special events, Bassam knows that with his brothers "Laith and Riyad gone there never would be special occasions in the house again".[27] Lastly, on the 999th night, Fatima's great grandchild Decimal enters the novel. She is the granddaughter of Fatima's third child, Hala. Hala is a successful gynaecologist at the University of Minnesota but expends most of her energy attempting to control Decimal's mother, Brenda, who has a proclivity for shoplifting. There are, of course, more characters and nightly tales than listed here, but what can be gleaned from this short overview is that the enumeration of Fatima's family is instrumental to the novel's structure. In this novel, much like Jarrar's, home and family are seen to signify one another but, unlike Jarrar's text, family is not used to facilitate a discussion of a house. Rather, in *The Night Counter*, family determines the structure of the novel, thereby illustrating how home is indeed embedded in narrative.

Yunis' novel is of course not the first to draw attention to the relationship between home and story. In fact the notion that domesticity can be constructed through story is reflected in the history of the development of the novelistic form. Alongside the claim made by Briganti and Mezei that the novel and the notion of a domestic abode emerged simultaneously in the eighteenth century is the equally valid suggestion that the very structure of the house is intertwined with the novel. The influence of houses on literature is best conveyed in Romantic and Victorian novels like Jane Austen's *Mansfield Park* (1814), Emily Brontë's *Wuthering Heights* (1847) and Henry James' *The Portrait of a Lady* (1881). The estates contained within these novels – Mansfield Park, Thrushcross Grange and Gardencourt – represent some of English literature's greatest homes and illustrate the "interactive relationship between home and the literary text".[28] Beyond this temporal affinity are the particular house-specific terms that critical or literary theory deploys when analysing novels. Philippa Tristram provides a preliminary list of such terms – "*structure, aspect, outlook,* even *character*" – while Mezei and Briganti append "*content* (contents of the house, content of the novel), *liminal, threshold, entry point, style, perspective, kitchen sink drama, aga sagas, country house mysteries* and *the domestic novel*".[29] Clearly, as these literary scholars suggest, the "house – and architecture – have served as foundational, powerful and recurring analogues" that have shaped both literary practice and interpretation.[30]

This mode of literary analysis, however, problematically favours a discourse of stasis. A house, as previously outlined, is highly symbolic of the stationary notion of home. According to Homi Bhabha this model of a fixed domestic structure is not only privileged in conventional domestic fiction but is also emphasised within "the traditions of Anglo-American liberal novel criticism".[31] The "image of the house" Bhabha argues, "has always been used to talk about the expansive, mimetic nature of the novel". But this form of liberal criticism does not "fit the political, cultural or chronological experience" of novels that deal with dislocation, exile and the loss of home.[32] While Bhabha's observations are made specifically in relation to three post-colonial texts, he inadvertently references the unconventional approach to home found in diasporic novels like *The Night Counter*.[33] Yunis' novel not only destroys the domestic structure contained within it, it is also, and most importantly, a novel that is dominated by what Bhabha describes as "cultural displacement and diasporic movement".[34] For this reason Western literary criticism, which analyses domestic novels primarily through the lens of domestic architecture, is not appropriate for application to this novel. In order to make sense of home in *The Night Counter*, one must move away from models of stasis and towards theories that take account of the movement and mobility that is embedded within migrant and diasporic literatures.

Mobility and Diaspora Literature

Such theories that incorporate movement are outlined by John Berger in *And Our Faces, My Heart, Brief as Photos* and Iain Chambers in

Migrancy, Culture, Identity. Both these scholars assume that modernity is steeped in instability and defined by the mass movement of peoples across the globe. In response to this movement Berger argues that home, once represented by the "roof over the head, the four walls [...] the traditional dwelling", no longer has any basis in a built structure.[35] This is especially the case for itinerant figures who recreate home through "memory [...] photos, trophies, souvenirs [...] [and] a set of practices".[36] Practices, which connote "words, jokes, opinions, gestures, actions", are repeated and memories are retold, thereby offering "more permanence [...] than any lodging" can. As a result Berger concludes that "Home is no longer a dwelling but the [...] story of a life being lived" in movement.[37] Similarly, Chambers stresses the importance of narrative in an age of movement. He argues that mobility complicates established definitions of home that insist upon "origins, traditions, linear movement" and the "fixed geometry of sites and roots".[38] In order to "interrogate and undermine any simple or uncomplicated sense of origins", Chambers examines the historical testimonies and chronicles of various diasporic groups.[39] In doing so he illustrates that "the migrant's tale [and] the nomad's story" contain the "other side of the authorized tale" of home as a fixed structure.[40] This alternate side of the official tale reveals that "an increasing number of people [...] are making a home in homelessness, there dwelling in diasporic identities" and in mobile "leaky habitats".[41]

This mobility is an integral part of *The Night Counter*, both in terms of the characters and the construction of the narrative. With regard to the former, it is clear that movement shapes the lives of several characters. This is especially the case with Fatima, whose migration is the subject of Yunis' book. When the novel begins, the protagonist is located in Los Angeles, but this is not her long-standing place of residence. In fact, it is revealed that she relocated there only 992 nights ago to live with her grandson. She arrives in Los Angeles from Detroit, the first American city she settled in after migrating from Lebanon. Los Angeles, then, is Fatima's second place of migration and the two upheavals she experiences indicate a life lived in movement and dislocation.

Likewise Fatima's husband, Ibrahim, is also a migrant to the US. Even though his relocation to Detroit is his only experience of migration, his life is nonetheless shaped by this move. In the one scene that concentrates most intensely on his story, he is shown travelling to Detroit airport as part of a bi-weekly routine to "wait for KLM Flight 6470" which contains many "Arabs, coming from Lebanon and Jordan and connecting through Amsterdam".[42] As the passengers greet their families at the arrivals gate Ibrahim is transported back to Lebanon through the particular Lebanese sounds and smells that are transferred with these visitors: he "hears the sound of his childhood dinners in [the passengers'] hyperbolic greetings [...] [and] smells his mother's evening gatherings in the heavy perfume of the overly made up grandmothers".[43] However, Ibrahim's nostalgia for Lebanon should not be seen as regressive. Rather, what this scene highlights is his capacity to recreate and retain a sense of his former home within his dislocated and mobile circumstances.

Beyond Ibrahim and Fatima, the Abdullah children are also engaged in itinerant practices. Born and raised in Detroit all of them, except for Laila, move away to various locations across America. Miriam lives in New Castle County in Delaware, Hala in Minnesota, Randa in Texas, Nadia in Washington, Bassam in Las Vegas and Lena in New York. Soraya, Amir's mother, resides in no particular place. Her profession as a fortune-teller determines her peripatetic lifestyle. On one of her occasional visits to Amir she indicates that she is moving "to Tijuana to work at a new spa hotel where everyone's going for cheaper cosmetic and dental surgery".[44] This movement also extends to the next two generations in the Abdullah clan. Dina, Randa's daughter, travels to Lebanon to deliver humanitarian relief in the Shatila refugee camp in Beirut.[45] She is the only one of Fatima's relatives to attempt to locate the Deir Zeitoon house. Decimal, Hala's granddaughter, although completely unknown to her great grandmother Fatima, journeys from Minneapolis to Los Angeles to meet Fatima for the first time.[46] Even Miriam's son, Rock, the most provincial of Fatima's grandchildren, periodically leaves his New Castle hometown. He enlists in the military and is stationed in Iraq as part of the effort to reconstruct the war ravaged state after the 2003 invasion.[47]

What these examples reflect is the degree of geographical mobility that pervades this text. Almost every character moves away, whether permanently or temporarily, from their place of birth. This movement is significant because it impacts upon the novel's plot and establishes various sub-plots. Dina's visit to Lebanon, for instance, is not primarily related to her grandmother's obsession with the Deir Zeitoon house. Going to Lebanon begins as a quest for Dina to provide humanitarian assistance to Palestinians in order to impress Jamal Masri, an activist to whom she is attracted. When this romance fails to develop Dina leaves the camp and before returning home to Texas makes a short trip to her grandmother's village. Her inability to locate the house foreshadows the news of its destruction that Fatima later learns about. Clearly, it is Dina's trip to Lebanon that brings her story and the overarching narrative of Fatima's house together and illustrates how movement to an alternate location helps to resolve the protagonist's intense nostalgia for the past. However, perceiving the relationship between mobility and the novel only in terms of plot development represents a rather limited way of assessing the function of movement in this text. In Yunis' novel mobility also undermines static concepts like origins and shows that roots are not always grounded in one place but are more complex and plural than the term assumes.

This is most acutely explored in the sections of the text that relate to Rock. Rock, whose story is revealed to Scheherazade on the 999th night, is a divorcée. His wife, Carla, leaves him with their daughter Brittany and marries Mike, Rock's closest friend. Carla, Brittany and Mike are members of an evangelical Christian faith that Rock does not share. In contrast to Carla and Mike's religious choice to be "born again", Rock inherited his religion by being born into a Muslim family. Rock's domestic and familial relations are indeed complicated, but he nonetheless manages to cling to a simple architectural conception of home. This is reflected in his work on the construction of template homes referred to as "subdivisions". These houses are consistent in style and what their conformity offers Rock is a standardised model of home that counters his complex domestic situation:

the subdivisions' conformity, never [...] [compelled Rock] to think about what shade the trim should be or even what door style to get. Rock couldn't pick a door style without overthinking. It would start with "What type of wood should I go with?" move on to "Which style would be too heavy for Brittany to open on her own?" shift to "Would Brittany know what to do if there was a fire in the house and she couldn't open the door?" go on to "Were Brittany's mother and stepfather thinking about her safety?" and end with "Why did my wife leave me for Mike?"[48]

Rock's particular view of home is replicated in the simplistic image he harbours of New Castle. His descriptions of his hometown reveal an insular and unchanging place containing supermarkets that remain unaltered for decades and people who never leave the town.[49] Yet despite this preliminary appearance of inertia, the town is neither static nor uninfluenced by external elements. The evangelical church conveys this most clearly. Initially Rock assumes that this church is a distinctly "New Castle thing". His opinion is altered during a service he attends to celebrate Brittany's confirmation. When the officiating minister reads a verse from the Old Testament that references Lebanon − "The righteous shall flourish like the palm tree: He shall grow like a cedar in Lebanon" − Rock questions why this American minister would mention Lebanon's cedars at all. Until this point Rock only perceives Lebanon in personalised terms, as the place "whose food he had grown up eating [...] [and] whose language came out of his mother's mouth", but this biblical reference forces him to connect Lebanon to New Castle: "This religion['s] [...] principles had come to New Castle from the Middle East with a stop in Europe, just as his grandparents had".[50] Rock's thoughts, even if historically reductive, reveal that the roots of this supposedly New Castle evangelical faith travelled from the Arab world with a detour through Europe before arriving in America. It is this travelling, this movement, that disrupts the insularity that Rock assumes of his hometown and exposes that New Castle is equally shaped by internal and external influences.

What Rock's narrative illustrates is the impact of mobility on how one conceives of home and how the "roots" of a certain place can originate elsewhere. Chambers, as outlined above, argues that mobility complicates definitions of home which privilege origins, traditions and roots and that it is only through narratives of movement that the "uncomplicated" definitions of home can be "undermined" and redrawn. While Rock's narrative certainly does this, his story merely represents how home is challenged through one of the many individual stories that Yunis' text interleaves. Beyond the individual story, *The Night Counter* is also a novel that consciously draws attention to narrative and storytelling. This is evident in the novel's intertextual dalliance with the literary world's quintessential storytelling text, *The Thousand and One Nights*. Given this investment in mobility and storytelling, it can be argued that the broader effect of *The Night Counter* is not simply to explore the theorisation of home through narrative but also, in a more complex manner, to examine how narrative theorises home in movement.

Nowhere is this more prevalent than in Scheherazade's character who manages to alter the narrative's direction through her mobility. This claim that Scheherazade has any bearing on the narrative's form may seem an unlikely one, given that she is the designated listener while Fatima is the appointed storyteller. Most reviewers of this text accept these role allocations without question. Even the author reinforces this position stating that "what I sort of did was reverse *The Thousand and One Nights* [...] [which has] Scheherazade telling a story to a king every night [...] and so I thought I wanted to reverse it and have Scheherazade be the story listener".[51] It is therefore assumed that Scheherazade mainly absorbs the stories she is told and if she has any influence over their selection it is merely to extract or encourage Fatima to recount certain tales. But if this is the case, if Fatima truly is the character who does all the narrating, why is it that *The Night Counter* does not simply advocate an idea of home that is based on the protagonist's perception of it? In this scenario a rather essentialist view of domesticity would prevail where it would be symbolically, if not literally, linked to a house and idealised as the original home that one must return to. This is not the case and, as I have argued, this view of the domestic that Fatima advocates is marginalised while a notion of home that is built through story is developed.

Evidently, despite her role as storyteller, it is not Fatima who manages to incorporate the individual stories of each of her offspring but Scheherazade who facilitates their inclusion. At the start of the novel it appears that Scheherazade has had to endure "993 stories of [Fatima's] house".[52] Even though she pleads for others from Fatima – "*Ya seit el beit*, oh lady of the house [. . .] *Wahayat deen el-nebi*, in the name of the prophet's religion, you've had ten children and two husbands. Surely something must have happened in the last sixty years?" – Fatima's reply, "I never told you about the week my grandfather's autumn grapevines trapped five bandit farmers", indicates that the subject of her stories will not change.[53] For this reason Scheherazade travels to each city or town that the Abdullah offspring are located in and observes their own tales of home and domesticity. While this does not mean that Scheherazade assumes the role of storyteller, it does free the narrative from Fatima's narrow depiction of domesticity and opens it up to broader considerations.

Scheherazade's journey to Randa's Texan residence illustrates this most effectively. Unlike Fatima's dominant home-as-house model, Scheherazade's observation of the Texan branch of the Abdullahs exposes what home means in a context of colonisation. Randa is uncomfortable with her Arab heritage and works "hard to make [. . .] [this] history irrelevant".[54] She does this by adopting a Westernised version of her name, Randy, and, most notably, by residing in a very American colonial-style house. Randa is extremely proud of her house but its colonial-style is not overlooked by the protagonist: "She [Randa] told me [Fatima] it was colonial-style, like British and French colonization hadn't destroyed the Arabs, like colonization was a good thing."[55] Even though Fatima's critical and unwittingly comical comments regarding colonialism are misapplied here, her words speak volumes in relation to the narrative of displaced Palestinians that Yunis skilfully intertwines into Randa's story.[56] It is through Randa's daughter, Dina, an aid worker in Lebanon's refugee camps, that the Palestinian stories of displacement are incorporated into the text. Dina quickly becomes privy to the Palestinian accounts of dispossession and their failure to have their past homes recognised. Alongside their oral accounts, the refugees also produce precious textual documentation of deed titles to the houses they were expelled from. The one deed title that Dina views is more than 50 years old and is handled by its owner "as if it had been spun from gold".[57] These papers are produced by refugees primarily for "foreigners because they think no one believes their stories" of displacement.[58] Such narratives and documents illustrate the ongoing legacy of colonialism to displaced peoples who, unlike the Americanised Randy, do not have the luxury to deny their past nor the legal rights to fashion alternative homes for themselves.

Scheherazade's role in extracting these other dimensions of home cannot be underestimated. Her capacity to independently travel across America ensures that Fatima's rather reductive version of the domestic is tempered by the inclusion of other stories that draw out aspects of home that Fatima's version neglects. Scheherazade's mobility disrupts the narrative's direction and consequently broadens and pluralises the novel's definition of home. The Scheherazade of Yunis' novel, then, is a destabilising and subversive figure, but the depiction of her in this way is not unusual. The supposedly original Scheherazade from the centuries-old *The Thousand and One Nights* is just as independent and disruptive. This Scheherazade is imprisoned by the misogynist and despotic King Shahryar. It is the king's intention to execute Scheherazade but she manages to circumvent her fate by wielding her storytelling prowess against him. Scheherazade's enticing nightly tales attract the king's attention because each story is intentionally left incomplete. The open-ended nature of her stories not only rescue her from the fate of execution, they also transform King Shahryar's tendency toward tyrannical rule. After 1,001 nights of suspenseful tales, the king elects to marry Scheherazade.

According to various literary critics, the king's supposed reassessment of his misogyny and despotism is widely attributed to Scheherazade's storytelling capabilities. Fedwa Malti-Douglas, in her article "Shahrazād feminist", argues that the "Arabic Shahrazād" is a "woman in control" and is "knowledgeable, intelligent, wise and an *adība* (a women learned in the arts of literature and society)".[59] This skill enables her to save "herself and her female kind" from the king's further tyranny.[60] Eva Sallis also emphasises Scheherazade's narrative power against the king and Suzanne Gauch suggests that Scheherazade is not only courageous for facing the king but also skilled and wise enough for the task.[61] Gauch argues that Scheherazade "employs her narrative skills to [...] divert the king from his obsession with women's infidelity, both entertaining him and altering the manner in which he looks on [female] human behaviour".[62]

What these literary critics expose is the proto-feminist agency that Scheherazade possesses. Her capacity to challenge and upend such patriarchal power complements other interpretations of *The Thousand and One Nights*. These interpretations emphasise the text's revolutionary and counter-hegemonic qualities. Saree Makdisi and Felicity Nussbaum note the political implications of this intervention, arguing that the *Nights* "changed the world on a scale unrivalled by any other literary text [...] and helped to inspire literary and ultimately cultural revolutions".[63] Those literary and cultural revolutions were most marked not in the Arab world from where the text emerged but in Europe.[64] Antoine Galland's eighteenth century compilation and French translation of a three-volume Syrian manuscript instigated Europe's interest in the *Nights*.[65] Since then "a chain of editions, compilations, translations, variations, and derivations [have] circled the globe".[66] Translators of the English editions of the *Nights* include Edward Lane (1801–76), John Payne (1842–1916) and Sir Richard Burton (1821–90).[67] These editions, each one deviating from or building on its predecessor, reflect why scholars of the *Nights* like Robert Irwin and Ibrahim Muhawi refer to it, respectively, as a "loose cluster of texts" and a "palimpsest".[68]

Such textual instability has determined the global appeal of the *Nights* and its adaptation. Ros Ballaster comments on this in relation to eighteenth century novels by European women. She argues that these novels "often made allusive reference to the enchantments of Oriental tales [i.e. *The Thousand and One Nights*] as a context for the explanation of the [...] power of the heroines".[69] Likewise, in the description to *The Arabian Nights: A Companion* its author, the eminent scholar of Arabic literature Robert Irwin, asserts that a "full understanding of the writings of Voltaire, Dickens, Melville, Proust and Borges [...] is impossible without some familiarity with the stories of the 'Nights'".[70] Shifting away from this European focus, Maher Jarrar has traced the impact of the *Nights* on Latin American and Arab writers. Various novels by Jorge Luis Borges, Gabriel Marquez, Emil Habibi and Elias Khoury incorporate elements or indicate inspiration from the *Nights*. By engaging with what they consider to be a transgressive text, these writers explore various contemporary political issues.[71] As Makdisi and Nussbaum explain, such writers "have found in the *Nights* a pre-text for a counter-narrative that interrupts [political issues like] colonialism and protests against it".[72]

The research of Ballaster, Jarrar, Makdisi and Nussbaum collectively demonstrates that the attraction of *The Thousand and One Nights* for a broad range of writers is determined by the text's capacity to challenge or engage with political issues like gender and imperialism. Yunis is no exception here. Scheherazade is used in *The Night Counter* as a way to overcome Fatima's rigid and nostalgic views of home. But apart from Scheherazade, *The Night Counter* further complicates the motif of home by redefining traditional notions of roots and by stressing the ways in which migration and communication technologies both facilitate and undermine the discourse of home. Narratives of roots have a clear connection to home and are often used by migrants to signify a natural or organic relationship to a past dwelling. Technology's connection to home may not be as immediately apparent but it is crucial nevertheless. This is because devices like the telephone, the internet, email, webcams, online chat sites as well as other forms of digital and social media facilitate contact and communication between differentially located peoples.

Telephonic Domesticity and Roots-as-Movement

While roots and communication technologies are connected to a domestic sensibility, their respective associations with it are generally expressed in conflicted terms. To begin with, communication devices are associated with movement because they disperse and destabilise conventional perceptions of home. Conversely, roots are synonymous with domestic stability and rely on the belief of an original home being located in a very specific place. Various scholars of diaspora and migration typically evaluate the fixity that roots encourage in disparaging terms. James Clifford, for instance, outlines the limitations of theorising diasporas only in relation to origins, Stuart Hall insists that an emphasis on one authentic site as home is a rather simplistic way of understanding how modern diasporas operate, and Salman Rushdie asserts that roots are "a conservative myth, designed to keep us in our places".[73] All of these writers believe that movement most accurately conveys what diaspora entails and argue that a focus on roots obscures the potential of mobility.[74] This is perhaps why James Clifford and Roger Rouse offer a much more positive appraisal of communication technologies. In fact, they argue that such devices are fundamental to the maintenance of home and illustrate how, in Clifford's words, certain forms of technology allow "displaced peoples [...] [to maintain] border relations with the old country" and enhance, according to Rouse, the "spatially extended relationships" between separated family members.[75] Despite this intersection of home, roots and technology in Clifford, Hall and Rouse's analysis of contemporary narratives of migration, these associations are contested and reordered by Yunis' novel. First, instead of depicting roots as a metaphor for regression or stagnation, Yunis shows that they are fundamental to mobility and second, instead of presenting an image of communication technology as a facilitator of a more mobile sense of home, Yunis illustrates how it can actually efface home.

In *The Night Counter* the principle communication device used by the Abdullahs is the telephone, and it is for this reason that the following discussion will focus entirely on this technological formation.[76] Invented in the 1800s, the telephone has always had two primary functions: to undermine distance and to enhance mobility. According to Ian Hutchby, the telephone "was the first technology for communication which enabled people to talk as if they were" co-present.[77] This illusionistic co-presence demonstrates that telephonic interaction is a form of "intimacy" fashioned specifically "across distance".[78] Colin Cherry makes a similar argument but also underscores that in the age of the telephone the experience of home need not be governed by ideas of stationariness or fixity. Indeed, he asserts that the invention of the telephone cultivated domestic social relations between family members that "no longer required [them] [. . .] to be located at a fixed point".[79] For this reason, the telephone increasingly "allows us to move about the country (or, today, over much of the world)" all the while maintaining a sense of home.[80] What these observations from Hutchby and Cherry suggest is that it is the intimate nature of telephone conversations that allows home to thrive in spite of distance and movement.

Yunis explores this kind of intimacy and the homely connections the telephone enables. In fact, in various instances it is the telephone that best allows the scattered Abdullah children to remain informed about various family issues like their mother's health, the prognosis of Laila's cancer and Bassam's alcoholism. The telephone is also the medium through which the movement of any one of the Abdullahs is transmitted between family members. For instance when Decimal leaves Minnesota to visit Fatima she reassures her grandmother, Hala, that she is safe through telephone contact.[81] Similarly Lena's business trip to Las Vegas is communicated to Bassam through a telephone conversation with Laila.[82] As a result of Laila's call Bassam and Lena meet and, even though it is only a brief encounter, Lena is able to ascertain the state of Bassam's sobriety on behalf of her concerned siblings.[83]

Evidently, in the daily lives of Fatima's family, the telephone not only mediates their geographical separation but also maintains their homely connections as they traverse the country. In these instances the function of the telephone echoes the arguments of various diaspora theorists and media researchers regarding the association between home and communication technologies. But what these scholars overlook is how telephonic communication can be interfered with and how such interference subsequently undermines the very homely functions for which the telephone is highly praised. Yunis' novel fills this gap because it illustrates how interruptions to telephone services can severely curtail the sustenance of home in situations where mobility dominates. The interference with telephone lines that takes place in *The Night Counter* is part of the surveillance efforts of two inept agents who seek to ingratiate themselves with the FBI. These agents initially focus on Amir mainly because they suspect that he is involved in some form of terrorist activity. They position themselves in an unmarked but nonetheless conspicuous utility vehicle outside Amir's duplex, eavesdropping on his conversations and taking compromising pictures of him wearing a jihadist outfit and *kefia*.[84] Their tips to the intelligence bureau arouse enough suspicion for an FBI operative, Sherri Hazard, to order "a wiretap [be put] in place on all the phones billed to [Amir's] address".[85] The telephone lines, however, are so inadequately tapped that background noise, static and abrupt line-drops determine that every telephone conversation is unintelligible, rendering the FBI spying tactics as a farce.

The interruptions to the telephone service have the most adverse impact on Fatima and Ibrahim's sense of home. As migrants to America, these two characters develop their feelings of homeliness and belonging predominately through their relationship. Ibrahim readily admits this when he explains how his wife helped him adapt to life in America: "When [Fatima] talked, she laughed a laugh – she bought Lebanon back to me."[86] The connection Ibrahim draws between Fatima and Lebanon is representative of how Ibrahim, after living in the US for over a decade, finally transforms it into his abode. He harshly abandons his "devoted first [American] wife after ten years of fairly pleasant marriage" because there "comes a time when you don't want to live with a stranger anymore".[87] Similarly, although it takes Fatima a long time to realise it, it is Ibrahim who anchors her sense of home. In the early stages of their marriage, the jokes he rehearses about a medieval fictional Arab character called Juha along with the Arabic newspapers he reads aloud to Fatima ease her alienation from her present circumstances.[88]

Fatima and Ibrahim's divorce certainly undermines their particular experience of home but what exacerbates this loss even further is their inability to converse on the telephone. In several episodes in the novel Ibrahim endeavours to restore his relationship with his wife via telephone contact. During these calls Ibrahim intends to inform Fatima about the destruction of the Deir Zeitoon house, something he has known about for approximately 20 years. At the time of his discovery, during a trip to Lebanon in the 1980s, Ibrahim conceals the truth from his wife and concocts an elaborate story about how he "spent his time [in Lebanon] repairing the house before [...] put[ting] the Mansour family in charge of taking care of it".[89] In the novel's present, precisely on the 998th night, Ibrahim stages what becomes his last attempt to tell his wife the truth, but as the following passage demonstrates his efforts to set the record straight are utterly futile:

> "Hello," [Fatima] said, and waited for a response on the other end.
> "Fatima?" Ibrahim said through the static and line glitches.
> "Ibrahim?" Fatima said, remarkably wordless.
> "Did you get my [...]" but Fatima could not make out the words through the interference on the line.
> "Get your what?"
> "Get my [...]" was all Fatima could make out [...]
> "I will try again [...]" Ibrahim said through the several clicks in the line. "When your phone is better".[90]

The potential of this conversation to restore Ibrahim and Fatima's relationship can only be measured against the protagonist's reaction when she does eventually learn the truth only three days later. The news of the house's destruction reorganises Fatima's view of home, transforming Detroit into its essential site rather than Deir Zeitoon.[91] In addition to this she embraces Ibrahim as a significant figure in her life and as instrumental to her realisation of home. He is, as she herself concedes, "the only person who was part of her past, present and future" and the only one "who could laugh [and commiserate] with her about [...] Deir Zeitoon" and Detroit.[92] At this point Fatima resolves to call Ibrahim "no matter how many times the telephone cut out" in order to salvage the homely sensibility she and her husband once shared.[93] However, Fatima's acceptance of a more honest vision of home occurs at the most inopportune moment because it coincides with Ibrahim's unexpected death. Poignantly, the last chance the couple had to restore their relationship and sense of home transpired a few days prior to Ibrahim's death, during his and Fatima's distorted and inaudible phone conversation. As this tragic failure of communication exemplifies, the telephone is vulnerable to manipulation and can alienate just as much as it can unite people across time and space.

The role that the FBI unwittingly plays here in this negation of homeliness also points to the broader issues related to the evolving discourse of homeland security post-9/11. The Bush administration's response to the attack on the Twin Towers was the immediate passage of the USA PATRIOT Act.[94] This Act strengthened the powers of the state against both foreigners deemed to be a threat to America's homeland security and its own citizen body. It gave legitimacy to racial profiling, torture in various circumstances, and increased the surveillance powers of intelligence agencies.[95] Yunis' novel documents this explicitly not just through the simple inclusion of a character that works for the FBI, but also through this agent's justification of her clandestine probing of the Abdullah clan. Sherri Hazard informs the Abdullahs that the "Patriot Act gives us [the FBI] the right to question and conduct sneak and peek searches" even if the intelligence that they unearth is as harmless as the employment of an undocumented domestic worker by Randa or the changing of Randa's husband's name from Bashar to Bud.[96] Agent Hazard suggests that her enforcement of the FBI's legal right to undertake these searches initially stems from suspicions regarding Amir's supposed jihadist leanings. This may be the case but it is not really Amir's Islamic or Arab heritage that troubles Agent Hazard. Rather, what concerns her is the Abdullah family's dispersal and mobility.

Agent Hazard never explicitly states that the itinerant nature of Fatima's family constitutes a threat worthy of investigation, but a particular scene between her and Fatima exposes this concern with mobility. Agent Hazard initially indicates to Fatima that she wishes "to talk about [. . .] Amir Abdullah [. . .] that's all" and insists that Fatima give her "information [only] about Amir".[97] However, this preoccupation with Amir readily expands to an interest in the location or movements of several of Fatima's other children and grandchildren. When, for example, it is mentioned that Amir's mother, Soraya, was once married to a Beiruti who now resides in Saudi Arabia, Agent Hazard cannot help but probe Fatima further about this man. Agent Hazard questions Fatima about any possible trips Amir may have taken to Saudi Arabia and wonders if "Amir ever go[es] to see [Soraya's ex-husband] there?"[98] There are also questions surrounding Soraya's current work in Tijuana and Dina's potential relocation to Gaza. Soraya and Dina's presence in places that are considered treacherous to US interests generate deep suspicions on the part Agent Hazard, namely with regard to the women's free movement across various borders.[99] Furthermore, it is after gathering this information from Fatima that Agent Hazard decides to monitor not only Amir's calls and his "comings and goings at strange times [. . .] in various disguises" but to also wiretap every phone number billed to Amir's landline.[100] Ultimately the intelligence she unearths about this family is not illegal in nature nor is it linked to any form terrorist activity; it simply describes a number of humiliating and personal indiscretions.

This surveillance and general suspicion surrounding the Abdullahs' mobility is, of course, entirely predictable given the political context of the novel. William Walters' article "Secure Borders, Safe Haven, Domopolitics" is particularly instructive here because it closely considers how the meaning of home changes in a context of governance and security. Even though he takes the British White Paper *Secure Borders, Safe Haven* (2002) as his main case study, his article nevertheless sheds light on what the discourse of homeland security entails in Western countries where migrant communities are prevalent. Walters argues that a state's sense of insecurity is "bound up with themes of mobility".[101] Insecurity is about the "movement, the circulation [and] the presence of unauthorized [or unlawful] bodies which have violated the borders of the nation-state".[102] In this context of migration and insecurity, Walters goes on to identify the two forms of domesticity that homeland security discourse engages with. The first is derived from the classical Greek word *oikos*, which is often taken to mean household but also refers to economic and utilitarian matters. *Oikos*, according to Walters, is "the need for an efficient migration system which can identify and harness the human skills and ambitions of migrants to promote the economic security of the state".[103]

In Yunis' book Fatima's two husbands, Marwan and Ibrahim, are the kind of migrants that fit this category. As Fatima reports to Scheherazade in one of her storytelling sessions, both men were employed in the 1940s and 1950s as factory workers for General Motors (GM), one of America's primary automobile manufacturers. Marwan in particular took a lead role in demanding rights for GM staff. Many workers sustained life-threatening injuries and were inadequately compensated. According to Fatima's version of events, Marwan unionised the car manufacturing plant and compelled "GM [. . .] to give the workers fair money and good treatment".[104] This activism highlights the degree to which Marwan was dedicated to supporting the US economy:

> Marwan's courage proved that we didn't just care about sending money back home, which is what most people thought about Arabs. I know because that's what Millie [Fatima's neighbour] told me her husband told her. He told her we'd just take off back to "garlic eater land" as soon as we made enough money.[105]

Despite this clear contribution to the American workforce and economy the Abdullahs are perceived as a threat because of their mobility. This is where Walters' second formulation of home – *domus* – is applicable because it registers the state's desire to control mobility. *Domus*, a Latin word that means house, "is closely related to the verb *domo* which can be literally translated as 'to tame' or 'break in' [. . .] [or to] domesticate".[106] Extending this meaning to security discourse, *domus* represents "the quest for domesticity and order: the protection of the homeland in a world of dangerous mobilities".[107] What this suggests is that the only domestic arrangement that the state conceives of in non-threatening terms is one of stasis. This presents a problem because the benefits of *oikos* are too great to arrest mobility entirely. Rather, as Walters contends, the aim of the state is "to tame" mobility, to monitor it and to bring it under state control.[108] This is what Agent Hazard has in mind when she decides to tap the phone lines of the Abdullahs. She does not simply seek to eavesdrop on conversations and gather intelligence but also to regulate the threat that the Abdullahs' itinerant lifestyles represent.

This threat to domestic mobility that the telephone surveillance exposes does not impede Yunis' promotion of a mobile and dislocated vision of home. Yunis' commitment to a broader definition of home is evident in her ability to transform what roots and trees are often seen to symbolise, that is stability and stasis, into a force of movement. This is rather innovative because to date, in diaspora theory at least, the concept of roots has never been conceived of in this way. While several scholars, like Stuart Hall, Paul Gilroy, Floya Anthias and James Clifford, have insisted upon the need to retain a discussion of roots in an analysis of diaspora, they also consistently caution against an overemphasis on origins and fixity at the expense of mobility. Roots therefore have, as Ghassan Hage explains, "a bad name in certain intellectual circles" because they "are associated with stasis, conservatism and narrow mindedness".[109] Hage argues that when "roots [are] experienced in this [negative] way" they drive "people [. . .] to bury [. . .] themselves in their roots [so that] their rootedness becomes territorial and [. . .] claustrophobic".[110] There is no doubt that Fatima exhibits this form of regressive attachment to her originary roots. This is demonstrated by her obsession with her childhood house. Linked to this house is the fig tree which was transplanted from Lebanon to America. It was planted in Detroit with seeds given to Fatima by her mother and then shipped from Detroit to Amir's Los Angeles garden.[111] Indeed, for the majority of the text the tree symbolises an adherence to a conservative view of roots.

But roots need not only manifest themselves in this negative or regressive way, and as the ending of Yunis' novel shows they can actually be the catalyst for feeling grounded in one's place of settlement. Hage explains this alternative function of roots. Witnessing the unkempt sight of three trees – fig, olive and pomegranate – planted by his Lebanese migrant grandfather, Hage, himself a migrant to Australia, remarks that the sight of these trees made him feel intensely Australian. This is a revealing moment for Hage because standing in the backyard of his grandfather's Bathurst home "next to these very Lebanese trees, planted by my very Lebanese grandfather" he realises just how rooted he is in Australia and how profoundly Australian he is.[112] What is most interesting about Hage's sentiment of rootedness is his categorisation of it in "non-paradoxical" and "non-ambivalent" terms.[113] He states that the "Lebanese trees did not make me feel Australian and Lebanese, although I do feel both at many moments of life. Nor did they make me feel torn between my Lebaneseness and my Australianness. They simply made me feel [. . .] more Australian."[114] As Hage goes on to qualify, however, this newly-found "sense of rootedness does not mean a sense of being locked in the ground, unable to move" but is more accurately, even if paradoxically, "experienced like an extra pair of wings".[115] This is, he finally argues, "exactly how I experienced my trees. *I felt them propelling me*".[116]

Not unlike Hage's epiphany in his grandfather's backyard, Fatima experiences a similar form of arboreal-induced propulsion to a new sense of home when she discovers that her tree, after 67 years of sterility, has finally produced its first fruit. The tree has not only rooted itself successfully in the soil of Amir's Los Angeles courtyard but also "found [itself] a home in America".[117] What is noteworthy here is that after this event, which coincides with the protagonist's discovery of her destroyed Deir Zeitoon home, Fatima makes a point of trying to call Ibrahim to talk to him not of her past or the house but only of the present miracle "of the fig tree fruiting".[118] Ibrahim's death, of course, means that Fatima is unable to communicate with him. Yet what Fatima is able to communicate to Scheherazade, and ultimately to the reader, is that she no longer wishes to be beholden to a past that has weighed her down for several decades. In the novel's closing pages Fatima accepts her own undeniable rootedness in

America and does so without being territorial. This is evident in her decision regarding the settlement of the Detroit house she inherits from her deceased husband. When Scheherazade asks "To whom will you leave this house in Detroit?" Fatima's reply of "Someone [...] Anyone" speaks volumes of her transformation with regard to houses and homes.[119] In this scene Fatima exhibits a form of rootedness that is, to borrow from Hage, "positive [in] character because [...] [it is] a mode of belonging that can stand in opposition to the [...] territorial", static and regressive manner of being rooted that several diaspora and migration theorists have criticised.[120]

Conclusion

The ending of Yunis' novel exemplifies that mobility is embedded within the discourse of home, especially in a context of displacement and migration. The text's many characters are itinerant beings and their sense of home is maintained through their distance and dispersal. Scheherazade's mobility reinforces this point and illustrates that narrative and storytelling facilitate the conception of "home-as-movement". Furthermore, Fatima's eventual acceptance of her longstanding rootedness in America at the novel's culmination overrides her essentialised view of home as being associated with her childhood house in Deir Zeitoon. Fatima's recognition of this transforms her vision of the domestic, where home has less to do with fixed architectural structures and more to do with fluidity across and between homes. This non-essentialised perception of home that *The Night Counter* advances is one that is taken up by Amin Maalouf in his important novel *Ports of Call*. Maalouf extends this view by focusing on the idea of a national home and the dangers inherent in the exclusivity that is deeply embedded within conceptions of the nation-state. Part III examines these issues in relation to the vexed conflict between Palestinians and Israelis, two peoples who both contend that their respective national homes are located in the same land.

PART III

CONTESTING THE
NATION-STATE

CHAPTER 7

NATION, STATE AND DIASPORA

This part focuses on *Ports of Call*, a novel by the Lebanese–French writer Amin Maalouf. Maalouf's text is one that resists the lure of a culturally homogenous national home that is traditionally associated with diaspora cultures and interrogates certain features that are used to define the nation-state. Traces of this interrogation of nationalism are evident in texts by numerous Lebanese writers, but *Ports of Call* is different.[1] What distinguishes Maalouf's novel from the rest is that it takes issue not with Lebanese nationalism, as one would perhaps expect, but examines the conflict between Jews and Palestinians prior to the partition of Palestine in 1948. Despite its subject matter, *Ports of Call* is still very much a novel that belongs to the Lebanese diaspora genre of literature. This is because what Maalouf does in his novel is apply the destabilising sensibility that is an inherent part of diaspora consciousness to a place that is not his immediate homeland. The discussion of *Ports of Call* in Chapter 8 will demonstrate this clearly, but first it is important to understand the complex relationship between diasporas and nations, to outline what the nation entails and to examine the established Lebanese literary tradition of engaging in representations of nation-states that emphasise difference and diversity.

The relationship between diasporas and nations is one that is often emphasised in theorisations of dispersal. In fact the nation-state is almost always part of any discussion related to diaspora because it is, on a broad scale, perceived as the authentic home of a dispersed community. Diana Brydon and Lily Cho argue that the very terms used to delineate a diaspora, such as the Chinese diaspora or the Irish diaspora, generally signal the nation that was left behind.[2] Even in Robin Cohen's text *Global Diasporas*, where he makes some effort to describe each diaspora he examines in terms that are independent of their homeland – the Lebanese, for example, are seen as a diaspora built through trade and commerce, while the transnational Armenians are represented as a victim diaspora – he nevertheless remains compelled to group these global communities in nationalist terms.[3] For Khachig Tölölyan, nations and diasporas maintain an antithetical relationship, but this does not diminish the centrality of the former. Indeed, as he argues, diasporas are the "Other" of the nation-state and should therefore be defined against it. This kind of definition is precisely what he makes the focus of *Diaspora*, a journal he has edited since 1991. In the inaugural issue he states that "Above all, this journal will focus on [how the] [...] processes [of nation-building] [...] shape and are shaped by the infranational and transnational Others of the nation-state".[4] Thus, as Brydon, Cho, Cohen and Tölölyan reflect, the nation-state is indispensable to understanding dispersal.

This, however, is a bold claim to make when considered in light of the fact that diasporas actually precede nation-states. In terms of chronology the nation-state emerged in the eighteenth and nineteenth centuries while certain diasporas, namely the Jewish and Greek varieties, can be dated respectively as far back as 586 BC and 800–600 BC.[5] Despite this it is not anachronistic for the nation-state to feature so heavily in theorisations of dispersal. As explained in the introductory chapter, the recent interest in diaspora studies within the academy, dating approximately from the 1990s, coincided with the rise in the appeal of the nation-state. Doreen Massey points out that the last two decades of the twentieth century were dominated by exclusivist and regressive forms of nationalism.[6] It is therefore understandable that diaspora would be defined against the notion of nationalism and why various theorists, especially Tölölyan, label-dispersed communities the "Others" of the nation-state.

Beyond this temporally-based rationale there is a further explanation for the close association between diaspora and the nation. This concerns the crucial role of the nation-state within the Jewish diaspora's perception of displacement. In *Diaspora: Jews Amidst Greeks and Romans*, Erich Gruen argues that at a theoretical level the Jewish assessment of their own diasporic "experience has been deconstructed from two quite divergent angles".[7] Certainly one of these angles is positive and purports that "Jews require no territorial sanctuary [. . .] [because] they are 'the people of the book' [. . .] [and] their homeland resides in the text".[8] In this construction "the book", the *Torah*, and various other Jewish texts, like the 13 books of the *Ketuvim* or the rabbinical writings found in the *Midrash*, are portable. So if Jewish writings rather than a territorial state define the nation, the "geographical restoration [of a Jewish homeland becomes] superfluous". This positive appraisal is countered by a negative one where "diaspora dissolves into *galut*, exile, a bitter and doleful image, offering a bleak vision that leads [. . .] to despair". Here diaspora is viewed as an abnormal state of being that requires correction. Yet, despite the persuasiveness of both arguments, it is the negative or "gloomy approach" that holds primacy and "dominates modern interpretations of the Jewish psyche" with regard to displacement.[9]

Eliezer Schweid reinforces this point in his examination of Zionistic attitudes towards dispersal. Focusing on Jewish thinkers and writers prior to the establishment of the state of Israel in 1948, Schweid argues that the "rejection of Jewish life in the Diaspora — *shlilat ha-gola* — is a central assumption in all currents of Zionist ideology".[10] This is true of the school of Zionist thought that stresses the negative impact of displacement on Jewish identity, advanced by Micha Josef Berdyczewski (1865–1921) and Yosef Haim Brenner (1881–1921). It also pervades the work of advocates of the positive lessons of diaspora, such as Ahad Ha'am (1856–1927) and Ahron David Gordan (1856–1922).[11] Collectively these Zionists were critical of a displaced existence because they were concerned that prolonged exile raised the risk of, firstly, "discrimination and extreme persecution from without" and, secondly, "decadence" from within.[12]

The remedy to these dangers was the establishment of a Jewish homeland, where the Jewish people could protect themselves from persecution and, more importantly, rejuvenate their cultural and religious practices. This was strongly supported by the most well-known Zionist, Theodor Herzl. As an assimilated and affluent Viennese journalist, it seemed unlikely that Herzl would emerge as the father of modern Zionism and in the process identify what form the Jewish homeland should take. According to Jacqueline Rose, Herzl's coverage of the 1894 Dreyfus Affair, where a French-Jewish army officer was falsely accused of spying for the Germans, transformed his political perspective. She argues that "Jewish *nationalism* would be the most important lesson of the Affair" for Herzl.[13] Soon after Dreyfus' trial Herzl published *The Jewish State* (1896), where he recognised the national status of the Jews – "We are one people – our enemies have made us one" – and argued that they should not simply seek a homeland but one that was shaped in terms of a nation-state – "we are strong enough to form a State, and, indeed, a model State".[14] As Schweid notes, "the Zionist solution in Herzl's political understanding of the term [was that the] Jewish people had to reorganise as a sovereign political nation in its own territory, *a modern nation like other nations*".[15]

What Gruen and Schweid's research clearly demonstrates is that Jewish culture overwhelmingly views diasporic existence as abnormal and the establishment of not just a homeland but a specific kind, in the form of a nation-state, as the best way that Jews can correct that abnormality. It is important to note this because while the Jews represent only one example of dispersal, their experience as well as their perception of displacement informs much diaspora theory.[16] William Safran's research reflects the centrality of Jewish dispersal most clearly. His work, compared to the scholarship of other diaspora theorists, unequivocally supports the idea that the Jewish diaspora is the prototype for all transnational communities.[17] I have in previous chapters and notably in the introduction identified and analysed various shortcomings of Safran's work, but one feature in particular, largely overlooked by critics and unmentioned in this book until now, is Safran's representation of the nation-state as the answer to displacement. This may seem an inaccurate assessment given that Safran hardly ever mentions or uses the phrase "nation-state" opting for the more general concept of "homeland". This is especially the case in the six criteria points that Safran uses to define diaspora. Points four through six place great emphasis on the homeland, namely its singularity and authenticity to diaspora cultures, its geographical necessity and its capacity to unite and galvanise the communities that claim to have been scattered from it.[18] Such criteria seemingly advance a generalist and non-specific view of diaspora but, upon closer examination, they reveal the intense particularity of Safran's work. Jon Stratton identifies this in his article "(Dis)placing the Jews: Historicizing the Idea of Diaspora", where he asserts that Safran's criteria "only make sense in Zionist terms, and [. . .] in relation to the Israeli nation-state".[19] What this means is that Safran's idea of diaspora is built not on "assumptions" that are broad-based and accommodating of a wide variety of communal displacements, but on conventions that "depend in crucial ways on modern constructions of the nation, the national people, and the space – the land – which the nation claims to belongs to it".[20]

The Nation and the State

It is difficult to pinpoint exactly what kind of nation-state Safran circuitously alludes to when he writes about the homeland; he certainly does not posit or establish a model of one in his article. This is hardly surprising given that nationalism itself has no standard or agreed-upon definition. Indeed the term is ambiguous and its uncertainty, according to Shlomo Sand, rests on the fact that nation and nationalism are not closely diagnosed and ultimately have been neglected by scholars.[21] What is ironic about Sand's claim is that there is an abundance of literature concerned with this topic from a range of disciplines, such as politics, anthropology, history and literary studies.[22] While it may be true, and even expected, that such a vast array of scholarly material has been unable to yield a definitive meaning of the nation-state, one can still point to a number of characteristics that recur in discussions of the term. Two of the most prominent which feature in the quote above from Stratton and are part of Safran's work are culture and land. Culture and land correlate with the nation-state, where the latter is adopted as a synonym of state and the former is used to frame national identity.

These two aspects of the nation-state are given particular distinction by the German historian Friedrich Meinecke (1862–1954). In *Cosmopolitanism and the National State* (1907), Meinecke develops the concepts civic nations – *Staatsnation* – and ethnic nations – *Kulturnation*. These remain relevant to contemporary scholars like David Brown, John Hutchinson and Désirée Kleiner-Liebau because they succinctly capture the significance of land and culture in theorisations of nationalism. Commenting on the political and territorial basis of *Staatsnation*, Brown argues that occupants of a state "constitute a nation because they have willingly come together to form a community of equal citizens irrespective of racial, religious or linguistic backgrounds".[23] *Kulturnation*, however, is "independent of the state and defines itself through supposedly objective cultural criteria, such as common ethnic origins, language, and religion".[24] For Hutchinson, the "essence of a nation" from the perspective of cultural nationalists "is its distinctive civilization, which is the product of its unique history [and] culture".[25] Based on these definitions, *Staatsnation* and *Kulturnation* are ideal-types in the Weberian sense and cannot be seamlessly applied to all nations.[26] Also, even though represented as mutually exclusive, the political nation and the cultural one are not so separate. In reality nationalism "is an existing or envisaged nation-state wherein cultural and political boundaries coincide".[27]

While both the cultural and political aspects are evident in all contemporary conceptions of the nation-state, the structure of these two parts raises crucial questions about national belonging and exclusivity. For example, in *Modern Nationalism* Hutchinson suggests that the most widely accepted understanding of nation-states is that they are "facets of nature that have differentiated humanity into distinctive cultural commodities, each of which has its own territorial habitat".[28] Even though Hutchinson's definition does not necessarily intend to be racially or ethnically exclusionary, it does highlight the potential and strong likelihood of nations to be so. In his seminal essay "Reflections on Exile", Edward Said focuses on the dangers of cultural exclusivity and argues that when cultural boundaries are drawn nationalism becomes an "assertion of belonging in and to a place, a people and a heritage".[29] Such acts are critically assessed by Said not just because he does not favour cultural exclusivity but because he, like Anthony D. Smith, contests the idea that nations are "naturally occurring units" that house particular ethnic groups in specific locations.[30] Similarly, Michael Shapiro takes issue with the idea of cultural uniformity. He challenges the popular and "primary understanding of the modern 'nation' segment of the nation-state" – "a nation embodies a coherent culture, united on the basis of shared descent or, at least, incorporating a 'people' with a historically stable coherence" – by pointing out that very few "if any states [actually] contain coherent historically stable communities".[31] In the absence of such coherence it becomes necessary to exercise the "maintenance of the nation-state [...] [through the] continuous management of historical narratives as well as territorial boundaries".[32]

The "management" that Shapiro refers to is reflected in the manner that territory and culture are manipulated by certain nationalists who wish to justify or legitimate their claims to a nation-state. Two interrelated examples, the myth of autochthony and the pursuit of cultural exclusivity, illustrate how such manipulation operates. Autochthony is used to describe the relationship between a given people and a particular plot of land. The concept has its roots in ancient Greek mythology where autochthons, mythical half-human half-serpent creatures, were believed to have emerged from the land itself. Citizens of ancient Athens referred to themselves as autochthons as a mark of their status as the original occupants of Athenian territory. Even though autochthony is related to the ancient world, it nonetheless remains a vital part of the production of contemporary national identity. Writing specifically about Western states, Eric Hobsbawm argues that such "modern nations [...] generally claim to be the opposite of novel, namely *rooted in the remotest of antiquity*, and the opposite of constructed, namely human communities so 'natural' as to require no definition".[33] In this regard, much like its ancient form, modern autochthony shows how the land and the nation are indivisible.

While many examples can be given to reflect how autochthony operates, the preoccupation with the establishment of Israel in Maalouf's text means that the more revelatory instances involve examining how it has been deployed by the Israeli state and its supporters in both its pre-existence and post-establishment periods. Not surprisingly, autochthony features heavily in Jewish myths of homeland, particularly among those Zionists, mentioned above, who stress the negative impact of diaspora. For instance, in the late nineteenth and early twentieth century writings of Micha Josef Berdyczewski autochthonous motifs are quite explicit. Assaf Sagiv reports that in his texts Berdyczewski sought to "create a 'new Jew', earthly and close to nature. He [Berdyczewski] urged the people to [...] return to 'the primeval past before the giving of the book', in which the Jew was united with nature in a [...] mythic embrace."[34] Israel's first Prime Minister, David Ben-Gurion, most actively promoted the autochthonous concept. For Ben-Gurion the "people of Israel, or the Hebrew people, was born in the land and raised in the land".[35] The implication of Ben-Gurion's statement is that the Jews possess an original entitlement to the land because they were born there "even before the days of Abraham [the father of Judaism], as one of the peoples of Canaan".[36] Furthermore, the Jewish people's entitlement is not diminished by their protracted exile. When local Arab populations, namely the Palestinians, argue that they are the land's indigenous inhabitants the Zionist response has been to refashion autochthony for the purpose of sustaining their claim of primacy. As Schweid explains:

> the Jewish people's claim that it had a historic right to its land rested upon [...] their statement that the bond between this people and its land had never been disrupted. Even if the people had perforce lived for generations in exile and its land had been conquered [or inhabited] by others, it had never relinquished their desire and hope to return there and wrest it from foreign domination.[37]

This reworking of autochthony introduces the notion of cultural exclusivity, the second of the two aspects used to justify a given people's claims to a nation-state. Such modification and exclusivity underlies the very text that gave birth to the Jewish state, the Israeli Declaration of Independence. As Daniel and Jonathan Boyarin point out, the "Declaration [...] begins with an imaginary autochthony – 'In the Land of Israel this people came into existence' – and ends with the triumphant return of the People to their natural Land, making them 're-autochthonized'" to the exclusion of all others on the land.[38] The point about autochthony in the context of the Declaration is, according to Stratton, that the nation-state can, first, always argue that it has an "original and unique claim to the Land on which it was formed" and, second, legitimate the "exclusivity of the national population" in racial and cultural terms.[39] Quite obviously one of Israel's challenges in legitimating its cultural exclusivity is the presence of the Palestinian other on the land. One method used to confront this challenge involved the Zionist negation of the prior presence of Arabs in historical Palestine. The popular early twentieth century Zionist slogan "a land for a people, for a people without a land" captures this sentiment to erase the other perfectly. In the early years of its establishment Israel also engaged in forms of ethnic cleansing against Palestinians. These events are well documented by both Zionists, like Benny Morris, and anti- or post-Zionists, like Ilan Pappé.[40] Charges of apartheid are also levelled at Israel by scholars like Jeff Halper or Uri Davis revealing another form of, if not denial exactly, then an advanced method of segregating the other.[41]

Such policies or actions are to be expected especially if Israel is contextualised as a settler-state. Australia, also a settler-state, provides a comparable example. Like Israel it practiced widespread ethnic cleansing of its indigenous population. It also denied the presence of the Aboriginal people on the land and dismissed all forms of indigenous sovereignty. This denial of sovereignty was later referred to by the term *terra nullius*.[42] Unlike Israel, however, Australia has not been able to adopt a concept of autochthonous origins in order to manage the ethnic composition of its own population. Since 1950, two years after Israel was established, the Law of Return has granted Jewish people across the globe the legal and historical right to settle in Israel. This statute is strategically termed the Law of Return rather than, for example, the Law of Immigration because Jewish settlement in Israel is perceived not as an act of relocation but as an act of "return" to the original birthplace of the Jews. It is, therefore, the Jewish people's "birthright" to attain Israeli citizenship and reside there. What is common to both the concepts of birthright and autochthony, at least in this context, is the notion that Israel is the birthplace of the Jews and the site of original habitation. It is in this manner that the two concepts are deployed to manage the kind of population the Israeli state desires.[43]

Cultural exclusivity and land are therefore key aspects that underpin the meaning of the nation-state. Nationalism understood in this mode is particularly rigid and unaccommodating of cultural plurality and territorial uncertainty. For several decades now, especially with the publication of Homi Bhabha's edited collection *Nation and Narration*, literary works have been implicated in the construction of nations. This does not mean that literature simply reinforces a nation-state's uniformity. In fact, Bhabha states that literature reflects how "national culture is neither unified nor unitary" but steeped in the "cultural difference" that he believes is inherent to all national spaces.[44] One chapter in Bhabha's collection, "Denaturalizing Cultural Nationalisms: Readings of 'Australia'" by Sneja Gunew, demonstrates this clearly. Of Gunew's contribution, Bhabha writes that her "portrayal of [...] Australian literature [is] split between an Anglo-Celtic public sphere and a multiculturalist counter-public sphere. It is the excluded voices of migrants [...] that Gunew represents, bringing them back to disturb [...] the writing of the Australian canon."[45]

Lebanese Literature

Lebanon and the literature its writers have produced has also undergone examination much along the same lines that Bhabha proposes. The most thorough of these examinations is Elise Salem's

Constructing Lebanon: A Century of Literary Narratives. In this text
Salem tracks the formation of the Lebanese state in order, as one
reviewer writes, to "see how the idea of Lebanon as a nation has been
constructed by its intellectuals in the twentieth century".[46] What
emerges in Salem's century-long literary study is a plural and diverse
image of Lebanon. This is illustrated, first, in the incongruous
depiction of rural Lebanon prior to and during the war and, second,
in the conflicted representations of Lebanon in the post-war era. With
regard to the former, Salem's analysis of the early twentieth century
writer Khalil Gibran exposes his over-determined romanticisation of
rural Lebanon. As suggested in a previous chapter, Gibran idealises
the simplicity of rural life and associates Lebanon with liberty and
justice. This particular image of Lebanon, however, is challenged in
the latter half of the same century by a group of writers that Salem
labels the Poets of the South. Writing of their experiences during the
civil war, these poets emphasise the plight of the Shi'a Muslim
villages that border Israel. Their Lebanon is afflicted by war,
injustice, occupation and poverty and is remarkably different to the
one advanced by Gibran several decades earlier. In terms of the post-
war literature, the disparity of representation is just as marked. Most
writers like Hanan al-Shaykh, Hoda Barakat and Elias Khoury
address what Salem and various other scholars identify as Lebanon's
war amnesia. Their post-war narratives wilfully and even dutifully
"disturb rather than entertain".[47] In contrast, Emily Nasrallah stresses
Lebanon's golden age and historical past because she believes that
readers need untainted national myths for nation-building purposes.

While Salem does not reference Amin Maalouf extensively in her
examination of how twentieth century Lebanese writers have
constructed Lebanon, she does note his contribution. For Salem,
Maalouf is an expatriate writer who helped develop a "global
Lebanese literature" and ensured that "Lebanon's story could and
would be told from abroad".[48] By focusing only on what Maalouf has
written about Lebanon primarily in one novel, *The Rock of Tanios*
(1994), Salem's appraisal of his contribution to the global Lebanese
literary scene remains limited.[49] What distinguishes Maalouf from
his peers is that he has not confined himself to simply writing about

Lebanon or making Lebanon the main subject of his novels. Where his main contribution lies is in his capacity as a diasporic Lebanese writer to destabilise various concepts or historical events. The narrative of *Ports of Call*, which deals with the partition of Palestine and the establishment of Israel, questions the two aspects that underpin the nation-state, outlined above as land and cultural exclusivity. In this novel, and especially through the relationship of its two protagonists, Maalouf skilfully illustrates what Boyarin and Boyarin have referred to as the "lessons of Diaspora". The first of these lessons is "that peoples and lands are not naturally and organically connected" and the second is that no state can successfully impose a model of cultural homogeneity or exclusivity.[50]

CHAPTER 8

ONE LAND OR TWO? ISRAEL AND PALESTINE IN AMIN MAALOUF'S *PORTS OF CALL*

In their reviews of *Ports of Call*, critics seem to focus on two aspects of the novel that they find difficult to reconcile. One is the tragic love story between the two protagonists, Ossyane Ketabdar and Clara Emden, and the other is the novel's array of political events, such as the Armenian genocide of 1915, the disintegration of the Ottoman Empire, the Nazi occupation of France during World War II and the partition of Palestine in 1948, all of which shaped the twentieth century. Jamal En-nehas suggests that the personal relationship between Ossyane and Clara is represented in terms of an idealised past while the political issues are situated in an unaccommodating present. Ossyane remembers his relationship with Clara in an intensely "nostalgic" manner but "a hostile present" marred by war and violence renders their love affair impossible.[1] En-nehas, while favourable to Maalouf's concern with weighty issues like identity and belonging, disapproves of the author's treatment of the personal and the political as a "clash between the old and the new".[2] Lucy Dallas also focuses on Maalouf's intertwining of the personal and the political, criticising the author's failure to strike the right representational balance. The subject-matter of Maalouf's novel, "people torn apart against a backdrop of bigotry and war", is simply not convincing because readers acquire too much information about the people and are left with "only a hazy picture of the conflicts".[3]

What Dallas finds most unconvincing is the 30-year separation the two main characters are forced to endure. The catalyst for this separation is the establishment of the state of Israel in May 1948. Ossyane is in Beirut visiting his father and Clara is in Haifa about to give birth to their daughter. The outbreak of the first war between the Arab states and Israel makes it impossible for Ossyane to return to Haifa. As Dallas concedes "the Arab-Israeli war separates the lovers initially" but this does not explain their protracted time apart.[4] On the strength of this assumption Dallas proceeds to argue that what keeps Ossyane and Clara from one another is "individual apathy and greed".[5] Such an accusation of indifference assumes that the protagonists possess a certain degree of agency and can, despite the violence that surrounds them, manoeuvre their way around the conflict. Dallas even makes this assertion despite the fact that for almost all of the years the characters spend in exile from one another Ossyane is virtually imprisoned in an asylum, drugged on a daily basis and forcibly restricted from leaving the compound.

The only way to explain this insistence that it is Ossyane and Clara's own disinterest that sustains their separation is to compare this part of the story with the characters' earlier exploits in Nazi occupied France. As members of the French Resistance, Clara and Ossyane undertake various dangerous missions, such as delivering secret documents to fellow comrades or disseminating pamphlets that denounce Nazism and the occupation.[6] Yet despite the heavy presence of fascist soldiers, neither character is permanently captured and Ossyane emerges as a key hero in the Resistance movement. Dallas finds these events convincing, noting that Maalouf's insertion of Ossyane into the French Resistance is "finely done; there are no big dramatic decisions or adventures [. . .] [Ossyane] acts according to his beliefs and becomes useful {to the Resistance} in a hundred discrete ways".[7] Even though Dallas does not state this explicitly, her approving comments here imply that if the protagonists were able to exercise a certain degree of agency during a world war then surely they should be able to navigate their way through a regional conflict.

The interpretative stress placed on the agency of characters reflects a rather narrow reading of the text. In fact it is entirely misguided to attribute Ossyane and Clara's separation to their own unwillingness to act. Such a reading overlooks the novel's broader agenda of countering the widely held assumptions that cultural or ethnic separation and the formation of two nation-states are the only viable living arrangements available to Palestinians and Israelis. Ossyane documents the limitations that the encroaching segregation involves. After he and Clara marry they elect to have two homes, one in Haifa and one in Beirut. They commute between the two cities and, like all people in the region, are able to "wander freely" across fluid borders.[8] Things change, however, as demands for the establishment of a Jewish state increase in the mid-1940s. The year 1947, Ossyane notes, "was the time when there was much talk about splitting Palestine into two states, one for the Jews and the other for the Arabs".[9] When this finally happens a year later the relatively easy passage between Lebanon and Palestine is completely compromised: "The frontiers became hermetically sealed. No travellers, no mail, no telegrams, no telephone."[10] As Gil Hochberg argues in her analysis of *Ports of Call*, while the 1948 Arab-Israeli war separates the protagonists at the outset, what keeps them "divided [. . .] [are] new national borders that are accompanied by a new segregated national-ethnic order".[11] What this means is that the newly-erected frontier is not just impassable for Ossyane and Clara in a literal sense but is also figuratively impenetrable because it instigates, as Hochberg notes, an enduring "national-ethnic order" of separation.

This national-ethnic order entails the division of land to accommodate what are considered to be two different national communities. In fact, for the duration of the Arab–Israeli conflict, such separation has been constantly reinforced in numerous peace proposals and is still perceived as the only way to end the protracted violence. Its first most notable mention came from the British administration during a time when it was losing power in its Palestinian colony. As Ali Abunimah argues it "was the British government [. . .] that had in the 1930s first given its official imprimatur to partition as *the* solution to the conflict between Jews and Arabs".[12] This endorsement took place specifically in 1937 and was part of the recommendations of the Peel Commission. Lord Peel headed the Palestine Royal Commission in order to deal with the escalating violence between Jews and Palestinians and the unrest caused by the Arab revolt. Peel, according to Ilan Pappé, "recommended the annexation of most of Palestine to Transjordan [. . .] [and awarded a] small portion of the land [. . .] as a future Jewish state".[13] Ultimately the commission failed, but it did set into place this notion of a two state solution that the global community increasingly coalesced around. This is why, a decade later in 1947, when the United Nations adopted its own plan for partition, Resolution 181, a majority in the General Assembly voted in favour of it. What this made clear, as Ali Abunimah, Ghada Karmi and Ilan Pappé confirm, is that the international community generally believed that partition was not only an answer to the conflict between Palestinians and Jews but also an achievable reality.[14]

The geographical gains Israel made after the 1967 war, where it effectively seized control of the Palestinian territories – the West Bank and the Gaza Strip – and established settlements there, meant that further peace initiatives became necessary. Again, these proposals simply assumed separation as the answer. The Russian plan in 1981, for example, called for the creation of a Palestinian state alongside Israel.[15] In other words, this plan sought the withdrawal of Israel from the territories it occupied a decade earlier. Similarly the 1982 Fez plan, put forward by King Fahd of Saudi Arabia, proposed that Palestine be established in the West Bank and Gaza and Israel withdraw its forces to the pre-1967 armistice lines.[16] The 1993 Oslo Accords reaffirmed this commitment to two states, as did President George W. Bush's 2003 Road Map for Peace and his pledge in 2007 to establish a viable Palestinian state within the occupied territories before he left office in 2009.[17] On the matter of partition, the Obama administration continued to support peace proposals based on a two state settlement, at least in its public rhetoric.[18] With regard to the international community, the UN organisation concerned with education, science and culture, UNESCO, voted in 2011 with an overwhelming majority to incorporate Palestine as a full member, thereby illustrating that most countries remain dedicated to recognising Palestine as an independent state that is separate from Israel.

Despite all the proposals for a settlement and the repeated commitment from the US and the international community of its support for a two state solution, none of the attempts to implement separation since 1948 have shown signs of success. There are numerous reasons for this and the most obvious explanations are politically derived. According to Abunimah the reason for repeated failure is simple: "There is no workable partition that is acceptable to a majority of Israelis and Palestinians" with regard to economic issues, security concerns and, most importantly, the distribution of land.[19] Virginia Tilley offers two explanations as to why the "two state option has been eliminated as a [politically] practical solution".[20] The first of these relates to geography. The extensive network of Jewish settlements in the West Bank has rendered Palestinian territory "into a vestige too small to sustain a viable national society".[21] Removing the settlements in the West Bank is an impossible task in Tilley's opinion not just because the number of settlements there far exceeds the amount dismantled during the Gaza withdrawal in August 2005, but also because "no power – internal or external – has the political capacity to effect any meaningful withdrawal of these urban communities".[22] What this ultimately means is that the settlements are a permanent part of the landscape, are under the jurisdiction of Israel and have transformed the potential Palestinian state into a "twisted [and discontinuous] scrap of land".[23]

The second reason why the two state solution is no longer an option relates to security. If a Palestinian state was to emerge it would be, as the previous point suggests, discontinuous and fragmented. In effect it would have to exist between and around the Jewish settlements. The state would be, as Tilley observes, "blocked off physically from the Israeli economy, its major cities would be cut off from each other, and its government would be unable to control the territory's water resources [...] or manage its trade".[24] This Palestine would be extremely unstable and would not only produce its own internal problems but also generate security concerns for its most immediate neighbour and perceived aggressor, Israel. Successive Israeli governments, and especially the recent administrations of Ariel Sharon, Ehud Olmert and Benjamin Netanyahu, have been aware of this and have sought to delay peace negotiations while creating what they believe are further security assurances. The construction of the Israeli "security fence", which began with Prime Minister Sharon, demonstrates Israel's determination to protect its citizen body.[25]

Beyond these political reasons there are also other explanations, related to culture, that explain why segregation is unachievable. These are difficult to categorise because they refer to the often overlooked cultural and filial affinities between the two peoples. Hochberg describes these connections as "a stubborn history of intimacy" and argues that Israelis and Palestinians "are forced to share an inextricably linked life" no matter how many checkpoints, fences or walls are put into place to keep them apart.[26] That linkage is ironically stimulated by the same efforts that drive the separation. Jewish settlements, for instance, located in the heart of Palestinian territory, although segregated and self-sufficient, nevertheless determine that the two peoples are in close proximity to one another. Palestinians and Israelis are also intertwined economically, not least because the hardships Palestinians face in terms of employment have forced many of them to seek work within Israel.[27] This increased proximity has, according to Hochberg, the potential to expose a "strange familiarity" between Jews and Arabs because it "furnishes our [. . .] imagination [. . .] for envisioning the relationship between [the] two peoples" in different or imperceptible ways.[28] Such imagining takes place not by marginalising the current practice of "othering" that both Israelis and Palestinians are guilty of, but by working within that very determination to differentiate.

This is best demonstrated by Edward Said in one of his earliest articles concerned with Arab and Jewish interaction. In its opening pages Said insightfully argues that neither the Israelis nor Palestinians "can develop without the other there". This is because no Arab today has an identity that can be unconscious of the Jew, that can rule out the Jew as a psychic factor in the Arab identity; conversely [...] no Jew can ignore the Arab in general, nor can he immerse himself in his ancient tradition and so lose the Palestinian Arab in particular and what Zionism has done to him. The more intense these modern struggles for identity become, the more attention is paid by the Arab or the Jew to his chosen opponent, or partner. *Each is the other.*[29]

This shared otherness of the Arab and the Jew resonates with Julia Kristeva's investigation, outlined earlier in the introduction, of the position of the foreigner within the nation-state. To recap briefly, Kristeva argues in *Strangers to Ourselves* that the figure of the foreigner disrupts the "assumed [national] unity of human beings" through "[his] *otherness*" while also occupying "an integral part of the *same*".[30] For Kristeva the foreigner is not an external being but is one that "lies within us: he is the hidden face of our identity, the space that wrecks our abode".[31] What this means is that the foreigner and the national are, like the Palestinian and the Israeli, each other's "other" while simultaneously being each other's equivalent or each other's "same". In that sense the distance between foreigner and national diminishes because if, as Kristeva declares, the "foreigner comes in when the consciousness of my difference arises" then "he [also] disappears when we all acknowledge ourselves as foreigners".[32]

Such ideas, theorised by Said and Kristeva, that complicate the assumed polarity of the Arab and the Jew or the foreigner and the national, are shared by Amin Maalouf. For Maalouf there can be no distance between the national and the foreigner because the author himself occupies both positions simultaneously. In his extended essay *On Identity* Maalouf declares "I don't have just one country" and in his memoir *Origins* confesses to never having "felt an overriding loyalty to one nation".[33] In fact, Maalouf feels that he is "poised between two countries, two or three languages and several cultural traditions".[34] He belongs not only to his native homeland of Lebanon but also his adopted home of France: "How many times, since I left Lebanon in 1976 to live in France, have people asked me [...] whether I felt 'more French' or 'more Lebanese'? And I always give the same answer: 'Both!'"[35] It is this lack of nationally-based loyalty, this wilful denial to identify with one state or homeland, that Maalouf makes the defining characteristic of his two protagonists in *Ports of Call*. Ossyane and Clara occupy opposing sides of the Arab–Israeli conflict; the former is a Lebanese-Muslim of Ottoman ancestry and the latter is a European-Jew. And yet despite the potential to be rivals, Ossyane and Clara not only marry but also work as activists for a single bi-national state that can accommodate both Jews and Arabs. While their efforts are ultimately unsuccessful and the partition that eventually does take place in 1948 tragically separates them, the novel remains committed to challenging the idea that two states are needed to accommodate these supposedly different peoples. This is evident in three ways. The first two involve undermining the features, land and cultural exclusivity, that are often used to define nationalism and the nation-state. The third, and perhaps most crucial, is the novel's attempt to posit a model of coexistence by highlighting that the identities of the Jew and the Arab are not opposed but are actually integral parts of a hybrid Levantine subjectivity.

Land and National Identity

The question of land ownership constitutes one of the most heated issues between Israeli-Jews and Palestinians because both have competing territorial entitlements. Within the Israeli sphere arguments of their autochthonous origins buttress their claims to the land, while in the Palestinian case it is issues surrounding indigeneity and recent experiences of dispossession.[36] *Ports of Call*, however, successfully disaggregates the link between national identity and land through its two protagonists. It does this despite luring the reader into assuming that each character, that is Ossyane and Clara, represents a particular national community. This is attested to in Hochberg's assessment of the protagonists' relationship. According to her, *Ports of Call* presents the "love affair" between Ossyane and Clara as a kind of "model in miniature" alternative to the hostile nature of Arab and Jewish or Palestinian and

Israeli relations.[37] Hochberg further suggests that the novel sets up a kind of "parallelism" between the "personal" and the "national" narratives, and it is this that encourages readers to conflate Ossyane with Palestine and Clara with Israel.[38] However, when one considers the complicated origins of each protagonist it becomes increasingly clear that neither can claim any essentialist or natural link to the land.

Clara is first introduced in the novel during the height of World War II as a member of the French Resistance stationed in Lyon.[39] She wilfully elects to go to France after being smuggled into the neutral state of Switzerland. Despite securing her own safety, Clara chooses not to remain in Switzerland because she "couldn't bear the idea of other people fighting, dying, her family included, while she remained snugly protected".[40] Her life, however, began in neither France nor Switzerland but in the small town of Graz in Austria. This is where she was born and where she spent her childhood and adolescence. Her initial travels to Palestine take place only after the culmination of World War II as she accompanies her maternal uncle, Stefan Termerles, to Haifa. Stefan decides to reside in Palestine for the remainder of his life but Clara admits to being "not at all sure that she would want to stay in Palestine".[41] Like Clara, Ossyane too is a migrant to Palestine and has an equally complex relationship to it and the Arab world. Ossyane is, as he indicates in the novel's opening pages, not entirely of Arab descent. His paternal grandmother is the daughter of an unnamed Ottoman prince and her husband, Ossyane's grandfather, an eminent nineteenth century Persian physician.[42] Ossyane's father, who spent much of his life in Adana, a province in southern Turkey, is recognised for his noble Ottoman origins while Ossyane's mother, despite spending the first decade of her life in Turkey and the remainder in Lebanon, is identified as an Armenian.[43] Of these three generations of the Ketabdar family it is Ossyane who is the first to be born in the Arab world, specifically on the outskirts of Beirut in Lebanon. His first encounter with Palestine only takes place after his marriage to Clara, when the couple decide to live in both Haifa and Beirut. Clearly, then, Clara and Ossyane are migrants to Palestine and neither are, nor do they claim to be, connected to the land in a mythic or, to borrow from Boyarin and Boyarin, an "organic" way.

This very rejection of the connection between identity and land is openly embraced by Ossyane. His cosmopolitan heritage is one explanation for this but it is also informed by the racist experiences of his Turkish and Armenian kin. One episode in particular, which takes place prior to Ossyane's birth, concerns his father and his maternal Armenian grandfather, Noubar. In the first decades of the twentieth century, as the Ottoman Empire was in decline, Turkish nationalists staged a series of attacks against minorities within the empire, namely the Armenians. By 1915 these attacks escalated into the Armenian genocide which lasted until 1923. An estimated one and a half million were killed and tens of thousands deported or forced to flee to adjacent countries.[44] Maalouf incorporates part of these events in his novel when Ossyane's grandfather and father are threatened by a mob of angry Turks "brandishing clubs and torches" in the Armenian quarter of their hometown Adana.[45] Even though this scene in the novel, which takes place in 1909, predates the 1915 genocide, there is no doubt that the intent of these rioters, with "their foreheads bound in cloth [and] faces bathed in sweat", is to ethnically cleanse the region of its Armenian inhabitants.[46] Ossyane indicates that while he did not experience these events himself – they occurred prior to his birth – he knows their details intimately because they are constantly rehearsed by his father and visually reinforced through photographic imagery.[47] The effect of this on Ossyane is twofold. The first and most obvious is that he comes to "loathe racial hatred and discrimination".[48] The second but more important effect is that he develops a unique sense of place and home that does not root itself in territory. This is evident when he indicates that "my inheritance" and "the place I come from" are not defined by the lands or nations that his parents migrated from, but by their ability to "hold hands" and remain "united" in the "midst of [...] massacres" that divided the Turks and Armenians.[49] What this illustrates is that Ossyane possesses what Jose Saldívar theorises as a "different cognitive map [...] in which the nation-state [...] and [national] belonging [...] [are]

distinguished from place".[50] To differentiate between land and national belonging, as Ossyane does, is to question the very foundation of nationalism because, as outlined earlier, territory is fundamental to the concept of the nation-state.

Ossyane's demonstrated lack of territorialism also defines the nature of his marital relationship. As previously mentioned, Ossyane and Clara live not in one city but across two or, as Ossyane indicates, "We chose to stay [...] between Haifa and Beirut".[51] To that end, the couple are able to maintain "two ports of call" facilitated by the relatively easy passage connecting the two cities. The novel makes a point of stressing the geographical and temporal proximity between Haifa and Beirut in several scenes. It is first mentioned when Ossyane explains how Clara's uncle, Stefan, is quickly transported to Beirut for their wedding celebration: "From Haifa to Beirut it is no more than a hundred and fifty kilometres; at the time it took about four hours by car, stops included."[52] He re-emphasises this twice at later stages in the novel: "In the days when the border was open, it wasn't far [to travel from Haifa to Beirut] if you took the coastal road" and "the [...] distance from one [city to] another [was] three or four hours by road".[53] The degree to which Clara and Ossyane are dedicated to their peripatetic lifestyle is also evident in their lack of home ownership. Ossyane confesses that although he and Clara "had [...] a number of houses" in the two cities, such as Uncle Stefan's in Haifa or his father's in Beirut, they had "none to call [their] own".[54] Such examples reveal that the ideal living arrangement for these two characters is constituted by "the *continuous* space open between the two locations".[55] Ossyane and Clara's multiple journeys and border crossings on the "open road" illustrate that national identity is not defined in terms of some form of land ownership and fixity but, rather conversely, through a sense of territorial detachment and mobility.

Alongside this favourable depiction of territorial detachment and itinerancy is the novel's adverse portrayal of fixity in a single place. For Ossyane and Clara such immobility is a consequence of the borders that demarcate the Jewish and Arab populations. Part of what these borders signify is, as Hochberg suggests, the apparent naturalisation of the link between national identity and territory.[56]

This naturalisation is, of course, challenged by the novel. When partition occurs in *Ports of Call* Ossyane is in Lebanon visiting his terminally ill father and is unable to travel back to Haifa. He is, therefore, contained in one place but his immobility is not depicted as a natural state of being. Soon after partition, and indeed as a result of it, Ossyane becomes mentally unstable and is eventually admitted into an asylum. The madness or pathological state that the protagonist is subject to mirrors the chaos of the nationalistic wars that are simultaneously waged between Jews and Arabs. The novel parallels these two examples of decline by juxtaposing descriptions of Ossyane's erratic behaviour with radio reports of the war. Reflecting on his own emerging neurosis, Ossyane recollects that he "started losing control over [...] [his] own behaviour", pursued "obstinate ideas" compulsively and spent "entire days roaming about the garden, thirty, forty times in quick succession".[57] Beyond the confines of his father's house, where Ossyane is protected from "unfolding events of the war" by refusing to listen "to the communiqués and the military marches", the text continues to document the erosion of stability and the escalation of violence.[58] This begins with the announcement of the outbreak of war in mid-May 1948 and quickly escalates into other events: "the British mandate in Palestine had come to an end [and] the Council of Jewish People, assembled in a museum in Tel Aviv, had proclaimed the birth of the State of Israel".[59] Also, before peaceful negotiation could prevail all "the Arab nations had gone to war" within hours of the Tel Aviv proclamation.[60] Ossyane's mental demise and the deteriorating political situation, both recorded as simultaneous events in the text, illustrate that the imposition of essentialist notions that link territoriality and nationality are not natural and produce little more than instability and hostility.

Cultural Homogeneity and the Nation-State

The madness that overcomes Ossyane is also a result of the cultural homogeneity that is imposed on the region with the inscription of the new national-ethnic borders. Ossyane is not accustomed to such insularity and his dedication to perceiving the world in non-racialist terms further highlights the text's commitment to undermining segregation. In other words, the feature of cultural exclusivity that is often part of a definition of the nation-state is not sustained by Maalouf's text. One of the first instances in the novel where this is evident is associated with Ossyane's membership to the French Resistance during World War II. His arrival in France, in Montpellier specifically, is driven by his desire to escape the intensely politicised atmosphere of his father's household. He promises himself that in France he will "not read daily papers" or involve himself in any form of political activity but simply concentrate on his passion to study medicine.[61] Initially he even perceives himself as a foreigner and embraces his status wholeheartedly: "Did I suffer from being an outsider [in France]? If the truth be told, no, I did not."[62] However, the impact of the Nazi occupation of France in June 1940 obliges Ossyane to shed his persona as an outsider:

> Like them [the French] [. . .] I wept after the German invasion. Suddenly I was no longer a foreigner, not at all. It was like being at a funeral, a member of the family of the deceased. I wept, and I tried to comfort the others just as the others tried to comfort me.[63]

As the above passage indicates, Ossyane is no longer able to function complacently as a stranger in France. He relates to France in the most intimate of terms, describing himself as a "member of the family". His affiliation is further affirmed when the French offer him solace. In short, Ossyane does not simply identify with the French but, more acutely, identifies himself as a besieged Frenchman.

His sudden embrace of French identity should not be construed as an acceptance of the codes of nationalism that stress cultural exclusivity. The novel makes a point of carefully explaining this in two consecutive scenes. The first takes place in a brasserie where an unnamed student challenges Ossyane about his views of the occupation and is followed by another where Ossyane is recruited into the Resistance by Bertrand, one of the movement's key leaders. What is notable about these scenes is how the two Frenchmen, Bertrand and the student, use language that is highly nationalistic to indicate their commitment to securing France's freedom while Ossyane resists staking his commitment to the liberation of France in such terms. In the first brasserie scene, the unnamed student defends the Vichy government's passage of a law which bans Jews from participating in various professional activities, such as teaching, as a shrewd political act. He "happily reasons" that "the Germans had demanded access to the 'Free Zone', to 'take care' of the Jews who lived there, and Pétain [the head of the Vichy administration], smelling a rat, had circumvented them by passing the law himself".[64] The student, constrained by his position as a French national, supports this law because its passage enables his state to retain a certain degree of autonomy. Ossyane, however, does not subscribe to such a view. His response to the student's support of the law is particularly revealing:

> If I've [Ossyane] understood you [the student] correctly, it's as if a man came now into this place, armed with a club to knock you down. I see him approaching, and I take up this bottle and bring it down on your head. Seeing that he's got no business here any longer, the man simply shrugs and leaves. I've foiled him.[65]

Ossyane's ridicule of his fellow student suggests that resisting the Germans cannot be confined to securing France's liberty. Rather, it entails a larger project of rejecting the violence and discrimination that is aimed at Europe's Jews.

This commitment to a broader project is further emphasised in the following scene where Bertrand recruits Ossyane into the Resistance. Again, as with the events detailed above, the language Ossyane employs is strikingly different from, or even opposed to, Bertrand's expressions of dedication to fighting the occupation. For Bertrand the main objective of the Resistance is to fight the Germans: "Our people [the French] mustn't mistake who the enemy is."[66] Ossyane, who is not concerned with such nationalistic issues, states that "the eternal quarrel between the French and the Germans left me indifferent [. . .]

it was not enough to make my blood boil".[67] Rather, as he goes on to explain, it is his distaste of the racism that is an inherent part of German fascism that motivates him: "I have hated Nazism not since the day it invaded France, but since the day it invaded Germany."[68] While Bertrand and the student in the brasserie fall into what Said describes as "the encompassing and thumping language of national pride, collective sentiments [and] group passions" there is no trace of the same in Ossyane's words.[69] Ossyane's decision to support France in its quest for liberation is defined not by submitting to the nationalist discourse and sentiments expressed by the French characters but, rather ironically, by resisting that very discourse. What these scenes make evident is that *Ports of Call* proposes no clear affinity between culture and nationality and in fact calls into question ideas that advocate a commitment to the nation-state in culturally specific terms.

This is no less the case in the instances where the novel turns its attention to contesting the notion of cultural exclusivity in relation to Israel–Palestine. There are several instances in *Ports of Call* where this takes place, but one of the more poignant examples concerns two relatively marginal characters, Uncle Stefan and Ossyane's brother-in-law Mahmoud Carmali. Mahmoud, at the time he is introduced in the novel, is located in Cairo but he is a Palestinian by birth, a "son of an old family from Haifa, the Carmalis".[70] He and his family were forced to leave Palestine due to the escalation of violence between Arabs and Jews. Mahmoud and Stefan's first and only encounter takes place at the wedding celebrations held in Beirut for Ossyane and Clara. Ossyane notes well the potential for friction between the two men: "Imagine the scene: on one side [the exile] Mahmoud [. . .] who knew in his heart that he would never be able to return; on the other Stefan, a Jew from Central Europe, who had come to settle in that very same city."[71] While Ossyane endeavours to keep the men apart his father, who is not as sensitive, encourages the two men to sit together and bond over their "common" interest of Haifa.[72]

After this awkward introduction the two men are left on their own. Ossyane and Clara return to check on them later and find them "still on their own, in the same place, laughing their heads off".[73]

The content of their extended conversation is never entirely revealed. Mahmoud is said to have "told [...] anecdotes, illustrating them with ample gestures, mimicking the characters, in several voices" and Stefan is noted to have received these stories while "sitting peacefully [...] in his [...] armchair" as if in a gentleman's club.[74] It is later suggested by Mahmoud's wife that the two men were sharing stories about Haifa – Stefan about current events and Mahmoud about his childhood. Their ability to bond, as Ossyane's father intends, over a contested and yet common city highlights their shared humanity. After all, as Ossyane's father points out, they do not "belong [...] to [a] different species".[75] In addition to their common humanity what the novel also illustrates is the fantasy that Israel and Palestine can ever be constituted of one people; there is, as Stefan and Mahmoud highlight, a history of the two peoples inhabiting the land prior to the very recent efforts to segregate the two.

Coexistence and "The Levantine Option"

Echoing Stefan and Mahmoud's entangled histories, ample attention is paid to the experiences that Jews and Arabs share throughout the novel. While the Stefan and Mahmoud scene exposes that Haifa has a history of being inhabited by a mixture of peoples and cultures, in other instances such shared experiences between Jewish and Arab characters are used to highlight alternatives to the policy of separation. This involves the often overlooked and discredited notion of coexistence which is explored in the novel through two means. One is culturally-based and pertains to Levantinism, a concept that was developed in the mid-twentieth century by Jacqueline Shohet Kahanoff (1917–79) and one that is, according to David Green, undergoing a recent resurgence in Israeli critical theory.[76] Levantinism refers to a kind of cultural hybridity or cosmopolitanism that proponents of the theory perceive as the defining feature of the Middle East. It also, particularly in Maalouf's novel, signifies a geographical region that is constituted by modern Lebanon, Israel, Palestine, Jordan, Syria, and Turkey. In that regard, it is a space that contains an inauthentic form of cultural identity rather than one framed by purity. Alongside these cultural issues the novel also examines coexistence through politically-based means which involves instances of organised cooperation between Jews and Arabs. This includes the political activism that the protagonist and his wife undertake in Palestine as members of a Jewish and Arab cross-cultural movement that advocates for a single state. Both the political and cultural aspects of the novel highlight that coexistence is a viable option, has historical precedence and provides an alternative to the failed attempts at segregation.

To commence with the political, Hochberg argues that Maalouf's novel details the activism that Ossyane and Clara undertake in Palestine as a form of "projected collaboration".[77] This is most clearly evident in their combined efforts to resist partition as members of the Palestine Arab and Jewish United Workers Committee. This begins with Clara's attempts to record Ossyane's heroism in the French Resistance. Her documentation of Ossyane's French experiences are part of a broader mission for the committee's newspaper which involves Clara's strategic decision to publish "the memoirs of both Jews and Arabs in the Resistance, who had [together] fought against the Nazis".[78] Her intention is not simply to record acts of bravery but to "convince both [Arab and Jewish communities] that they should be on the same side, fighting for a common cause" in Palestine.[79] Ossyane replicates Clara's act approximately 30 years later in 1976. This is possible because *Ports of Call* – Maalouf's novel – doubles as Ossyane's life story, a memoir that the protagonist narrates to an unnamed character he meets in Paris just after his escape from the asylum. Ossyane hopes to be reunited with Clara, but in the four days he has between his arrival in Paris and the designated date of his meeting, he provides a "testimony" to the unnamed Parisian that he believes will be a useful historical document of inter-racial and inter-religious cooperation in Palestine.[80] Curiously the text does not record many details of the committee's exploits but it is suggested by Ossyane that the committee's activities were akin to those that he and Clara practised in France.[81] These activities and the careful attempts by the protagonists to document the joint efforts of Arabs and Jews during World War II, as well as in Palestine, illustrates the novel's investment in providing an alternative to the discourse of partition.

Clara and Ossyane's public activism is also echoed in their private lives. This is portrayed in the "quarrels [...] [and] heated discussions" that the protagonists partake in with regard to the political issues that surround Jews and Arabs.[82] Their conduct during these disagreements is rather unique and is in fact the "opposite to what might reasonably have been expected".[83] As Ossyane describes: "When Clara contradicted me, it was to side strongly with the Arabs, to say that I should understand them better; with me, when I retaliated, it was to tell her she was being too hard on her own people."[84] Ossyane describes these arguments as "morally elegant" and explains that what is required of each feuding participant is that they put "[them]selves [...] in the other's place" and, to a certain degree, become the other.[85] Such "moral elegance" is not simply the preserve of creative literature but is reflected in the contemporary political criticism related to Israel–Palestine. This is evident in much of Said's work especially in his article "Arabs and Jews" where he recognises that "each [the Jew and the Arab] is the other".[86] Another notable figure on these issues is the Israeli-Jewish historian Ilan Pappé. In his article "The Exilic Homeland of Edward W. Said", Pappé argues for collective forms of mutual understanding. He believes that Jews and Arabs share a destiny that is forever intertwined and are therefore compelled to build a sense of "mutual understanding of [each other's] tragedies, national traumas and collective fears".[87] It is only by doing this, Pappé argues, that Palestinians and Israelis can recognise the irrationality of partition and the inevitability of coexistence. Thus, the "moral elegance" that Maalouf attributes to his protagonists, much like Pappé's "mutual understanding", undermines the logic of separation that dominates the discourse of the Israel–Palestine conflict and instead provides an alternative model that stresses the possibility of coexistence.

Apart from these political strategies there are also cultural considerations that provide even stronger justifications for coexistence. This comprises the concept of Levantinism which is used in *Ports of Call* to contest the partition of Israelis and

Palestinians and the supposed need to establish separate nation-states. References to the Levant and Levantine culture are evident throughout the novel, but its most notable application is in *Ports of Call*'s original French title, *Les Échelles du Levant*. The literal translation of *Les Échelles du Levant* is "The Scales of the Orient", where "*échelle*" (scale) is derived from the Turkish word *iskele*. *Iskele* describes a type of pier constructed on stilts with stairs to assist with the loading and unloading of cargo onto ships. Given *iskele*'s association with sea trade, *Les Échelles du Levant* can certainly be translated as "The Ports of the Levant". While the current English title *Ports of Call* speaks to the protagonists' two homes in the port cities of Haifa and Beirut, the omission of "Levant" from the English title obscures two things. The first is the significance of the Levant region within France's imperial history. From the sixteenth to the eighteenth century the ruling French and Ottoman authorities came to a series of agreements referred to as the Capitulations. The first took place in 1536 between Sultan Suleiman the Magnificent and King Francis I and officially granted France the privilege to trade freely in all Ottoman ports.[88] This is why the phrase *les échelles du Levant* in the French vernacular refers specifically to several port cities of the Ottoman Empire, like Constantinople (modern Istanbul), Adana, Haifa, Beirut, Cairo, Alexandria, Aleppo and Damascus. As indicated earlier, Ossyane's story is narrated from the vantage point of France and so, in this context, the title "The Ports of the Levant" is a register of the historical interactions between France and the Middle East. The second feature that the omission of Levant from the English title conceals, or at least does not make immediately obvious, is Maalouf's wilful engagement with Levantinism as a concept that stresses the multi-ethnic reality of the region. This is evident when the term is used to describe a region that is indifferent to race and religion and where "men of all origins lived side by side in the ports of the Levant, mingling their many tongues".[89] Such descriptions suggest that the Levant cannot be defined as a place of cultural stability but is a site that induces and encourages what Hochberg designates as "a state of in-betweenness".[90] This is how the region was appreciated by the British and French colonisers who at first, in the sixteenth century, saw the Levant as a transitional space between East and West and its inhabitants as "capital mediators" for European sea merchants. Later by the nineteenth century the term was understood as an indication of "racial, national and cultural [...] impurity" and uncertainty.[91] What is reflected in these evolving connotations is that the term "Levant" is evocative of both culture and geography. This is how the concept is theorised by various scholars, like Jacqueline Kahanoff and David Shasha, and also represented in the novel. In both instances the cultural and geographical attributes of Levantinism undermine the premise of separation.

It is in the work of Kahanoff that the cultural and geographical features are most evident. This is, in many ways, a result of her personal circumstances. Kahanoff is a Mizrahi or Eastern Jew who was born in Egypt in 1917 to a Tunisian mother and Iraqi father and migrated to Israel in 1954. Her upbringing in the interwar period in Egypt was marked, as she explains, by an interaction with a range of peoples of diverse cultural backgrounds. Reflecting on her life in Egypt, Kahanoff writes that "When I was a child, it seemed natural that people understood each other although they spoke different languages, and were called by different names – Greek, Moslem, Syrian, Jewish, Christian, Arabs, Italian, Turkish, Armenian".[92] That world "was a friendly" one for Kahanoff and formed the basis for her theory of the Levant. This is attested to in Deborah Starr and Sasson Somekh's recent anthology of Kahanoff's writings. In their joint introduction Starr and Somekh write that "Kahanoff draws upon her experiences of cultural interaction in [...] Egypt to form the basis of a social model she terms Levantinism".[93] Culturally speaking, then, the Levant is deeply plural and is described as such by Kahanoff:

Here [in the Levant] Europe and Asia have encroached on one another, time and again, leaving their marks [...] in the shadowy memories of the Levant's peoples. Ancient Egypt, ancient Israel, and ancient Greece, Chaldea and Assyria, Ur and Babylon, Tyre and Sidon, and Carthage, Constantinople, Alexandria, Jerusalem are all dimensions of the Levant. So are

Judaism, Christianity, and Islam, which [...] [constitute] the multilayered identity of the Levant's people. It [the Levant] is not exclusively Western or Eastern, Christian, Jewish, or Moslem.[94]

Such cultural diversity and the ability of the Levant region to be at once Western and Eastern, Jewish and Muslim cannot be divorced from its geographical setting. According to Hochberg, who provides a rather extensive assessment of Kahanoff's oeuvre, "Kahanoff never ceased to believe that the geographic location of the emerging Jewish nation, and the nation's mixed population [...] present a rare opportunity to revive the great Levantine multilingual and cross-ethnic culture" of the past.[95] Unlike Nissim Rejwan, who argues that culture rather than geography is the most meaningful aspect of Levantinism, Kahanoff is unable or unwilling to separate the two.[96] This perhaps explains why she is rather proscriptive regarding Israel's assessment of its own position in the Middle East region. Israel's Jewish population should not view themselves as entirely European and should not seek to "Westernise" their state. "No matter how many [European] Jews settle this land" she argues, "Israel will still be in this part of the world" and needs to rectify its association with the "people in the area".[97] In order to do this the Jewish state must embrace a "modernized Levantine framework comprising of people who are different, equal, and equally native" because it this framework that will "provide a [...] pattern for coexistence".[98]

In more recent theorisations of the Levantine concept, this blending of culture and geography is just as important. For David Shasha, a Syrian-Jewish scholar based in New York, the assumption that "Jews are culturally different from Arabs" is a claim to be rejected.[99] This is because, as history records, there have been instances, in Andalusia and in the Ottoman Empire, where "Jews lived productively in the Middle East [or amongst Arabs] and developed a [robust] [...] culture".[100] He labels this culture "the Levantine Option" and insists it be urgently restored against the current "spurious binarism" that continues to separate Jews and Arabs.[101] This option would not only draw out the "commonalities in culture" between the Middle East's three main religions but it "would [also] become a means to create a shared [. . .] space for Jews and Arabs".[102] As Shasha claims, the "walls and barriers that are endemic" in the region can be overcome with the re-introduction of Levantine culture.[103]

Such Levantinism is embedded within *Ports of Call* and is used to advance the novel's position against the partition of Jews and Arabs. This is reflected in a number of instances but the most notable include the rationale used to explain why Ossyane's paternal and maternal families select Mount Lebanon as their place of exile and how that place becomes the model for what Ossyane and Clara hope to create in Palestine. When Ossyane's family leaves Turkey in 1909, as a result of the pogroms against the Armenian community, Mount Lebanon is their chosen destination because it, unlike the province Adana, retains the "fraternity between the peoples of the [Ottoman] Empire, Turks, Armenians, Arabs, Greeks and Jews".[104] In other words, Lebanon still contains, in Maalouf's fictional construction, the features of coexistence and hybridity that Levantine culture is defined by. This world is formative for Ossyane and he states that he wishes the twentieth century retains all the features of the nineteenth century that his father lived through and praised. To that end, what Clara and Ossyane seek to instigate in Palestine is a replica of that era where "all differences of race, tongue and faith" are "brushed aside" in favour of humanity, civility and commonality.[105] These attempts to instil "the Levantine Option" within Palestine from Ossyane and Clara constitute another example of how the novel argues against segregation and erects a model of coexistence that challenges nationalism's territoriality and cultural insularity.

The final testimony to the text's relentless advocacy for coexistence is found in two of its closing scenes. These take place in the novel's present, in precisely June 1976, and include Ossyane's re-entry into his father's home and his reunification with Clara. When Ossyane finally leaves the asylum and returns to his father's house he finds the place in complete ruins and riddled with bullets due to the Lebanese civil war. Ossyane salvages none of his personal possessions from the wreckage but does make a point of collecting all the keys contained in the house. These amount to approximately "two hundred" and consist of keys from "the cupboards, the trunks, the drawers, the doors and the gates" and even "the keys that had been left rusting for centuries in ancient tin boxes".[106] The novel provides no explanation as to why he does this and merely indicates that the importance of doing so is "clear" to Ossyane.[107] However, while the novel obscures explanations, the reasoning for such acts are distinct within the context of Palestinian culture. Edward Said explains that holding on to objects like keys and, as already seen in relation to Yunis' *The Night Counter*, title deeds relates immediately to Palestinian experiences of loss and dispossession. In *After the Last Sky*, an evocative account of the lives of contemporary Palestinians, Said conveys the importance to Palestinians of what he refers to as "intimate mementoes of a past irrevocably lost":

When A.Z.'s father was dying, he called his children, one of whom is married to my sister, into his room for a last family gathering. A frail, very old man from Haifa he had spent his last thirty-five years in Beirut in agitated disbelief at the loss of his house and property. Now he murmured to his children the final, faltering words of a penniless, helpless patriarch. "Hold on to the keys and the deed" he told them, pointing to a battered suitcase near his bed.[108]

These objects are therefore politically-charged signifiers of loss that are not surprisingly recurring motifs in Palestinian literature.

As signifiers of loss or dispossession, such items are used to draw together narratives of Palestinian exile. Keys, deed titles, photographs and national costumes "circulate among" Palestinians and, as Said illuminates, are "much reproduced, enlarged, thematized, embroidered [...] and passed around [so that] they [become the] [...] strands in the web of affiliations we Palestinians use to tie ourselves to our identity and to each other".[109] This, however, cannot apply to Ossyane because, as described earlier, he possesses a complex subjectivity that is neither simply Arab nor Palestinian. Given this, the function of the keys in *Ports of Call* cannot be circumscribed by a usage that reinforces narratives of dispossession primarily among and within the Palestinian community. The keys' transportation to France, the site where their owner reunites with his former lover, indicates that in Maalouf's text these items have a significance that extends beyond the Palestinian sense of loss.

In the novel's final scene Ossyane is reunited with Clara in Paris. This, as various reviewers note, represents the culmination of their personal and tragic separation.[110] At a broader level it also demonstrates the novel's relentless commitment to championing the coexistence of Arabs and Jews. But even this broader consideration is more substantially attested to than simply through the reunification of two characters who were once co-activists engaged in campaigns to curtail the partition of Palestine. The keys are pivotal here and the novel makes this undoubtedly clear by linking Ossyane's "need to assemble" the keys with his need to "take them with him on his voyage" to France.[111] As outlined earlier, various theories have been put forward that confirm the historical and circumstantial intimacy of Jews and Arabs. Hochberg refers to a "strange familiarity" that defines these two peoples and Said more strongly contends that Palestinian and Jewish identities are indistinct because "each is the other". For Hochberg and Said, one's narrative of dispossession is simultaneously and undeniably the other's. The keys that Ossyane carries with him to Paris, then, are put into circulation between him and his supposed adversary implicating the "other" who is also the "self" in the experience of loss and displacement. The fact that this takes place in France does not diminish the novel's critical stance regarding segregation. Rather, it reinforces it because from the geographical vantage point of Paris, Israel–Palestine becomes the Levant. In that regard Maalouf, a diasporic writer who resides in France, reasserts "the Levantine Option" and the coexistence that is inherent to Levantinism.

CONCLUSION

PLACE AND DIASPORA
LITERATURE

Mourning the loss of his homeland through his own experience of exile, Theodor Adorno argued that writing becomes a place to live.[1] For the displaced or diasporic author, writing is not just a substitute home but is also the site where place is, as Bill Ashcroft states, "uttered into being and maintained by narrative".[2] It is no surprise, then, that diaspora literature should be so fundamentally concerned with constructions of place. This book suggests that this preoccupation with place is a consequence of the fact that it is a literature written from a position of deracination. This reasoning, however, is at odds with a key aspect of diaspora theory. Despite the fact that diaspora "references the theme of location" that theme is often overlooked because diaspora is seen as equivalent to displacement and dislocation.[3] What this means is that certain scholars of diaspora relegate place as marginal or irrelevant. It is notable that this marginalisation of place generally occurs when diaspora is distinguished from exile. In Nico Israel's *Outlandish: Writing Between Exile and Diaspora* and Hamid Naficy's *An Accented Cinema: Exilic and Diasporic Filmmaking*, exile is "circumscribed [by a] limited conception of place"[4] and involves a view of home that is "binaristic" and "dualistic".[5] Conversely, in their definitions of diaspora, place is rarely mentioned. For Naficy, while diasporic consciousness involves "the homeland" it is really "compatriot communities" that matter because it is these communities that produce the "multiplicity" and "hybridity" that shape the diasporic subject.[6] Similarly, in Israel's conception, the "hybridity" and "performativity" of the displaced subject are key features of dispersal.[7]

Such comparative definitions not only negate the importance of place in diaspora, they also suggest that diaspora can only be understood in terms of its transformative impact on the subject. In these constructions diaspora involves a subject who has transcended the "exilic" feelings of solitariness, melancholia and deracination and is instead reconciled to or not debilitated by an "out of place" existence.[8] This notion that diaspora is tied up with the settled subject rather than with one that is fixated by a loss of place constitutes Syrine Hout's distinction between it and exile. Hout's article, "*The Last Migration*: The First Contemporary Example of Lebanese Diasporic Literature", charts this distinction conceptually by analysing a number of Lebanese diaspora novels. Drawing on Israel and Naficy's work, Hout argues that a particular novel, *The Last Migration: A Novel of Diaspora and Love* by Jad El Hage, is the first post-war text by an expatriate Lebanese writer that can be described as diasporic.[9] Other texts, such as Tony Hanania's *Unreal City*, Nada Awar Jarrar's *Somewhere, Home*, Patricia Sarrafian Ward's *The Bullet Collection* and Rabih Alameddine's *Koolaids*, are considered examples of exilic literature.[10] Hout argues that El Hage's novel "is a prototype of Lebanese diasporic literature" because it "offers a balanced perspective on the effects of living abroad on personal and collective identities, by contrast to other [exilic] novels [that are] permeated by unsettled responses towards one's origins".[11]

In Hout's assessment, then, a diasporic novel's classification depends on its representation of "living abroad" which must be "balanced" rather than "unsettled". In order to prove her thesis, Hout focuses solely on El Hage's protagonist, Ashraf Saad, and shows that this character harbours no "unresolved feelings towards his homeland" which, if he did, would "foster a mental condition of exile".[12] Instead Ashraf, who resides in London and travels periodically to Sydney to visit his daughters, elects to "belong to a self-devised [...] 'home'" that is framed not by a distant homeland but by his quest for love, both romantic and familial.[13] This, however, can be also said about the protagonists in Jarrar's *Somewhere, Home*, a text that Hout rejects as diasporic.[14] Salwa, for instance, the third of Jarrar's main characters, indicates that the love she has for her family allows her to develop homely feelings in America and Australia, her two places of migration.[15] Hout further asserts *The Last Migration*'s diasporic status by highlighting that unlike "other Lebanese Anglophone post-war narratives [. . .] [it] offers a moving account of the *interactions* [. . .] between East and West".[16] But Hout fails to elaborate what this "moving account" constitutes and why it is particular to El Hage's novel. Given the multiple movements between East and West of the protagonists in *Somewhere, Home* (Aida moves between Beirut and several European cities, Salwa from a Lebanese village to America and later Australia) and in *Unreal City* (the protagonist spends time in Beirut, Madrid and London) it is impossible to distinguish why this criterion excludes Jarrar and Hanania's texts from being classified as diasporic.

These examples from Hout's article reflect that a focus on character forms the basis of her definition of a diasporic novel. While this may constitute one determining aspect of diaspora literature, Hout's intense concentration on character means that she overlooks or minimises the importance of other features. One of these is the author's own diasporic sensibility. As outlined in the introduction, this sensibility is constituted by features that designate diaspora not as a typology but as a lived condition or a subjective position. Most importantly, diasporic subjectivity is marked by a loss of place and "genealogies of displacement".[17] As a result of displacement, members of a dispersed community exhibit what Samir Dayal refers to as a "diasporic sensibility" and a "deterritorialized critical consciousness".[18] Such features are only evident when place's importance to diaspora is acknowledged, and when the loss of place is seen as a fundamental aspect of dispersal. Examining novels by Lebanese diaspora writers in light of these features exposes the limitations of relying solely upon character analysis to determine a text's diasporic status.

Unreal City by Tony Hanania provides a good example. Hout writes that it contains "a young, privileged Lebanese man" who not only yearns for his war-torn home city, but is also "driven by guilt to

Islamic political fanaticism in the form of a suicide mission".[19] This means that the central character's suffering and longing produces acute "loneliness of physical and psychological displacement which is typical of exilic literatures".[20] Hout's characterisation of the protagonist casts this novel as exilic, but an examination of Hanania's representation of place reveals an alternate way of classifying this novel. As a displaced writer Hanania exhibits a "deterritorialised critical consciousness" and his representation of Beirut reflects this in the following ways. First, his effort to depict the war-riven and decimated urban space is provocative because it coincides with the current suppression of the war that dominates post-war Beirut. Second, it is not mere coincidence that the central character of Hanania's novel becomes a member of a particular Islamic organisation – *Jihad al-Binaa* – whose reconstruction projects are welfare-focused rather than commercially driven. This posits a sharp criticism against the post-war reconstruction programme headed by Solidere. Solidere may have delivered what Jamal Abed, borrowing from Saskia Sassen, refers to as an urban "glamour zone" but it has failed to alleviate water shortages, electricity outages and unaffordable healthcare services.[21] Hanania is therefore able to cast doubt over the much celebrated reconstruction projects of Solidere and to trouble the amnesia that dominates post-war Beirut.

Beyond *Unreal City*'s significance in the Lebanese context, this novel also demonstrates how the character of a place is illuminated when its interactions with another place are recognised. Places, as Doreen Massey states, do not possess "single, essential, identities", nor are they constructed in an "introverted, inward-looking" manner.[22] Rather, their construction and formation is determined through open and porous networks of interconnection.[23] One of the ways that Hanania expresses the gravity of Beirut's war situation is to mobilise T. S. Eliot's *The Waste Land* as a comparative literary reference. Eliot's modernist poem is acclaimed for its reflection of urban entropy in post-war London. Hanania transposes this European topos onto a contemporary Lebanese scenario in order to stress the particular political context of post-war Beirut. This illustrates that places within diaspora texts are not enclosed or inward-looking but are open to all kinds of intertextual references and comparisons, even when the places in question are as divergent as London and Beirut. From the displaced position of London where Hanania now resides, he is able to unsettle the conventional conception of place as an introverted site and to highlight that places are constructed by their interactions with other places.

In a similar manner, this reflexive interaction between politically-charged representations of place is also true of Rawi Hage's *De Niro's Game*. According to Hage, his grave depiction of Beirut was contingent upon his geographical and temporal distance from his home city and, most importantly, his relocation to Canada.[24] Since his receipt of the prestigious literary IMPAC award, as well as being nominated for several Canadian-based literary prizes, Hage has been marked out as a distinctly Canadian writer. In an interview he explains that when "people ask what's Canadian about the book, I say the fact that I wrote it here in Canada, in a free atmosphere and with financial support [. . .] Had I stayed in New York, it would have been a case of survival, and, in Beirut, I may not still be alive."[25] In other words, what Hage describes as his own diasporic subjectivity as a writer is bound by a renewed sense of place. Canada provides Hage with a "free atmosphere" and the necessary critical distance from East Beirut to write about the costly exercise of unquestioned "tribal" affiliation.

France also shapes Hage's depiction of Beirut and Lebanon. This is just as true for Amin Maalouf in *Ports of Call*. France's colonial legacy is at the forefront of the two texts but is depicted in strikingly different ways. In *De Niro's Game*, France is shown as a key player in a Zionist alliance that undermines the Lebanese state and the historical association between it and Lebanon's Christians. Conversely in Maalouf's *Ports of Call*, the undesirable aspects of France's colonial relationship towards Lebanon are irrelevant. Maalouf himself is indifferent towards colonialism and has been criticised by Robert Fisk and Gil Hochberg for this oversight.[26] In his novel he even has the protagonist Ossyane declare that "that the words 'occupier' and 'occupied' do not raise my hackles".[27] By leaving the negative qualities of colonialism aside, Maalouf is able to unambiguously portray France as the vantage point from which to imagine the coexistence of Jews and Arabs in Palestine. He traces Levantinism to its French origins and instils it with the capacity to liberate Palestinians and Israelis from the spurious policies of segregation. Hence, from their displaced residences in Canada and France, Hage and Maalouf illustrate the ambivalent relations between Lebanon and its former colonial master. While Hage casts doubt over France's role in the region and highlights its deception of the Lebanese, Maalouf venerates France as the saviour of the Levant.

Despite this erasure of France's colonial legacy, Maalouf continues to exhibit the critical disposition that characterises diasporic consciousness. This is evident in his interrogation of the concept of the nation-state in relation to the partition of Palestine and the creation of Israel. As previously outlined, the nation-state is often identified as territorially bound and culturally exclusive. With regard to the Jewish and Arab populations that inhabit Israel– Palestine, the general consensus from the international community has overwhelmingly leaned towards segregation. This vision of a two state solution reinforces the nationalistic principles of cultural homogeneity and geographic separation and is proposed as the only viable living arrangement available to the Palestinians and Israelis. *Ports of Call*, however, does not support this view and assiduously undermines it in two interrelated ways. The first involves the novel's concentration on the historically-based coexistence of Jews and Arabs in the Levant region. The second is reflected in the efforts of the text's two protagonists to resist the encroaching segregation and to preserve coexistence. It is therefore separation and the creation of two nation-states that are depicted as unnatural and irrational in Maalouf's novel rather than the inverse.

Such dynamic portrayals of place from Hanania, Hage and Maalouf are not just confined to literary depictions of urban or national spaces but are also evident in texts that focus on the intimate space of the home. In Jarrar and Yunis' novels, home is an extremely unsettled and evolving site. It is true that in *Somewhere, Home* domesticity conforms to a more basic principle of "home-as-house", but even within this text there is an effort by Jarrar to unfold the plurality of the domestic. Home is equated with family and is used to convey the intimate sentiments a migrant harbours towards their homeland. Where this novel fails to reach the feminist-driven text it is critically acclaimed for is by depending heavily on the female characters to narrate the stories rather than addressing how the domestic sphere can be mobile and emancipatory. This, however, is what Yunis achieves in her novel. Like *Somewhere, Home*, *The Night Counter* is narrated by female characters, Fatima and Scheherazade, but unlike Jarrar's novel Yunis' is not framed by a limited conception of domesticity. Fatima's dominant view of home, which is singular and bound up with a house, is overturned by Scheherazade. The mobility that Yunis extends to Scheherazade, a character who traverses America to collect the domestic stories of the Abdullah clan, allows the author to illustrate that in diasporic cultures home is inherently mobile and cannot be governed by a simple architectural structure located in a distant homeland.

Ultimately, place is fundamental to understanding diaspora literature. This is true not just because place is reconfigured by such texts but also because it is through place that diaspora literatures are most likely to reveal their revolutionary capacity. In Lebanese diaspora fiction the experience of location does not dissolve into an absence. Rather than obscure place's significance and centrality, diaspora novels both focus on and challenge normative constructions of place. Most crucially, diaspora literature provides alternate ways to conceive of place, where it is defined in terms of its multiplicity, its interactions with other places and its mobility.

NOTES

Introduction   Diaspora Literature and Place

1. Tony Hanania, *Unreal City* (1999; London: Bloomsbury, 2000), p. 221.
2. Avtar Brah, *Cartographies of Diaspora: Contesting Identities* (London; New York, NY: Routledge, 1996), p. 177.
3. Ibid., p. 177.
4. William Safran, "Diasporas in Modern Societies: Myths of Homeland and Return", *Diaspora: A Journal of Transnational Studies* 1.1 (1991), pp. 83–95.
5. Ibid., pp. 83–4. Despite publishing a revised and slightly longer version of his six criteria in 2005, very little has changed in Safran's model of diaspora. The more recent list simply documents the original criteria and appends another, all the while retaining strict markers like originary roots and return to the homeland as key features of diaspora. See Safran, "The Jewish Diaspora in a Comparative and Theoretical Perspective", *Israel Studies* 10.1 (2005), pp. 37–8. The scant alteration between the two articles means that Safran's 1991 piece continues to be the most cited of the two and is used by more progressive diaspora scholars, like Stuart Hall and James Clifford, as a key indicator of conservative definitions of dispersal. The seminal nature of Safran's 1991 article and the fact that his work is seen to typify more conservative definitions of dispersal indicate why I revisit his diaspora typology throughout this book.
6. Safran, "Diasporas in Modern Societies", p. 84.
7. Gérard Chaliand and Jean-Pierre Rageau, *The Penguin Atlas of Diasporas* (New York, NY: Viking Books, 1991), p. 4.
8. The title of the first chapter in Cohen's book is "Classical Notions of Diaspora: Transcending the Jewish Tradition". See Robin Cohen, *Global Diasporas: An Introduction* (Seattle, WA: University of Washington Press, 1997).
9. Floya Anthias, "Evaluating 'Diaspora': Beyond Ethnicity?", *Sociology* 32.3 (1998), p. 562.
10. Michelle Reis, "Theorizing Diaspora: Perspectives on 'Classical' and 'Contemporary' Diaspora", *International Migration* 42.2 (2004), p. 4. For other examples that privilege Jewish dispersal see Nancy Green, *Jewish Workers in the Modern Diaspora* (Berkeley, CA: University of California Press, 1998); Charles King and Neil Melvin, "Diaspora Politics: Ethnic Linkages, Foreign

Policy, and Security in Eurasia", *International Security* 24.3 (1999), pp. 108–38; Kate Gillespie, Liesl Riddle, Edward Sayre and David Sturges, "Diaspora Interest in Homeland Investment", *The Journal of International Business Studies* 30.3 (1999), pp. 623–34.

11. Reis, "Theorizing Diaspora", p. 45.
12. Ibid., p. 44.
13. James Clifford, "Diasporas", in J. Clifford, *Routes: Travels and Translation in the Late Twentieth Century* (Cambridge, MA: Harvard University Press, 1997), p. 249.
14. Safran, "Diasporas in Modern Societies", p. 83.
15. Judith Shuval, "Diaspora Migration: Definitional Ambiguities and a Theoretical Paradigm", *International Migration* 38.5 (2000), p. 43.
16. Clifford, "Diasporas", p. 269.
17. Ibid., p. 250.
18. Ibid., p. 269.
19. Ibid., p. 250.
20. Safran, "Diasporas in Modern Societies", p. 83.
21. Safran's portrayal of the Jewish diaspora is politically framed. He does not, for example, take into account the complicated religious teachings regarding diaspora, nor does he incorporate views from within the Jewish transnational community that assess dispersal in cultural terms. See, for example, Daniel Boyarin and Jonathan Boyarin, "Diaspora: Generation and the Ground of Jewish Identity", *Critical Inquiry* 19.4 (1993), pp. 693–725 for cultural and theological appreciations of the Jewish dispersal and Erich Gruen, *Diaspora: Jews Amidst Greeks and Romans* (Cambridge, MA: Harvard University Press, 2002) for a historically-based assessment. The ideas presented by these scholars are developed in Chapter 7.
22. Ephraim Nimni (ed), *The Challenge of Post-Zionism: Alternatives to Israeli Fundamentalist Politics* (London: Zed Books, 2003); Ilan Pappé, *A History of Modern Palestine: One Land, Two Peoples* (Cambridge: Cambridge University Press, 2004); Tanya Reinhart, *Israel/Palestine: How to End the War of 1948* (New York, NY: Seven Stories Press, 2005).
23. Amitav Ghosh, "The Diaspora in Indian Culture", in A. Ghosh, *The Imam and the Indian: Prose Pieces* (Delhi: Orient Longman, 2002), p. 248.
24. Paul Gilroy, *The Black Atlantic: Modernity and Double Consciousness* (Cambridge, MA: Harvard University Press, 1993).
25. Stuart Hall, "New Cultures for Old", in D. Massey and P. Jess (eds), *A Place in the World? Places, Cultures and Globalization* (Oxford: Oxford University Press, 1995), p. 206.
26. Safran, "Diasporas in Modern Societies", pp. 91–2.
27. Stuart Hall, "Cultural Identity and Diaspora", in P. Williams and L. Chrisman (eds), *Colonial Discourse and Post-Colonial Theory: A Reader* (New York, NY: Columbia University Press, 1994), p. 401.
28. Clifford, "Diasporas", pp. 1–6.

29. Amin Maalouf, *Origins: A Memoir* (New York, NY: Farrar, Straus and Giroux, 2008), np. This memoir was published in 2004 as *Origines* (Paris: Bernard Grasset) and translated by Catherine Temerson in 2008. All references are taken from the English edition.

30. Ghassan Hage, "Under the Global Olive Tree: A Review of Amin Maalouf's *Origines*", *Griffith Review* 6 (2004), p. 220.

31. Russel Potter, "Black Modernisms/Black Postmodernisms", *Postmodern Culture* 5.1 (1994), par. 21. Available at http://pmc.iath.virginia.edu/text-only/issue.994/review-1.994 (accessed 28 October 2013).

32. Hall, "Cultural Identity and Diaspora", p. 402.

33. Ibid., p. 402.

34. Maalouf, *Origins*, p. 21.

35. Hage, "Under the Global Olive Tree", p. 219.

36. Anthias, "Evaluating 'Diaspora'", pp. 561–5. Cohen and Safran do not present a coeval view of diaspora. They are in fact adversaries of each other's work. Cohen rejects the Jewish specificity of Safran's model and targets Safran in *Global Diasporas*. Safran responds to Cohen's criticisms in his lengthy review essay "Comparing Diasporas: A Review". My point here is that despite the political and ideological differences of their work, the models of diaspora they each establish are presented as "types" that consist of descriptive criteria and definitional lists. See Cohen, *Global Diasporas* and William Safran, "Comparing Diasporas: A Review", *Diaspora: A Journal of Transnational Studies* 8.3 (1999), pp. 255–91.

37. For constructions of diaspora as a subjective condition see Lily Cho, "The Turn to Diaspora", *Topia* 17 (2007), pp. 11–30, as a social condition see Anthias, "Evaluating 'Diaspora'", and as a mode of thinking and acting see Clifford, "Diasporas".

38. Khachig Tölölyan, "The Nation-State and its Others: In Lieu of a Preface", *Diaspora: A Journal of Transnational Studies* 1.1 (1991), pp. 4–5.

39. Hamid Naficy, *An Accented Cinema: Exilic and Diasporic Film Making* (Princeton, NJ: Princeton University Press, 2001), p. 14.

40. Nico Israel, *Outlandish: Writing Between Exile and Diaspora* (Stanford, CA: Stanford University Press, 2000), p. 3.

41. Cho, "Turn to Diaspora", p. 14; emphasis added.

42. Samir Dayal, "Diaspora and Double Consciousness", *The Journal of the Midwest Modern Language Association* 29.1 (1996), p. 58.

43. Edward Said, *Representations of the Intellectual: The Reith Lectures* (1994; New York, NY: Vintage Books, 1996), p. 60.

44. Israel, *Outlandish*, pp. ix, 3.

45. Dayal, "Diaspora", p. 46.

46. Hall, "New Cultures for Old", p. 206.

47. Hall, "Cultural Identity and Diaspora", pp. 401–2.

48. Doreen Massey and Pat Jess, "Introduction", in D. Massey and P. Jess (eds), *A Place in the World? Places, Cultures and Globalization* (Oxford: Oxford University Press, 1995), p. 1.

49. Doreen Massey, "A Place Called Home?", *New Formations* 17 (1992), p. 7.
50. Ibid., p. 3.
51. Tim Cresswell, *Place: A Short Introduction* (Malden, MA: Blackwell Publishing, 2004), p. 8.
52. Doreen Massey, *Space, Place and Gender* (Cambridge: Polity, 1994), p. 146.
53. Ibid., p. 151.
54. Ibid., p. 152.
55. Bill Ashcroft, *Post-Colonial Transformation* (London; New York, NY: Routledge, 2001), p. 156.
56. Massey, *Space, Place*, p. 120.
57. Ashcroft, *Post-Colonial Transformation*, p. 161.
58. Massey, *Space, Place*, p. 121.
59. Yi-Fu Tuan, *Space and Place: The Perspective of Experience* (London: Edward Arnold, 1977), p. 3.
60. Cresswell, *Place*, p. 7.
61. Douglas J. Porteous, "Home: The Territorial Core", *Geographical Review* 66.4 (1976), p. 383.
62. Tuan, *Space and Place*, p. 147.
63. Massey, *Space, Place*, p. 7; Gillian Rose, *Feminism and Geography: The Limits of Geographical Knowledge* (Cambridge: Polity, 1993), pp. 57–9.
64. Rose, *Feminism and Geography*, p. 57.
65. Ibid., p. 59.
66. Porteous, "Home", p. 384.
67. bell hooks, *Yearning: Race, Gender, and Cultural Politics* (London: Turnaround, 1991), p. 47.
68. Ghassan Hage, "At Home in the Entrails of the West: Multiculturalism, Ethnic Food and Migrant Home-Building", in H. Grace, G. Hage, L. Johnson, J. Langsworth and M. Symonds (eds), *Home/World: Space, Community and Marginality in Sydney's West* (Annandale: Pluto Press, 1997), p. 104.
69. Ibid., pp. 104–5.
70. Ibid., p. 101.
71. Ibid., p. 108.
72. Diana Brydon, "Canadian Writers Negotiating Home Within Global Imaginaries". Keynote address for *Moving Cultures, Shifting Identities* conference at Flinders University, Australia (2007), p. 8. Available at http://myuminfo.umanitoba.ca/Documents/1169/Negotiating%20Home.pdf (accessed 23 March 2013).
73. Margaret Atwood, "Approximate Homes", in C. Rooke (ed), *Writing Home* (Toronto: McClelland and Stewart, 1997), p. 7.
74. Roger Rouse, "Mexican Migration and the Social Space of Postmodernism", *Diaspora: A Journal of Transnational Studies* 1.1 (1991), p. 9.
75. Angelika Bammer, "Editorial", *New Formations* 17 (1992), p. ix.
76. Eric Hobsbawm, "Introduction", *Social Research* 58.1 (1991), p. 66.

77. Homeland and nation are not synonymous terms but, as Nico Israel explains, while *heimat* does indeed signify homeland it can also be understood as "home nation". See Israel, *Outlandish*, p. 180.

78. Bammer, "Editorial", p. ix.

79. Ibid., p. x.

80. Sudesh Mishra, *Diaspora Criticism* (Edinburgh: Edinburgh University Press, 2006), p. 131.

81. Jana Braziel and Anita Mannur, "Nation, Migration, Globalization: Points of Contention in Diaspora Studies", in J. Braziel and A. Mannur (eds), *Theorizing Diaspora: A Reader* (Malden, MA: Blackwell Publishers, 2003), pp. 3–4, 7–10.

82. John Hutchinson and Anthony D. Smith, "Introduction", in J. Hutchinson and A.D. Smith (eds), *Nationalism* (Oxford: Oxford University Press, 1994), p. 5.

83. Ato Quayson and Girish Daswani, "Introduction – Diaspora and Transnationalism: Scapes, Scales and Scopes", in A. Quayson and G. Daswani (eds), *A Companion to Diaspora and Transnationalism* (Malden, MA: Blackwell Publishers, 2013), p. 7.

84. Braziel and Mannur, "Nation, Migration, Globalization", p. 2.

85. Tölölyan, "The Nation-State and its Others", p. 4.

86. Massey, *Space, Place*, pp. 4, 151.

87. Hutchinson and Smith, "Introduction", pp. 3–4. Hutchinson and Smith identify two problems that account for this inadequacy. The first relates to the fact that "the field of nationalist phenomena [...] is vast and ramified". Nationalism can take on many forms – "religious, conservative, liberal, fascist, communist, cultural, political" – and confront a number of related subjects – "race and racism, [...] ethnic conflict, international law, [...] minorities, gender, immigration genocide". The second problem identified by these scholars relates to "interdisciplinarity". Historians who once dominated the field are now rivalled by anthropologists, political scientists, sociologists, international relations theorists and philosophers.

88. Stephanie Lawson, *Culture and Context in World Politics* (Basingstoke: Palgrave Macmillan, 2006), p. 104.

89. Michael Shapiro, *Methods and Nations: Cultural Governance and the Indigenous Subject* (New York, NY: Routledge, 2004), p. 45; Anthony D. Smith, *The Ethnic Origins of Nations* (Oxford: Blackwell, 1986), p. 12.

90. Tölölyan, "The Nation-State and its Others", p. 5.

91. Brian Axel, "National Interruption: Diaspora Theory and Multiculturalism in the UK", *Cultural Dynamics* 14.3 (2002), pp. 236–7.

92. Julia Kristeva, *Strangers to Ourselves* (New York, NY: Columbia University Press, 1991), p. 96.

93. Homi Bhabha, *The Location of Culture* (London; New York, NY: Routledge, 2004), p. 200.

94. Ibid., p. 204; emphasis added.

95. Sigmund Freud, "The 'Uncanny'", in S. Freud, *The Penguin Freud Library Volume 14: Art and Literature* (London: Penguin Books, 1985), pp. 339–76. Orig. pub. 1919.

96. Ibid., p. 345. Freud quotes Friedrich Schelling in order to confirm this peculiar relationship between the *heimlich* and the *unheimlich*. Schelling says that "the 'unheimlich' is the name for everything that ought to have remained [. . .] secret and hidden but has come to light".

97. Ibid., pp. 363–4.

98. Kristeva, *Strangers*, p. 181.

99. Ibid., p. 181.

100. Ibid., p. 191.

101. Virinder S. Kalra, Raminder Kaur and John Hutnyk, *Diaspora and Hybridity* (London; Thousand Oaks, CA: SAGE Publications, 2005), p. 32.

102. Ibid., p. 32.

103. Benedict Anderson, "Western Nationalism and Eastern Nationalism: Is There a Difference That Matters?", *New Left Review* 9 (2001), p. 42.

104. Gilles Deleuze and Félix Guattari, *Kafka: Toward a Minor Literature* (Minneapolis, MN: University of Minnesota Press, 1986), p. 17.

105. Ibid., p. 16.

106. Ibid., p. 17.

107. Said, *Representations of the Intellectual*, p. 49.

108. Bhabha, *Location of Culture*, p. x.

109. Mikhail M. Bakhtin, *The Dialogic Imagination: Four Essays*, M. Holquist (ed), C. Emerson and M. Holquist (trs), (Austin, TX: University of Texas Press, 1981).

110. Ashcroft, *Post-Colonial Transformation*, p. 153.

111. Theodor Adorno, *Minima Moralia: Reflections from Damaged Life* (London: New Left Books, 1974), p. 87.

112. Ashcroft, *Post-Colonial Transformation*, p. 155.

113. Clifford, "Diasporas", p. 264.

114. Cho, "Turn to Diaspora", p. 16.

115. Clifford, "Diasporas", p. 264.

116. Michael Humphrey, "Lebanese Identities: Between Cities, Nations and Trans-nations", *Arab Studies Quarterly* 26.1 (2004), p. 32.

117. Ibid., p. 32.

118. Dalia Abdelhady, "Representing the Homeland: Lebanese Diasporic Notions of Home and Return in a Global Context", *Cultural Dynamics* 20.1 (2008), p. 57.

119. Ibid., p. 58.

120. Gabriel Sheffer, *Diaspora Politics* (Cambridge: Cambridge University Press, 2003), p. 105.

121. Humphrey, "Lebanese Identities", p. 33.

122. Arend Lijphart, *Democracy in Plural Societies: A Comparative Exploration* (New Haven, CT: Yale University Press, 1977). Lijphart defines consociationalism as "both the segmental cleavages typical of a plural society and the political

co-operation of the segmented elites" (p. 5). The idea of political cooperation is a pivotal feature in these sorts of democracies. Lijphart argues that "political leaders of all significant segments of plural society co-operate in a grand coalition to govern" in order to ensure a strong process of conflict management (p. 25). Thus, civil disintegration in Lebanon should be seen as a failure of the system to provide viable avenues for conflict resolution between various communal groups.

123. Humphrey, "Lebanese Identities", p. 47.

124. Ibid., p. 33.

125. Saree Makdisi, "Beirut, City Without History?", in P. Silverstein and U. Makdisi (eds), *Memory and Violence in the Middle East and North Africa* (Bloomington, IN: Indiana University Press, 2006), p. 210.

126. Solidere is a Lebanese company responsible for the reconstruction of the war-damaged city. It was founded in May 1994 by the then Prime Minister Rafiq al-Hariri. Before his assassination in 2005 he remained the major stakeholder within the company and many have noted a conflict of interest in his dual positions as "father" of the reconstruction programme and Prime Minister of the state.

127. S. Makdisi, "Beirut", p. 210.

128. Ibid., p. 212.

129. For further details on the lack of a historical narrative of the war see Hannah Wettig, "Is Latest Version of National History Fit to Print?", *The Daily Star* (Beirut), 2 August 2004 and Dalal Mawad, "Lebanon's History Awaits its Textbook", *The Daily Star* (Beirut), 20 November 2009. Wettig outlines the politics involved in the production of new history textbooks for secondary schools. The first post-war government mandated these texts after a review of school curricula. Some books were delivered to schools but were recalled because particular factions were displeased. Mawad also stresses the need for new texts but suggests that it is erroneous to aim for history books that focus on one "national" narrative of the war. She argues that "Each of the different communities in Lebanon is attached to its own culture, memory and martyrs. Political parties have their own reading of history. Why look for one story in a country whose history has been crafted by the stories of different cultures and communities? Wouldn't that represent a negation of Lebanon's pluralistic identity?" Given this complexity Mawad suggests the Lebanese "work on a non-political, non-ideological book compiling a chronology of facts, figures and events".

130. Authors who write critically about the war from inside Lebanon include Rashid al-Daif, Jean Said Makdisi and Elias Khoury. These writers and their texts are examined in Elise Salem's *Constructing Lebanon: A Century of Literary Narratives* (Gainesville, FL: University Press of Florida, 2003).

131. Maalouf's novel was originally published in 1996 in French as *Les Échelles du Levant* (Paris: Bernard Grasset) and translated as *Ports of Call* in 1999 by Alberto Manguel. I deal with aspects of the translation of this text in Chapter 8. All page references to *Ports of Call* pertain to the English edition.

Chapter 1   The Urban Space: Beirut at War

1. Iman Khalil, "Writing Civil War: The Lebanese Experience in Juseuf Naoum's German Short Stories", *The German Quarterly* 67.4 (1994), p. 549.
2. Jad Tabet, "Towards a Master Plan for Beirut", in S. Khalaf and P. S. Khoury (eds), *Recovering Beirut: Urban Design and Post-War Reconstruction* (Leiden: E. J. Brill, 1993), p. 88.
3. Richard Sennett, "An Introduction", in R. Sennett (ed), *Classic Essays on the Culture of Cities* (New York, NY: Appleton-Century-Crofts, 1969), pp. 3–19; William Sharpe and Leonard Wallock, "From 'Great Town' to 'Nonplace Urban Realm': Reading the Modern City", in W. Sharpe and L. Wallock (eds), *Visions of the Modern City: Essays in History, Art, and Literature* (1983; Baltimore, MD: Johns Hopkins University Press, 1987), pp. 1–50.
4. Sennett, "An Introduction", p. 3.
5. Sharpe and Wallock, "From 'Great Town'", p. 3.
6. Sennett, "An Introduction", p. 6; emphasis added.
7. Ibid., p. 7.
8. Max Weber, "The City (Non-Legitimate Domination)", in M. Weber, *Economy and Society: An Outline of Interpretive Sociology*, G. Roth and C. Wittich (eds), E. Fischoff, H. Gerth, A. M. Henderson, F. Kolegar, C. W. Mills, T. Parsons, M. Rheinstein, G. Roth, E. Shils and C. Wittich (trs), (Berkeley, CA: University of California Press, 1978), p. 1212. Orig. pub. 1913.
9. Ibid., p. 1213.
10. George Simmel, "The Metropolis and Mental Life", in R. Sennett (ed), *Classic Essays on the Culture of Cities* (New York, NY: Appleton-Century-Crofts, 1969), p. 59. Orig. pub. 1903.
11. Ibid., pp. 59–60.
12. Ibid., p. 60.
13. Sennett, "An Introduction", p. 12.
14. This essay was first published in 1915 in *The American Journal of Sociology*. A revised and updated version with the same title later appeared in Robert Park and Ernest Burgess' co-authored book *The City* (1925).
15. Robert Park, "Chapter I: The City: Suggestions for the Investigation of Human Behavior in the Urban Environment", in R. Park and E. Burgess, *The City* (Chicago, IL: University of Chicago Press, 1925), p. 1.
16. Robert Park, "The City: Suggestions for the Investigation of Human Behavior in the Urban Environment", *The American Journal of Sociology* 20.5 (1915), p. 578.
17. Park, "Chapter I: The City", pp. 9–10.
18. Samir Kassir, *Beirut*, M.B. DeBovoise (tr), (Berkeley, CA: University of California Press, 2011), p. 111.
19. Ibid., pp. 112, 427.
20. Ibid., pp. 427, 428; Samir Khalaf, *Lebanon's Predicament* (New York, NY: Columbia University Press, 1987), p. 220.

21. Samir Khalaf and Guilain Denoeux, "Urban Networks and Political Conflict in Lebanon", in N. Shehadi and D.H. Mills (eds), *Lebanon: A History of Conflict and Consensus* (London: I.B.Tauris, 1988), p. 181.

22. Samir Khalaf, *Lebanon's Predicament*; "Urban Design and the Recovery of Beirut", in S. Khalaf and P. S. Khoury (eds), *Recovering Beirut: Urban Design and Post-War Reconstruction* (Leiden: E. J. Brill, 1993), pp. 11–62; *Heart of Beirut: Reclaiming the Bourj* (London: Saqi, 2006); Fuad Khuri, *From Village to Suburb: Order and Change in Greater Beirut* (Chicago, IL: University of Chicago Press, 1975); John Gulick, *Tripoli: A Modern Arab City* (Cambridge, MA: Harvard University Press, 1967).

23. Samir Khalaf and Per Kongstad, *Hamra of Beirut: A Case of Rapid Urbanisation* (Leiden: E. J. Brill, 1973), p. 120.

24. Mike Davis, *Planet of Slums: Urban Involution and the Informal Working Class* (London: Verso, 2006).

25. Louis Wirth, "Urbanism as a Way of Life", *The American Journal of Sociology* 44.1 (1938), p. 3.

26. Arend Lijphart, "Consociational Democracy", *World Politics* 21.2 (1969), p. 208.

27. Imad Salamey and Paul Tabar, "Consociational Democracy and Urban Sustainability: Transforming the Confessional Divides in Beirut", *Ethnopolitics* 7.2–3 (2008), p. 245.

28. Ibid., p. 245.

29. See Theodor Hanf, *Coexistence in Wartime Lebanon: Decline of a State and Rise of a Nation* (London: I.B.Tauris, 1993), especially Chapter 2 where Hanf emphasises the role of sectarian friction within the urban space as a cause for civil unrest.

30. Ester Charlesworth, *Architects Without Frontiers: War, Reconstruction and Design Responsibility* (Oxford: Architectural Press, 2006), p. 61.

31. Ibid., p. 61.

32. Michael Davie, "City as Excavation? Notes for the Excavation of Beirut: A Quest for National Identity?" Paper delivered at *City Debates Seminar* at the American University of Beirut, 3 June 2002.

33. Mona Fawaz, Mona Harb and Ahmad Gharbieh, "Living Beirut's Security Zones: An Investigation of the Modalities and Practice of Urban Security", *City and Society* 24.2 (2002), pp. 188–9.

34. Ibid., p. 187.

35. Charlesworth, *Architects Without Frontiers*, p. 61.

36. Miriam Cooke, "Beirut Reborn: The Political Aesthetics of Auto-Destruction", *The Yale Journal of Criticism* 15.2 (2002), p. 408.

37. Angus Gavin and Ramez Maluf, *Beirut Reborn: The Restoration and Development of the Central District* (London: Academy Editions, 1996), p. 29.

38. Ibid., p. 28.

39. Caroline Nagel, "Ethnic Conflict and Urban Redevelopment in Downtown Beirut", *Growth and Change* 31.2 (2000), p. 224.

40. The consensus among literary scholars (Miriam Cooke, Syrine Hout and Saree Makdisi), historians (Ussama Makdisi), and social scientists (Samir Khalaf and

Hashim Sarkis) is that Lebanon's post-war scene is dominated by amnesia. A recently published study by Sune Haugbolle challenges this consensus. Haugbolle contends that while the civil war is still seen as a "taboo" subject in Lebanon, a discussion of the war did emerge at the start of the twenty-first century. This discussion, however, differs between those who experienced the war "and have memories of guilt and suffering" and those who escaped it by emigrating (p. 72). The former group have accepted "amnesia [. . .] as a means to keep the traumatic experiences at a distance" while the latter group have reacted against it (p. 72). Haugbolle, therefore, does not deny that amnesia continues to mar contemporary Lebanon but adds further nuance as to who is engaged in this forgetting. His point that migrant Lebanese are rejecting the practice of forgetting addresses the argument I make here in relation to diaspora writers, which is that most writers displaced by the war are consciously invested in remembering it through narrative. See Sune Haugbolle, *War and Memory in Lebanon* (Cambridge: Cambridge University Press, 2010). For arguments that stress post-war amnesia in Lebanon see Miriam Cooke, "Beirut Reborn", pp. 393–424; Syrine Hout, *Post-War Anglophone Lebanese Fiction: Home Matters in the Diaspora* (Edinburgh: Edinburgh University Press, 2012); Saree Makdisi, "Beirut, City Without History?", in P. Silverstein and U. Makdisi (eds), *Memory and Violence in the Middle East and North Africa* (Bloomington, IN: Indiana University Press, 2006), pp. 201–14; Ussama Makdisi, "From Sectarianism to Lebanese Nationalism: Has the Lebanese War Unequivocally Ended?", *Adab* 11–12 (2001), p. 49; Samir Khalaf, "Contested Space and the Forging of New Cultural Identities", in P. Rowe and H. Sarkis (eds), *Projecting Beirut: Episodes in the Construction and Reconstruction of a Modern City* (Munich; London; New York, NY: Prestel, 1998), pp. 140–64; Hashim Sarkis, "Territorial Claims: Architecture and Post-War Attitudes Toward the Built Environment", in S. Khalaf and P. S. Khoury (eds), *Recovering Beirut: Urban Design and Post-War Reconstruction* (Leiden: E. J. Brill, 1993), pp. 101–27.

41. U. Makdisi, "From Sectarianism to Lebanese Nationalism", p. 49.

42. S. Makdisi, "Beirut", p. 202.

43. The war amnesia that the postcards explicitly reinforce has been challenged by two Lebanese artists, Joana Hadjithomas and Khalil Joreige. In *Wonder Beirut: The Story of the Pyromaniac Photographer* the artists created a series of prints that are based on the pre-war postcards. Each postcard was modified and distressed with burn marks in order to capture the impact of the war on the Lebanese landscape. In this way, "Hadjithomas and Joreige transform [. . .] the original postcards from clichéd tourist souvenirs into dreamscapes, pseudo-ravaged by iridescent bubbles of melted color and glowing ruptures". The image on the cover of this book is taken from this series – *Wonder Beirut #22 (General View with Mountains)*. See Kelly Baum, *Nobody's Property: Art, Land, Space, 2000–2010* (Princeton, NJ: Princeton University Art Museum, 2010), pp. 112–7 for further details on this artwork.

44. S. Makdisi, "Beirut", pp. 203–4.

Chapter 2   The Destruction of West Beirut in Tony Hanania's *Unreal City*

1. Ruth Padel, "Illicit Love in a War-Torn Land", *The Daily Telegraph*, 6 March 1999. Available at www.telegraph.co.uk/culture/4716981/Illicit-love-in-a-war-torn-land.html (accessed 31 August 2013).
2. Luke Vinten, "Out of his Head". *Times Literary Supplement* 5007 (1999), p. 22.
3. Tony Hanania, *Unreal City* (1999; London: Bloomsbury, 2000), pp. 62–3.
4. Ibid., p. 22.
5. Vinten, "Out of His Head", p. 22.
6. Ibid., p. 22.
7. Michel de Certeau, *The Practice of Everyday Life* (Berkeley, CA: University of California Press, 1984), p. 96.
8. Richard Lehan, *The City in Literature: An Intellectual and Cultural History* (Berkeley, CA: University of California Press, 1998), p. 128.
9. T. S. Eliot, *The Waste Land* (1922; London: Hogarth Press, 1923), lines 374–7.
10. Lehan, *The City in Literature*, p. 134.
11. Hanania, *Unreal City*, p. 167.
12. Lehan, *The City in Literature*, p. 129.
13. Akram Khater, *Inventing Home: Emigration, Gender, and the Middle Class in Lebanon, 1870–1920* (Berkeley, CA: University of California Press, 2001), p. 119.
14. Ibid., pp. 120–3.
15. Hanania, *Unreal City*, pp. 50–1.
16. Ibid., p. 61.
17. Ibid., p. 61.
18. Ibid., p. 60.
19. Ibid., p. 249.
20. Ibid., p. 248.
21. Ibid., p. 249.
22. Ibid., p. 192.
23. Ibid., p. 246.
24. Ibid., p. 246.
25. Ibid., p. 53.
26. Ibid., p. 194.
27. Ibid., p. 167.
28. Tony Hanania quoted in Syrine Hout, "The Predicament of In-Betweenness in the Contemporary Lebanese Exilic Novel in English", in Y. Suleiman and I. Muhawi (eds), *Literature and Nation in the Middle East* (Edinburgh: Edinburgh University Press, 2006), p. 200.
29. Hanania, *Unreal City*, p. 216.
30. Ibid., p. 216.
31. Ibid., p. 216.

32. Ibid., p. 216.
33. Salim Nasr, "The Political Economy of the Lebanese Conflict", in N. Shehadi and B. Harney (eds), *Politics and the Economy in Lebanon* (Oxford: Centre for Lebanese Studies, 1989), p. 47.
34. Ibid., p. 48.
35. Samir Makdisi and Richard Sadaka, "The Lebanese Civil War, 1975–1990", *American University of Beirut, Institute of Financial Economics: Lecture and Working Paper* Series 3 (Beirut: American University of Beirut Press, 2003), p. 48.
36. Hanania, *Unreal City*, p. 44.
37. Ibid., p. 217.
38. Ibid., p. 128.
39. Ibid., p. 107.
40. Ibid., p. 128.
41. Ibid., p. 143.
42. Ibid., pp. 234–5.
43. Ibid., p. 235.
44. Ibid., p. 235.
45. Angelika Neuwirth, "Introduction", in A. Neuwirth, B. Embalo, S. Gunther and M. Jarrar (eds), *Myths, Historical Archetypes and Symbolic Figures in Arabic Literature: Towards a New Hermeneutic Approach* (Beirut: In Kommission bei Franz Steiner Verlag Stuttgart, 1999), p. xx.
46. Hanania, *Unreal City*, p. 118.
47. Ibid., p. 78.
48. Ibid., pp. 160–1.
49. Ibid., p. 145.
50. Brigit Embalo, "The City, Mythical Images and their Deconstructions: The Image of Beirut in Contemporary Works of Arab Fiction", in A. Neuwirth, B. Embalo, S. Gunther and M. Jarrar (eds), *Myths, Historical Archetypes, and Symbolic Figures in Arabic Literature: Towards a New Hermeneutic Approach* (Beirut: In Kommission bei Franz Steiner Verlag Stuttgart, 1999), p. 589.
51. Hanania, *Unreal City*, p. 145.
52. Ibid., p. 166.
53. Ibid., p. 205.
54. Neuwirth, "Introduction", p. xx.
55. Embalo, "The City, Mythical Images and their Deconstructions", p. 592.
56. Mahmoud Darwish quoted in Embalo, "The City, Mythical Images and their Deconstructions", p. 592.
57. Hanania, *Unreal City*, p. 221.
58. Ibid., p. 222.
59. Ibid., p. 222.
60. Ibid., p. 223.
61. Embalo, "The City, Mythical Images and their Deconstructions", p. 588.
62. Neuwirth, "Introduction", p. xvii.
63. Eliot, *The Waste Land*, p. 29.

64. Jessie L. Weston, *From Ritual to Romance* (Cambridge: The University Press, 1920), pp. 35–6.
65. George Frazer, *The Golden Bough: A Study in Magic and Religion* (London: Macmillan, 1922), p. 325.
66. Lehan, *The City in Literature*, p. 135.
67. Saddik Gohar, "Towards a Hybrid Poetics", *InterCulture: An Interdisciplinary Journal* 4.2 (2007), p. 1.
68. Ibid., p. 1.
69. Ibid., p. 2.
70. Shmuel Moreh, *Modern Arabic Poetry 1800–1970: The Development of Its Forms and Themes Under the Influence of Western Literature* (Leiden: E. J. Brill, 1976), p. 216.
71. Neuwirth, "Introduction", p. xii.
72. Frazer, *The Golden Bough*, p. 325.
73. Ibid., p. 325.
74. Issa Boullata, *Modern Arabic Poets: 1950–1975* (London: Heineman, 1976), p. xii.
75. Hanania, *Unreal City*, pp. 63–4.
76. Ibid., p. 65.
77. Ibid., p. 65.
78. Ibid., p. 82.
79. Frazer, *The Golden Bough*, p. 335.
80. Hanania, *Unreal City*, p. 96.
81. Ibid., p. 80.
82. Ibid., p. 50.
83. Ibid., pp. 199–200.
84. Ibid., p. 129.
85. Ibid., p. 213.
86. Ibid., p. 213.
87. Ibid., p. 213.
88. Ibid., pp. 213–14.
89. Ibid., p. 191.
90. Frazer, *The Golden Bough*, p. 326.
91. Hanania, *Unreal City*, p. 117.
92. Ibid., pp. 141, 151, 154.
93. Ibid., p. 229.
94. Ibid., p. 230.
95. See the introduction for an outline the commercial focus of the Solidere reconstruction programme.
96. Paul Tabar, "*Ashura* in Sydney: A Transformation of a Religious Ceremony in the Context of a Migrant Society", *Journal of Intercultural Studies* 23.3 (2002), pp. 285–6.
97. Hanania, *Unreal City*, p. 98.
98. Ibid., pp. 99–100.

99. Ibid., p. 100.

100. Zeina Maasri, "The Aesthetics of Belonging: Transformations in Hizbullah's Political Posters", *Middle East Journal of Culture and Communication* 5 (2012), p. 166.

101. Maasri, "The Aesthetics of Belonging", p. 166.

102. Tabar, "*Ashura* in Sydney", pp. 290–5.

103. Hanania, *Unreal City*, p. 54.

104. Ibid., p. 55.

105. Ibid., p. 168.

106. Ibid., p. 259.

107. Ibid., p. 193.

108. Ibid., p. 195.

109. Abul Ezzati, "The Concept of Martyrdom in Islam", *Al-Serat: A Journal of Islamic Studies* xii (1986), par. 2. Available at www.al-islam.org/al-serat/ concept-ezzati.htm (accessed 31 August 2013).

110. Maher Jarrar, "The Martyrdom of Passionate Lovers: Holy War as a Sacred Wedding", in A. Neuwirth, B. Embalo, S. Gunther and M. Jarrar (eds), *Myths, Historical Archetypes and Symbolic Figures in Arabic Literature: Towards a New Hermeneutic Approach* (Beirut: In Kommission bei Franz Steiner Verlag Stuttgart, 1999), p. 88.

111. Hanania, *Unreal City*, p. 30.

112. Ibid., p. 56.

113. Ibid., p. 253.

114. Syrine Hout, *Post-War Anglophone Lebanese Fiction: Home Matters in the Diaspora* (Edinburgh: Edinburgh University Press, 2012), p. 48.

115. Ibid., p. 49.

116. Hanania, *Unreal City*, p. 22.

117. Michael Long, "Eliot, Pound, Joyce: 'unreal city'", in E. Timms and D. Kelley (eds), *Unreal City: Urban Experience in Modern European Literature and Art* (New York, NY: St. Martin's Press, 1985), p. 146.

Chapter 3   Undermining the Christian City in Rawi Hage's *De Niro's Game*

1. M. Wayne Cunningham, "Ten Thousand Plaudits", *January Magazine*, May 2007. Available at www.januarymagazine.com/fiction/denirosgame.html (accessed 31 August 2009).

2. Eibhlín Evans quoted in "Lord Mayor of Dublin unveils winner of International IMPAC Dublin Literary Award", *Dublin City Council Website*, 12 June 2008. Available at www.dublincity.ie/PRESS/PRESSRELEASES/

PRESSRELEASES2008/PRESSRELEASESJUNE2008/Pages/impac_dubli
n_literary_award_announced.aspx (accessed 31 August 2013).

3. Ibid.

4. Rawi Hage, *De Niro's Game* (Canada: Anansi, 2006), pp. 12, 124, 256.

5. Daniel Campi, "Book Review: *De Niro's Game*", *Barcelona Metropolitan Magazine 1.0*, 2006. Available at www.barcelona-metropolitan.com (accessed 9 June 2009). Link no longer working.

6. Ibid.

7. Syrine Hout, *Post-War Anglophone Lebanese Fiction: Home Matters in the Diaspora* (Edinburgh: Edinburgh University Press, 2012), p. 129.

8. Najat Rahman, "Apocalyptic Narrative Recalls and the Human: Rawi Hage's *De Niro's Game*", *University of Toronto Quarterly* 78.2 (2009), p. 811.

9. Rawi Hage quoted in Sarah L'Estrange, "The Book Show: Rawi Hage's *De Niro's Game*", *ABC Radio National*, 12 June 2007, par. 31. Available at www. abc.net.au/radionational/programs/bookshow/rawi-hages-de-niros-game/ 3248206#transcript (accessed 4 May 2009).

10. Nouri Gana, "Rawi Hage: *De Niro's Game*", *The International Fiction Review* 34 (2007), p. 196.

11. Salah Hassan, "UnStated: Narrating War in Lebanon", *PMLA* 123.5 (2008), p. 1621.

12. Hage, *De Niro's Game*, p. 13.

13. Dina Georgis, "Masculinities and the Aesthetics of Love: Reading Terrorism in *De Niro's Game* and *Paradise Now*", *Studies in Gender and Sexuality* 12.2 (2011), p. 139.

14. Robert Park, "Chapter I: The City: Suggestions for the Investigation of Human Behavior in the Urban Environment", in R. Park and E. Burgess, *The City* (Chicago, IL: University of Chicago Press, 1925), p. 4.

15. Ibid., p. 3.

16. Robert Park quoted in John Brewer, *Ethnography* (Buckingham: Open University Press, 2000), p. 13.

17. Hashim Sarkis, "Beirut, the Novel", *Parachute: Contemporary Art Magazine* 108 (2002), p. 107.

18. Ibid., p. 107.

19. Samir Khalaf, "Contested Space and the Forging of New Cultural Identities", in P. Rowe and H. Sarkis (eds), *Projecting Beirut: Episodes in the Construction and Reconstruction of a Modern City* (Munich; London; New York, NY: Prestel, 1998), p. 141.

20. For further details on the ongoing commemoration of Gemayel see Sune Haugbolle, "The Secular Saint: Iconography and Ideology in the Cult of Bashir Jumayil", in A. Bandak and M. Bille (eds), *Politics of Worship in the Contemporary Middle East: Sainthood in Fragile States* (Leiden: Brill, 2013), pp. 191–211.

21. Estimates of the number of the Palestinians who perished vary. The Lebanese government records a number of 2,000, the International Committee of the

Red Cross, 2,750, and the Lebanese Red Cross, 3,000. See Bayan al-Hout, *Sabra and Shatila: September 1982* (London: Pluto Press. 2004), p. 296.

22. Robert Worth and Franklin Lamb have reported that Samir Geagea, a leading figure in the party during the war, issued an apology to the Palestinians. At best it was, as Worth suggests, "a kind of apology" because of its nebulous nature. Delivered in the same week that the Sabra and Shatila massacres were commemorated in September 2008, Geagea did not explicitly refer to these violent events but instead sought absolution for all the "mistakes" his party made during the war. He also diluted the sincerity of his approach by immediately categorising his militia's acts as part of their unavoidable "national duties". Finally, he ordered "those who are exploiting our past mistakes {i.e. rival parties and Palestinian activists} to stop doing so because only God can judge us". Geagea's evasive and non-specific approach reinforces the fact that no official apology has been issued to the Palestinians by a Christian leader. See Robert Worth, "10 Years After a Mea Culpa, No Hint of a 'Me, Too'", *The New York Times*, 16 April 2010. Available at www.nytimes. com/2010/04/17/world/middleeast/17lebanon.html (accessed 13 December 2011). See also Franklin Lamb, "Why Lebanon's Palestinians are Hopeful about an Election in Which They Cannot Vote: The Palestinians 26 Years After the Massacre at Sabra-Shatila – Part Three", *thepeoplesvoice.org*, 25 September 2008. Available at www.thepeoplesvoice.org/cgibin/blogs/voices. php/2008/09/25/p28996 (accessed 13 December 2011).

23. al-Hout, *Sabra and Shatila*, p. 12.

24. Jim Quilty, "Confronting Demons to Banish them like Sabra and Shatilla, 'Massaker' is a Political Creature and Should be Handled as Such", *The Daily Star* (Beirut), 21 October 2005. Available at www.dailystar.com.lb/Culture/ Arts/Oct/21/Confronting-demons-to-banish-them-like-Sabra-and-Shatilla-Massaker-is-a-political-creature-and-should.ashx#axzz1aHS4VFcH (accessed 11 October 2011).

25. Hobeika was assassinated in 2002 only days after agreeing to testify in a Belgian court that Ariel Sharon was directly involved in the 1982 siege against the Palestinians.

26. Not all Maronites are represented by the political parties of the Phalange or LF. There are other Maronite political groups that are critical of these two. With regard to the Palestinians, however, there is very little disagreement about their role in the civil war. What this means is that rival Maronite factions do not insist on an apology nor do they seek to expose the wrong done to the Palestinians in September 1982.

27. Sarkis, "Beirut, the Novel", p. 107.

28. Miriam Cooke, "Beirut Reborn: The Political Aesthetics of Auto-Destruction", *The Yale Journal of Criticism* 15.2 (2002), p. 422.

29. The first memorial to mark the massacres in Sabra and Shatila was erected in 1999, 17 years after the event. Even this memorial can hardly be described as state-sponsored because it was established by Hezbollah for politically

strategic purposes. This issue is discussed in further detail in Chapter 5 in relation to Nada Awar Jarrar's novel.

30. Sarkis, "Beirut, the Novel", p. 107.

31. See Elizabeth Renzetti, "The Search for Rawi Hage", *The Globe and Mail*, 4 August 2008. Available at www.theglobeandmail.com/news/arts/the-search-for-rawi-hage/article308056/ (accessed 23 April 2009). See also Genevieve Swart, "10,000 Reasons to Revisit His Youth", *The Sydney Morning Herald*, 28 May 2007. Available at www.smh.com.au/news/books/10000-reasons-to-revisit-his-youth/2007/05/27/1180205060755.html?page=fullpage#contentSwap1 (accessed 9 June 2008).

32. L'Estrange, "The Book Show: Rawi Hage's *De Niro's Game*", par. 4.

33. Edward Said, "Identity, Authority, and Freedom: The Potentate and the Traveller", *Transition* 54 (1991), p. 18.

34. Ibid., p. 18.

35. Hout, *Post-War Anglophone Lebanese Fiction*, p. 130.

36. Hage, *De Niro's Game*, p. 98.

37. Gana, "Rawi Hage", p. 196.

38. Hage, *De Niro's Game*, p. 11.

39. Ibid., p. 12.

40. Gérand Genette, *Narrative Discourse*, J.E. Lewin (tr), (Oxford: Blackwell, 1980), pp. 189–90. The other two kinds of focalisation that Genette identifies are *"variable"* where the focal character oscillates between two protagonists and *"multiple* [. . .] where the same event may be evoked several times according to the point of view of several [. . .] characters".

41. Hage, *De Niro's Game*, p. 78.

42. Ibid., p. 78.

43. Ibid., p. 78.

44. Ibid., p. 67.

45. Ibid., p. 67.

46. Ibid., p. 68.

47. Ibid., p. 68.

48. Ibid., p. 78.

49. In the mid-twentieth century, as Arab nationalism was gaining momentum, the majority of Maronite leaders and several scholars of Maronite history, such as Matti Moosa or Walid Phares, sought to distance the community from collective notions of Arab identity. At this point, as Moosa explains, it was not only Islam that Maronites defined themselves against but also Arabism. The struggle for Maronites to locate their history or culture outside of Arab forms has been much more difficult than differentiating themselves from Islam. It is clear that Maronite Christians are not Muslim but it is not as clear that they are not Arab, given that the Christian presence in the Middle East pre-dates Islam and that the Arabic language is not exclusive to Muslims. For further details on this issue see Matti Moosa, *The Maronites in History* (Syracuse, NY: Syracuse University Press, 1989) and Walid Phares, *Lebanese Christian*

Nationalism: The Rise and Fall of an Ethnic Resistance (Boulder, CO: Lynne Rienner Publishers, 1995).

50. Sami Ofeish and Sabah Ghandour, "Transgressive Subjects: Gender, War, and Colonialism in Etel Adnan's *Sitt Marie Rose*", in L. S. Majaj and A. Amireh (eds), *Etel Adnan: Critical Essays on the Arab American Writer and Artist* (North Carolina, NC: McFarland & Company Inc. Publishers, 2002), p. 126.

51. Moosa, *The Maronites in History*, p. 303; emphasis added.

52. Ibid., p. 279. This claim made by Moosa is highly inaccurate and one that has been refuted by the eminent historian Kamal Salibi. Salibi notes that the Maronites retained Syriac as the language of their liturgy well into the ninth century, after the conquest and the Umayyad invasion, but suggests that this is an irrelevant marker of their cultural origins. He argues that "Syriac, which is the Christian literary form of Aramaic, was originally the liturgical language of all the Arab and Arameo-Arab Christian sects, in Arabia as well as in Syria and Iraq". See Kamal Salibi, *A House of Many Mansions: The History of Lebanon Reconsidered* (London: I.B.Tauris, 1988), p. 90.

53. Ghassan Hage, "Nationalist Anxiety and the Fear of Losing Your Other", *Australian Journal of Anthropology* 7.2 (1996), p.128. The work of Ghassan Hage and Kamal Salibi explores the conflicts between Maronites and Muslims and provides details of the historical relationship of these two communities. Both Hage and Salibi undertake archival research and reveal that certain scholars, like Bishop Jiba'il ibn al-Qilai (1450–1516) and Patriarch Istphan al-Duwayhi (1629–1704), document Maronite history in order to stress the persecution of Christians at the hands of Muslims and to insist upon Lebanon as an essentially Christian land. For further details see Ghassan Hage, "Religious Fundamentalism as a Political Strategy: The Evolution of the Lebanese Forces' Religious Discourse during the Lebanese Civil War", *Critique of Anthropology* 12.27 (1992), pp. 27–45 and Kamal Salibi, *Maronite Historians of Mediaeval Lebanon* (Beirut: American University of Beirut, 1959).

54. Walid Phares quoted in G. Hage, "Nationalist Anxiety", p. 123.

55. The arguments of Moosa and Phares represent a particular, although not necessarily obscure, characterisation of Maronite culture and history. The community's position with regard to Islam and Arabism is more complex than presented by these two scholars and not all historians of the Maronites subscribe to the notions of non-Arab identity and historical persecution. See, for instance, John P. Entelis, "Belief-System and Ideology Formation in the Lebanese Katâ'ib Party", *International Journal of Middle East Studies* 4.2 (1973), pp. 148–62 for more complex views of Maronite identity. My focus on the arguments made by Moosa and Phares stems from the ideological stance Hage's novel takes against the form of Maronite culture they depict.

56. G. Hage, "Nationalist Anxiety", p. 123.

57. Kamal Salibi, "Introduction: The Historical Perspective", in N. Shehadi and D. H. Mills (eds), *Lebanon: A History of Conflict and Consensus* (London: I.B.Tauris, 1988), p. 7.

58. Bashir Gemayel quoted in G. Hage, "Religious Fundamentalism", p. 34.
59. Ibid., p. 34.
60. Hage, *De Niro's Game*, p. 130.
61. Ibid., p. 131.
62. Ibid., p. 123.
63. Ibid., p. 277
64. Ibid., p. 128.
65. Hashim Sarkis, "Territorial Claims: Architecture and Post-War Attitudes Toward the Built Environment", in S. Khalaf and P. S. Khoury (eds), *Recovering Beirut: Urban Design and Post-War Reconstruction* (Leiden: E. J. Brill, 1993), p. 120.
66. Hage, *De Niro's Game*, p. 12.
67. Ibid., p. 154.
68. Theodor Adorno, "Commitment", *New Left Review* I 87–88 (1974), p. 85.
69. Hage, *De Niro's Game*, p. 175.
70. Ibid., p. 174.
71. Ibid., p. 174.
72. Ibid., p. 178.
73. Ibid., p. 174.
74. Unnamed former militiaman quoted in Jalal Toufic, *Undeserving Lebanon* (Beirut: Forthcoming Books, 2007), p. 51. Available at http://www.jalaltoufic. com/downloads/Jalal_Toufic_Undeserving_Lebanon.pdf (accessed 10 May 2014).
75. Hage, *De Niro's Game*, pp. 51, 53.
76. Toufic, *Undeserving Lebanon*, p. 53.
77. Adorno, "Commitment", p. 85.
78. Conor Cruise O'Brien, *Camus* (London: Fontana, 1970), p. 26.
79. English Showalter, Jr., *The Stranger: Humanity and the Absurd* (Boston, MA: Twayne Publishers, 1989), p. 5.
80. Ibid., p. 5.
81. Ibid., p. 71.
82. David Carroll, *Albert Camus, the Algerian: Colonialism, Terrorism, Justice* (New York, NY: Columbia University Press, 2007), pp. 28, 33.
83. Gana, "Rawi Hage", p. 198.
84. O'Brien, *Camus*, p. 84.
85. Philip Thody, "Camus's *L'Étranger* Revisited", *Critical Quarterly* 21.2 (1979), p. 63.
86. Edward Said, *Culture and Imperialism* (New York, NY: Viking, 1994), p. 209.
87. Hilal Khashan, "The Political Values of Lebanese Maronite College Students", *Journal of Conflict Resolution* 34 (1990), p. 725.
88. Ofeish and Ghandour, "Transgressive Subjects", p. 124.
89. Nancy W. Jabbra and Joseph G. Jabbra, "Education and Political Development in the Middle East", in S. G. Hajjar (ed), *The Middle East: From Transition to Development* (Leiden: E. J. Brill, 1985), p. 89.

90. Yasir Suleiman, *The Arabic Language and National Identity: A Study in Ideology* (Edinburgh: Edinburgh University Press, 2003), p. 205.
91. Ofeish and Ghandour, "Transgressive Subjects", p. 126.
92. Hage, *De Niro's Game*, p. 199.
93. Ibid., pp. 191, 225.
94. Ibid., pp. 215–16.
95. Ibid., p. 216.
96. Walid Phares, "Whose Lebanon? Parallels of Arab Occupation", *B'tzedek Online*, 1998. Available at http://www.btzedek.co.il/lebanon.htm (accessed 12 April 2008). Link no longer working.
97. G. Hage, "Religious Fundamentalism", p. 39.
98. Hage, *De Niro's Game*, p. 136.
99. Ibid., p. 144.
100. Ibid., p. 144.
101. Hassan, "UnStated", p. 1627.
102. Hage, *De Niro's Game*, p. 175; emphasis added.
103. Ibid., p. 218.
104. Ibid., p. 265.
105. Ibid., p. 266.
106. Rawi Hage, "To Roam a Borderless World", *The Globe and Mail*, 13 June 2008. Available at www.theglobeandmail.com/commentary/to-roam-a-borderless-world/article720197/ (accessed 31 August 2013).

Chapter 4   Domicile and Diaspora: Women Write the Home

1. Avtar Brah, *Cartographies of Diaspora: Contesting Identities* (London; New York, NY: Routledge, 1996), p. 181.
2. William Safran, "Diasporas in Modern Societies: Myths of Homeland and Return", *Diaspora: A Journal of Transnational Studies* 1.1 (1991), p. 83.
3. Paul Tabar, "Lebanese Diaspora: Hybrid, Complex and Contentious", in P. Tabar (ed), *Lebanese Diaspora: History, Racism and Belonging* (Beirut: Lebanese American University Press, 2005), p. 7.
4. Ibid., p. 8.
5. Dalia Abdelhady, "Representing the Homeland: Lebanese Diasporic Notions of Home and Return in a Global Context", *Cultural Dynamics* 20.1 (2008), p. 53.
6. See Dalia Abdelhady, "Beyond Home/Host Networks: Forms of Solidarity Among Lebanese Immigrants in a Global Era", *Identities: Global Studies in Culture and Power* 13.3 (2006), pp. 427–53; "Cultural Production in the Lebanese Diaspora: Memory, Nostalgia and Displacement", *Journal of Political and Military Sociology* 35.1 (2007), pp. 39–62; *The Lebanese Diaspora: The Arab Immigrant*

Experience in Montreal, New York, and Paris (New York, NY: New York University Press, 2011).

7. Angelika Bammer, "Editorial", *New Formations* 17 (1992), p. x.

8. Ibid., p. vii.

9. Ibid., p. x.

10. Ibid., pp. ix–x.

11. Eric Hobsbawm, "Introduction", *Social Research* 58.1 (1991), p. 65.

12. Peter Somerville, "Homelessness and the Meaning of Home: Rooflessness or Rootlessness?", *International Journal of Urban and Regional Research* 16.4 (1992), p. 532.

13. See Somerville, "Homelessness and the Meaning of Home", p. 532 for further details of the material dimensions of home. Here Somerville explains that while shelter and abode respectively reflect home as "a roof over one's head" and "anywhere one happens to stay", the characteristic of privacy suggests "the power to control one's boundaries".

14. Hobsbawm, "Introduction", p. 66.

15. See Somerville, "Homelessness and the Meaning of Home", pp. 532–3 for a discussion of the nostalgic aspects of home. Where home is viewed as hearth and heart, terms like warmth, cosiness, security, stability and health are used to describe the emotional satisfaction one derives from being "at home". The paradisiacal home is achieved when "the idealization of all the positive features of home [are] fused together".

16. Hobsbawm, "Introduction", p. 65.

17. Ibid., p. 67.

18. Ibid., p. 61.

19. Ibid., p. 66.

20. Ibid., p. 66.

21. Ibid., p. 66.

22. Alison Blunt, *Domicile and Diaspora* (Malden, MA: Blackwell Publishers, 2005), p. 2.

23. Ibid., p. 2.

24. Ibid., p. 2.

25. Ibid., pp. 3–4.

26. Ibid., p. 4.

27. Ibid., p. 5.

28. Alison Blunt and Robyn Dowling, *Home* (London: Routledge, 2006), p. 2.

29. See Blunt, *Domicile and Diaspora*; Blunt and Dowling, *Home*; Rosemary George, *The Politics of Home: Postcolonial Reformations and Twentieth-Century Fiction* (Cambridge: Cambridge University Press, 1996); and the collection of articles in the special editions on "Home" in *New Formations* 17 (1992) and *Social Research* 58.1 (1991).

30. Nigel Rapport and Andrew Dawson, "The Topic and the Book", in N. Rapport and A. Dawson (eds), *Migrants of Identity: Perceptions of Home in a World of Movement* (Oxford, UK; New York, NY: Berg, 1998), p. 6.

31. Ibid., p. 6.
32. Joseph Rykwert, "House and Home", *Social Research* 58.1 (1991), p. 54.
33. Mary Douglas, "The Idea of a Home", *Social Research* 58.1 (1991), p. 289.
34. Ibid., p. 290.
35. Rykwert, "House and Home", p. 54.
36. Nigel Rapport and Andrew Dawson, "Home and Movement – A Polemic", in N. Rapport and A. Dawson (eds), *Migrants of Identity: Perceptions of Home in a World of Movement* (Oxford, UK; New York, NY: Berg, 1998), p. 21.
37. Safran, "Diasporas in Modern Societies", p. 83; emphasis added.
38. Ibid., pp. 83–4.
39. On the whole Diana Brydon, working within a contemporary and postcolonial context, actually embraces a model of home that strongly leans towards movement and mobility rather than stasis. My point here is that when she views home from the perspective of diaspora she reduces it to a fixed category.
40. Diana Brydon, "Canadian Writers Negotiating Home within Global Imaginaries". Keynote address for *Moving Cultures, Shifting Identities* conference at Flinders University, Australia (2007), p. 6. Available at http://myuminfo.umani toba.ca/Documents/1169/Negotiating%20Home.pdf (accessed 23 March 2013).
41. Ibid., p. 7.
42. Rapport and Dawson, "The Topic and the Book", p. 7.
43. James Clifford, "Diasporas", in J. Clifford, *Routes: Travels and Translation in the Late Twentieth Century* (Cambridge, MA: Harvard University Press, 1997), p. 269.
44. Ibid., p. 269.
45. Roger Rouse, "Mexican Migration and the Social Space of Postmodernism", *Diaspora: A Journal of Transnational Studies* 1.1 (1991), p. 13.
46. Ibid., p. 13.
47. Ibid., p. 14.
48. Ibid., p. 13.
49. Ibid., p. 14.
50. Brah, *Cartographies of Diaspora*, p. 180.
51. Ibid., p. 193.
52. Svetlana Boym, *The Future of Nostalgia* (New York, NY: Basic Books, 2001), p. 252.
53. Gillian Rose, *Feminism and Geography: The Limits of Geographical Knowledge* (Cambridge: Polity, 1993), pp. 59–60.
54. bell hooks, *Yearning: Race, Gender, and Cultural Politics* (London: Turnaround, 1991), p. 47. These ideas regarding the multiple functions of home from a feminist perspective are also discussed in the introductory chapter.
55. Brydon, "Canadian Writers Negotiating Home", p. 4.

Chapter 5   Stasis and Domesticity in Nada Awar Jarrar's *Somewhere, Home*

1. Chris Brice, "Home is Where the Culture is", *The Advertiser* (Adelaide), 26 June 2004, p. 9; May Farah, "Lebanese Writer Returns to Her *Somewhere, Home*", *The Daily Star* (Beirut), 12 April 2003, p. 6.

2. Rayyan al-Shawaf, "*Somewhere, Home*: An Evocative Look at Our Need to Belong", *The Daily Star* (Beirut), 6 January 2004, p. 8.

3. Nada Awar Jarrar quoted in Brice, "Home is Where the Culture is", p. 9.

4. For further details on author's perception of her life both pre- and post-war see Brice, "Home is Where the Culture is", p. 9 and Farah, "Lebanese Writer Returns", p. 6.

5. Nada Awar Jarrar quoted in Toby Eady Associates, "Top Titles: *Somewhere, Home*", 7 July 2003. Available at www.tobyeadyassociates.co.uk/top_titles/s omewhere_home.htm (accessed 25 June 2013). Link no longer working.

6. Jarrar quoted in Brice, "Home is Where the Culture is", p. 9.

7. Jarrar quoted in Farah, "Lebanese Writer Returns", p. 6.

8. Jarrar quoted in Brice, "Home is Where the Culture is", p. 9.

9. Ibid., p. 9.

10. Syrine Hout, *Post-War Anglophone Lebanese Fiction: Home Matters in the Diaspora* (Edinburgh: Edinburgh University Press, 2012), p. 71.

11. Ibid., p. 63.

12. al-Shawaf, "*Somewhere, Home*", p. 8.

13. Joseph Rykwert, "House and Home", *Social Research* 58.1 (1991), p. 52.

14. Nada Awar Jarrar, *Somewhere, Home* (2003; London: Vintage; 2004), p. 3.

15. Ibid., p. 3.

16. Ibid., p. 12.

17. Ibid., p. 47.

18. Hout, *Post-War Anglophone Lebanese Fiction*, p. 66.

19. Jarrar, *Somewhere, Home*, p. 10.

20. Ibid., p. 40.

21. Rosemary George, *The Politics of Home: Postcolonial Reformations and Twentieth-Century Fiction* (Cambridge: Cambridge University Press, 1996), p. 11.

22. Dawn Mirapuri, "Meditations on Memory and Belonging: Nada Awar Jarrar's *Somewhere, Home*", in L. Al Maleh (ed), *Arab Voices in Diaspora: Critical Perspectives on Anglophone Arab Literature* (Amsterdam: Rodopi, 2009), p. 475.

23. Jarrar, *Somewhere, Home*, p. 83.

24. Ibid., p. 83.

25. Ibid., pp. 83–4.

26. Peter Somerville, "Homelessness and the Meaning of Home: Rooflessness or Rootlessness?", *International Journal of Urban and Regional Research* 16.4 (1992), p. 532.

27. Hout, *Post-War Anglophone Lebanese Fiction*, pp. 66–7.

28. Jarrar, *Somewhere, Home*, p. 90.

29. Ibid., p. 91.

30. Ibid., p. 91.

31. Ibid., p. 180.

32. Ibid., p. 189.

33. Hout, *Post-War Anglophone Lebanese Fiction*, p. 70.

34. Ibid., p. 203.

35. Ibid., p. 203.

36. Gillian Dooley, "Review: *Somewhere, Home*", *Writer's Radio, Radio Adelaide*, 12 July 2004. Available at http://dspace.flinders.edu.au/jspui/bitstream/2328/474/1/SomewhereHome.pdf (accessed 20 August 2012).

37. al-Shawaf, "*Somewhere, Home*", p. 8.

38. This movement from city to mountain during heightened periods of violence was not open to all Lebanese but biased in favour of the middle classes. Unlike the poor and working class residents, these wealthier inhabitants were mobile because they had access to furnished family homes in their ancestral villages and could leave behind their occupations until the violence relented. In the memoir *A World I Loved*, Wadad Makdisi Cortas, the principal of a school for girls in West Beirut, writes about her family's need to finally escape the city. Also, in *Beirut Fragments* Jean Said Makdisi documents the degree of urban destruction and the periodic move to the mountain home in Broumana to safeguard the family. See Wadad Makdisi Cortas, *A World I Loved: The Story of an Arab Woman* (New York, NY: Nation Books, 2009) and Jean Said Makdisi, *Beirut Fragments: A War Memoir* (New York, NY: Persea Books, 1990).

39. Jarrar, *Somewhere, Home*, pp. 4, 7.

40. The most information that the text imparts with regard to the impact of the war on the daily lives of Beirut's residents takes place when Maysa asks Wadih "Are things alright in the city these days?" and he replies "The fighting flares up and calms down again. We manage to live during the gaps in between." Jarrar, *Somewhere, Home*, pp. 47–8.

41. Ibid., p. 87.

42. Raymond Williams, *The Country and The City* (London: Chatto and Windus, 1973), p. 297.

43. Shmuel Moreh, *Studies in Modern Arabic Prose and Poetry* (Leiden: E. J. Brill, 1987), p. 136.

44. Ibid., p. 136.

45. Ibid., p. 141.

46. Ibid., p. 141.

47. Samir Khalaf, *Heart of Beirut: Reclaiming the Bourj* (London: Saqi, 2006), p. 22.

48. Christopher Stone, *Popular Culture and Nationalism in Lebanon: The Fairouz and Rahbani Nation* (London: Routledge, 2008), p. 26.

49. Ibid., p. 26.

50. Ibid., p. 27.

51. Robert George and Michael Owen Jones, *Folkloristics: An Introduction* (Bloomington, IN: Indiana University Press, 1995), p. 4.

52. Ibid., p. 1.

53. Samir Khalaf, *Civil and Uncivil Violence in Lebanon: A History of the Internationalization of Communal Conflict* (New York, NY: Columbia University Press, 2002), p. 206.

54. Anis Frayha quoted in Stone, *Popular Culture*, p. 27.

55. Ibid., p. 27.

56. Khalaf, *Civil and Uncivil Violence*, p. 206.

57. Stone, *Popular Culture*, p. 64.

58. Muhammad Abi Samra, "Assi Rahbani in Fairouz's voice", *An-Nahar* (Beirut), 22 May 1999, p. 7.

59. *Hala and the King* quoted in Stone, *Popular Culture*, p. 78.

60. Ibid., p. 79.

61. Richard Terdiman, *Present Past: Modernity and the Memory Crisis* (Ithaca, NY: Cornell University Press, 1993), p. 5.

62. In 1967, the year *Hala and the King* was first staged, the Arab countries suffered a collective defeat in the Six-Day War. In Arabic this defeat is referred to as *al-naksa* ("the setback"). One of its consequences in the arts is that the vision of the mountain became less prominent in the Rahbani plays. This, however, does not diminish the perfected image of the village that had been the hallmark of pre-1967 theatre. The pervasiveness of the mountain village can be attributed to the fact that the Rahbani Brothers never undertook to revise the exclusive image of the mountain they helped foster. When it was subject to scrutiny, principally by Assi and Fairouz's son Ziad, a critic of his parents' oeuvre and of leftist persuasions, his musical theatre proved unable to challenge the bucolic images the previous Rahbani generation established. Stone attributes this to Ziad's "novelisation" of "Rahbani Lebanon" and the inability of audiences to process his parody of village life, heritage and mountain essentialism. See Stone, *Popular Culture*, pp. 110–38 for further details.

63. Jarrar, *Somewhere, Home*, p. 31.

64. Ibid., p. 70.

65. Ibid., p. 5.

66. Ibid., p. 5.

67. Ibid., p. 5.

68. Ibid., p. 48

69. Ibid., p. 49.

70. Ibid., p. 28.

71. Ibid., p. 28.

72. In Part III of the novel which features Salwa's story, the house is not pronounced enough to warrant attention. Salwa views the house in a photograph and assumes it is her childhood home. For Gillian Dooley, the house's remoteness in the novel's final instalment is a flaw in the narrative as it

weakens the unifying link between the three stories. See Dooley, "Review: *Somewhere, Home*".

73. Jarrar, *Somewhere, Home*, p. 127.
74. Ibid., p. 127.
75. Ibid., pp. 140, 141.
76. Ibid., p. 142.
77. Ibid., p. 142.
78. Jacques Derrida, *Archive Fever: A Freudian Impression*, E. Prenowitz (tr), (Chicago, IL: Chicago University Press, 1996), p. 7.
79. al-Shawaf, "*Somewhere, Home*", p. 8.
80. Ibid., p. 8.
81. Derrida, *Archive Fever*, pp. 1, 2.
82. Jarrar, *Somewhere, Home*, p. 8.
83. Derrida, *Archive Fever*, p. 1.
84. Jarrar, *Somewhere, Home*, pp. 13–14.
85. Ibid., p. 29.
86. Dooley, "Review: *Somewhere, Home*".
87. Doris Lessing quoted in Christopher Bigsby, "The Need to Tell Stories", in E. Ingersoll (ed), *Doris Lessing: Conversations* (Princeton, NJ: Ontario Review Press, 1994), p. 71.
88. Nomology expresses certain principles such as "laws of nature" that are neither logically necessary nor theoretically explicable but are simply assumed to be true.
89. Antoinette Burton, *Dwelling in the Archive: Women Writing House, Home, and History in Late Colonial India* (Oxford: Oxford University Press, 2003), p. 143.
90. Ibid., pp. 143–4.
91. Derrida, *Archive Fever*, p. 3.
92. Ibid., p. 3.
93. Jarrar, *Somewhere, Home*, p. 3.
94. Ibid., p. 3.
95. Derrida, *Archive Fever*, p. 2.
96. Ibid., p. 2.
97. Jarrar, *Somewhere, Home*, p. 13.
98. Ibid., p. 30.
99. Ibid., p. 30.
100. Ibid., pp. 25–6.
101. Ibid., p. 63.
102. Derrida, *Archive Fever*, p. 2.
103. Ibid., p. 2.
104. Jarrar, *Somewhere, Home*, p. 44.
105. Ibid., p. 45.
106. Derrida, *Archive Fever*, p. 11.
107. Ibid., p. 11.
108. Mirapuri, "Meditations on Memory and Belonging", p. 471.
109. Jarrar, *Somewhere, Home*, pp. 27, 57–8.

110. See Fawaz Traboulsi, *A History of Modern Lebanon* (London: Pluto Press, 2007), namely "Part I: Ottoman Lebanon" for a history of the pivotal role the Druze played in the early founding of Lebanon. Pages 5–15 provide details of the political careers of Fakhr al-Din II and Bashir Shihab, especially the vexed relationship the former had with the Sultanate.

111. In Lebanon the Prime Minister must be Sunni Muslim and Speaker of the House Shi'a Muslim.

112. Mithu Banerji, "Back to Where They Belong – A Lyrical Debut Novel Tells of Three Civil War Exiles' Return", *The Observer* (London), 23 June 2003, p. 17.

113. Nada Awar Jarrar, "Family at War", *The Times*, 27 July 2006. Available at www.timesonline.co.uk/article/0,,7-2286676_2,00.html (accessed 2 August 2006).

114. Jarrar, *Somewhere, Home*, p. 73.

115. Ibid., p. 67.

116. There is one reference made regarding the presence of other religious communities in the mountain in Part I. This takes place when Alia, requiring assistance from a priest, makes "her way to the small church that stood at the heart of the Christian area of the village". See Jarrar, *Somewhere, Home*, pp. 24–6. Apart from this no details about this "Christian area" are developed. While Jarrar inserts a Christian enclave within the mountain, she does so minimally and therefore maintains the village's religious and cultural exclusivity.

117. Stone, *Popular Culture*, p. 80.

118. Rabih Alameddine quoted in Kieron Devlin, "A Conversation with Rabih Alameddine", *Blip Magazine*, 16 October 2002, par. 31. Available at http://newworldwriting.net/backissues/2002/leilani-devlin-alameddine.html (accessed 26 August 2010).

119. Edward Said, "Reflections on Exile", in E. Said, *Reflections on Exile and Other Essays* (Cambridge, MA: Harvard University Press, 2002), p. 173.

120. Ibid., pp. 175–6.

121. Ibid., p. 174.

122. Jarrar, *Somewhere, Home*, p. 93.

123. Ibid., p. 94.

124. Ibid., p. 94.

125. Ibid., pp. 96–7.

126. Ibid., p. 94.

127. Ibid., pp. 86–7.

128. Ibid., p. 121.

129. Ibid., p. 92.

130. Ibid., p. 92.

131. Ibid., p. 85.

132. Ibid., p. 145.

133. Mahmoud Darwish, "The Earth is Closing on Us", in Adonis, M. Darwish and S. al-Qasim, *Victims of a Map: A Bilingual Anthology of Arabic Poetry*, A. al-Udhari (tr), (London: Saqi, 1984), lines 12–13.

134. Edward Said, *After the Last Sky* (New York, NY: Pantheon Books, 1986), p. 11.

135. Laleh Khalili, "Places of Memory and Mourning: Palestinian Commemoration in the Refugee Camps of Lebanon", *Comparative Studies of South Asia, Africa and the Middle East* 25.1 (2005), p. 44.

136. Ibid., p. 42.

137. Ibid., p. 44.

138. Ibid., p. 42.

139. Ibid., p. 44.

140. Mirapuri, "Meditations on Memory and Belonging", p. 464; emphasis added.

Chapter 6   Home and Movement in Alia Yunis' *The Night Counter*

1. Kathryn Kysar, "1,001 Nights with Modern Family Twist", *StarTribune*, 8 August 2009. Available at www.startribune.com/entertainment/books/52617702.html (accessed 11 October 2009).

2. Carolyn See, "Book World: Carolyn See Reviews *The Night Counter* by Alia Yunis", *The Washington Post*, 14 August 2009. Available at www.washingtonpost.com/wpdyn/content/article/2009/08/13/AR2009081303267.html (accessed 10 October 2009).

3. Kysar, "1,001 Nights with Modern Family Twist".

4. Alia Yunis, *The Night Counter* (New York, NY: Shaye Areheart Book, 2009), p. 79.

5. Rola Zaarour, "Chasing the American Dream, Arabian Style", *Egypt Independent*, 10 January 2010. Available at www.almasryalyoum.com/en/node/10160 (accessed 12 October 2010).

6. Emily Holman, "Humorous, Humane and Readable. But Charming?", *The Daily Star* (Beirut), 2 December 2009. Available at www.dailystar.com.lb/Culture/Arts/Dec/02/Humorous-humane-and-readable-But-charming.ashx#axzz1iZNuuPox (accessed 11 October 2010).

7. Kysar, "1,001 Nights with Modern Family Twist".

8. Holman, "Humorous, Humane and Readable".

9. Alia Yunis quoted on *Kitab Book Show*, "Alia Yunis – Part 1", 1 December 2009, 3:06–3:45 mins. Available at www.youtube.com/watch?v=fiIEKvStxxk&feature=related (accessed 12 May 2011). This interview was broadcast on the Lebanese television station Murr TV in 2009. The interview was conducted in Arabic and the translations are my own.

10. Alia Yunis quoted at Frankfurt City Library, "Alia Yunis Presents *The Night Counter*", *US Consulate Frankfurt Channel*, 24 November 2010, 0:29–0:51 mins. Available at www.youtube.com/watch?v=7o7s6QssY10 (accessed 12 May 2011).

11. Yunis, *The Night Counter*, p. 5.

12. Ibid., p. 5.

13. Ibid., p. 12.

14. Ibid., p. 12.

15. Nada Awar Jarrar, *Somewhere, Home* (2003; London: Vintage; 2004), pp. 3, 12; 48–9.

16. Yunis, *The Night Counter*, pp. 294, 353.

17. Ibid., p. 358.

18. Ibid., pp. 353–4.

19. Ibid., p. 354.

20. Angelika Bammer, "Editorial", *New Formations* 17 (1992), p. viii; Roger Rouse, "Mexican Migration and the Social Space of Postmodernism", *Diaspora: A Journal of Transnational Studies* 1.1 (1991), pp. 13–14.

21. Chiara Briganti and Kathy Mezei, *Domestic Modernism, the Interwar Novel, and E.H. Young* (Hampshire: Ashgate, 2006), p. 18.

22. Ibid., p. 23. Philippa Tristram makes a similar argument when she states that the eighteenth century not only "saw the rise of the novel, [but] was also the great age of the English house". See Philippa Tristram, *Living Space in Fact and Fiction* (London: Routledge, 1989), p. 2.

23. Yunis quoted on *Kitab*, 6:33–7:00 mins.

24. Yunis, *The Night Counter*, p. 45.

25. Ibid., pp. 105–6.

26. Ibid., p. 308.

27. Ibid., p. 308.

28. Kathy Mezei and Chiara Briganti, "Reading the House: A Literary Perspective", *Signs* 27.3 (2002), p. 837.

29. Tristram, *Living Space in Fact and Fiction*, p. 2; Mezei and Briganti, "Reading the House", p. 838.

30. Mezei and Briganti, "Reading the House", p. 837.

31. Homi Bhabha, "The World and the Home", *Social Text* 31–32 (1992), p. 142.

32. Ibid., p. 142.

33. The three texts that Bhabha refers to in his article are *A House for Mr. Biswas* (1961) by V.S. Naipaul, *Beloved* (1987) by Toni Morrison and *My Son's Story* (1990) by Nadine Gordimer.

34. Bhabha, "The World and the Home", p. 142.

35. John Berger, *And Our Faces, My Heart, Brief as Photos* (1984; New York, NY: Vintage International, 1991), pp. 63–4.

36. Ibid., p. 64.

37. Ibid., p. 64.

38. Iain Chambers, *Migrancy, Culture, Identity* (London: Routledge, 1994), p. 16; Iain Chambers, "Leaky Habits and Broken Grammar", in G. Robertson, M. Mash, L. Tickner, J. Bird, B. Curtis and T. Putnam (eds), *Travellers Tales: Narratives of Home and Displacement* (London: Routledge, 1994), p. 246.

39. Chambers, *Migrancy*, pp. 16–17.

40. Chambers, "Leaky Habits", p. 246.

41. Ibid., p. 246.
42. Yunis, *The Night Counter*, p. 19.
43. Ibid., pp. 19–20.
44. Ibid., p. 128.
45. Ibid., p. 182.
46. Ibid., p. 271.
47. Ibid., p. 242.
48. Ibid., pp. 242–3.
49. Ibid., pp. 243, 259.
50. Ibid., p. 253.
51. Yunis quoted at Frankfurt City Library, 0:55–1:14 mins.
52. Yunis, *The Night Counter*, p. 29.
53. Ibid., pp. 29–30.
54. Ibid., p. 161.
55. Ibid., p. 193.
56. The links between the plight of the Palestinians and colonialism are not overstated in the novel but events like the Balfour Declaration in 1917, the British mandate of Palestine post-World War I, the United Nations vote in favour of partition in 1947, the dispossession of Palestinians in 1948 and 1967 and the construction of Jewish-only settlements in the occupied territories all point to a long history of colonial practices that the Palestinians have had to endure.
57. Yunis, *The Night Counter*, p. 182.
58. Ibid., p. 182.
59. Fedwa Malti-Douglas, "Shahrazād feminist", in R. G. Hovannisian and G. Sabagh (eds), *The Thousand and One Nights in Arabic Literature and Society* (Cambridge: Cambridge University Press, 1997), p. 51.
60. Ibid., p. 50.
61. Eva Sallis, *Sheherazade Through the Looking Glass: The Metamorphosis of the Thousand and One Nights* (England: Curzon, 1999), p. 87; Suzanne Gauch, *Liberating Shahrazad: Feminism, Postcolonialism, and Islam* (Minneapolis, MN: University of Minnesota Press, 2007), p. ix.
62. Gauch, *Liberating Shahrazad*, pp. ix–x.
63. Saree Makdisi and Felicity Nussbaum, "Introduction", in S. Makdisi and F. Nussbaum (eds), *The Arabian Nights in Historical Context: Between East and West* (Oxford: Oxford University Press, 2008), p. 1.
64. Ibid., p. 2.
65. I say "compilation" because it is suggested that Galland assimilated stories into his translation that were not part of the Syrian manuscript. The tale of the sailor Sindibad is one that was added by Galland, according to Mia Gerhardt. Apparently a Maronite Christian from Aleppo passed on various stories to Galland, which include *Alâ Ed-Dîn and The Marvellous Lamp* and *Ali Baba*. These two tales "are universally known" and "to the general public represent the perfect example of a '1001 Nights'-story" despite not existing in the

244 NOTES TO PAGES 156–159

supposed master text. See Mia Gerhardt, *The Art of Story-Telling: A Literary Study of The Thousand and One Nights* (Leiden: E. J. Brill, 1963), pp. 12–14.

66. Makdisi and Nussbaum, "Introduction", p. 1.

67. Gerhardt provides a comprehensive list of translations in various European languages (Danish, Dutch, German, Italian) and the variety of "original" manuscripts they were based on. See Gerhardt, *The Art of Story-Telling*, pp. 67–9.

68. Robert Irwin, *The Arabian Nights: A Companion* (London: Allen Lane, 1994), pp. 2–3; Ibrahim Muhawi, "The Arabian Nights and the Question of Authorship", *Journal of Arabic Literature* 36.3 (2005), p. 323.

69. Ros Ballaster, "Playing the Second String: The Role of Dinarzade in Eighteenth-Century English Fiction", in S. Makdisi and F. Nussbaum (eds), *The Arabian Nights in Historical Context: Between East and West* (Oxford: Oxford University Press, 2008), p. 97.

70. Irwin, *The Arabian Nights*.

71. Maher Jarrar, "*The Arabian Nights* and the Contemporary Arabic Novel", in S. Makdisi and F. Nussbaum (eds), *The Arabian Nights in Historical Context: Between East and West* (Oxford: Oxford University Press, 2008), p. 297.

72. Makdisi and Nussbaum, "Introduction", p. 23.

73. James Clifford, "Diasporas", in J. Clifford, *Routes: Travels and Translation in the Late Twentieth Century* (Cambridge, MA: Harvard University Press, 1997), p. 269; Stuart Hall, "Cultural Identity and Diaspora", in P. Williams and L. Chrisman (eds), *Colonial Discourse and Post-Colonial Theory: A Reader* (New York, NY: Columbia University Press, 1994), p. 400; Stuart Hall, "New Cultures for Old", in D. Massey and P. Jess (eds), *A Place in the World? Places, Cultures and Globalization* (Oxford: Oxford University Press, 1995), p. 206; Salman Rushdie, *Shame* (London: Cape, 1983), p. 86.

74. In the introductory chapter I outline in some detail the dangers of privileging movement or "routes" at the expense of "roots". I do not mean to suggest here that Clifford, Hall or Rushdie dismiss roots completely. What they do seem to express, however, is a partiality towards mobility and argue that strict narratives of roots deny this.

75. Clifford, "Diasporas", p. 247; Rouse, "Mexican Migration", p. 13.

76. In various scenes email is used by Amir to convey to the Abdullahs issues related to Fatima. This form of communication is confined to Amir and, unlike the telephone, is not subject to the same level of scrutiny by the FBI in the novel.

77. Ian Hutchby, *Conversations and Technology: From the Telephone to the Internet* (Cambridge: Polity Press, 2001), p. 85.

78. Ibid., p. 85.

79. Colin Cherry, "The Telephone System: Creator of Mobility and Social Change", in I. de Sola Pool (ed), *The Social Impact of the Telephone* (Cambridge, MA: MIT Press, 1977), p. 115.

80. Ibid., p. 114.

81. Yunis, *The Night Counter*, p. 279.

82. Ibid., p. 311.
83. Ibid., p. 319.
84. Ibid., p. 190. A *kefia* is the traditional headscarf worn by Arab and Kurdish men.
85. Ibid., p. 191.
86. Ibid., p. 99.
87. Ibid., p. 17.
88. Ibid., p. 199.
89. Ibid., p. 302.
90. Ibid., p. 194.
91. Ibid., p. 361.
92. Ibid., p. 359.
93. Ibid., p. 360.
94. The USA PATRIOT Act is an acronym that stands for Uniting and Strengthening America by Providing Appropriate Tools Required to Intercept and Obstruct Terrorism Act of 2001. It is most commonly known as the Patriot Act.
95. For information on the Patriot Act and its limitations on civil liberties see Amitai Etzioni, *How Patriotic is the Patriot Act? Freedom Versus Security in the Age of Terrorism* (New York, NY: Routledge, 2005) and Jean-Claude Paye, *Global War on Liberty*, J. Membrez (tr), (New York, NY: Telos Press Publishing, 2007).
96. Yunis, *The Night Counter*, p. 346.
97. Ibid., p. 147.
98. Ibid., p. 149.
99. Ibid., pp. 148, 151.
100. Ibid., p. 347.
101. William Walters, "Secure Borders, Safe Havens: Domopolitics", *Citizenship Studies* 3.3 (2004), p. 247.
102. Ibid., p. 247.
103. Ibid., p. 248.
104. Yunis, *The Night Counter*, p. 85.
105. Ibid., p. 85.
106. Walters, "Secure Borders", p. 241.
107. Ibid., p. 248.
108. Ibid., p. 248.
109. Ghassan Hage, "With the Fig, the Olive and the Pomegranate Trees: Thoughts on Australian Belonging", in P. Tabar and J. Skulte-Ouaiss (eds), *Politics, Culture and the Lebanese Diaspora* (Newcastle: Cambridge Scholars Press, 2011), p. 157.
110. Ibid., p. 157.
111. Yunis, *The Night Counter*, p. 78.
112. G. Hage, "With the Fig", p. 156.
113. Ibid., p. 156.
114. Ibid., p. 156.

115. Ibid., p. 157.
116. Ibid., p. 157; emphasis added.
117. Yunis, *The Night Counter*, p. 331.
118. Ibid., p. 360.
119. Ibid., p. 363.
120. G. Hage, "With the Fig", p. 158.

Chapter 7   Nation, State and Diaspora

1. See Elise Salem, *Constructing Lebanon: A Century of Literary Narratives* (Gainesville, FL: University Press of Florida, 2003) for examples of authors who complicate nationalism, especially Chapters 3 and 6.
2. Diana Brydon, "Canadian Writers Negotiating Home Within Global Imaginaries". Keynote address for *Moving Cultures, Shifting Identities* conference at Flinders University, Australia (2007), p. 6. Available at http://myuminfo.um anitoba.ca/Documents/1169/Negotiating%20Home.pdf (accessed 23 March 2013); Lily Cho, "The Turn to Diaspora", *Topia* 17 (2007), p. 12.
3. Robin Cohen, *Global Diasporas: An Introduction* (Seattle, WA: University of Washington Press, 1997), pp. 94–100, 42–53.
4. Khachig Tölölyan, "The Nation-State and its Others: In Lieu of a Preface", *Diaspora: A Journal of Transnational Studies* 1.1 (1991), p. 3.
5. Cohen, *Global Diasporas*, pp. 3, 2.
6. Doreen Massey, *Space, Place and Gender* (Cambridge: Polity, 1994). Also see the introduction to this text for further information on the historically-based reasons behind the centrality of the nation-state to dispersal and with regard to the regressive forms of nationalism that Massey describes.
7. Erich Gruen, *Diaspora: Jews Amidst Greeks and Romans* (Cambridge, MA: Harvard University Press, 2002), p. 232.
8. Ibid., p. 232.
9. Ibid., p. 232.
10. Eliezer Schweid, "The Rejection of the Diaspora in Zionist Thought: Two Approaches", *Studies in Zionism* 5.1 (1984), p. 43.
11. See Schweid, "The Rejection of the Diaspora in Zionist Thought", especially pages 46–50 and 57–68 for further details about these early Zionists and their writings.
12. Schweid, "The Rejection of the Diaspora in Zionist Thought", p. 43.
13. Jacqueline Rose, *Proust Among the Nations: From Dreyfus to the Middle East* (Chicago, IL: University of Chicago Press, 2011), p. 10; emphasis added.
14. Theodor Herzl, *The Jewish State* (Minneapolis, MN: Filiquarian Publishing, 2006), p. 24. Orig. pub. 1896.
15. Schweid, "The Rejection of the Diaspora in Zionist Thought", p. 53; emphasis added.

16. See the introduction for details on the centrality of the Jewish model in diaspora theory.

17. William Safran, "Diasporas in Modern Societies: Myths of Homeland and Return", *Diaspora: A Journal of Transnational Studies* 1.1 (1991), p. 83.

18. Ibid., pp. 83–4.

19. Jon Stratton, "(Dis)placing the Jews: Historicizing the Idea of Diaspora", *Diaspora: A Journal of Transnational Studies* 6.3 (1997), p. 307.

20. Ibid., p. 307.

21. Shlomo Sand, *The Invention of the Jewish People*, Y. Lotan (tr), (London; New York, NY: Verso, 2009), p. 31.

22. A few texts from these disciplines include the anthropologist Ernest Gellner's *Nations and Nationalism* (Oxford: Blackwell, 1983), the historian Eric Hobsbawm's *Nations and Nationalism Since 1780* (Cambridge: Cambridge University Press, 1990), the literary critic Homi Bhabha's edited collection *Nation and Narration* (New York, NY: Routledge, 1990) and the professor of politics and international studies Benedict Anderson's *Imagined Communities: Reflections on the Origins and Spread of Nationalism* (London; New York, NY: Verso, 1991).

23. David Brown, *The State and Ethnic Politics in South-East Asia* (London: Routledge, 1994), p. 181.

24. Désirée Kleiner-Liebau, *Migration and the Construction of National Identity in Spain* (Madrid: Iberoamericana, 2009), p. 32.

25. John Hutchinson, *The Dynamic of Cultural Nationalism: The Gaelic Revival and the Creation of the Irish Nation State* (London: Allen and Unwin, 1987), p. 13.

26. Lloyd Cox, "Nation-State and Nationalism", in G. Ritzer (ed), *Blackwell Encyclopedia of Sociology* (Malden, MA: Blackwell Publishing, 2007), p. 3144; Kleiner-Liebau, *Migration*, p. 32.

27. Cox, "Nation-State and Nationalism", p. 3143.

28. John Hutchinson, *Modern Nationalism* (London: Fontana Press, 1994), p. 1.

29. Edward Said, "Reflections on Exile", in E. Said, *Reflections on Exile and Other Essays* (Cambridge, MA: Harvard University Press, 2002), p. 176.

30. Anthony D. Smith, *The Ethnic Origins of Nations* (Oxford: Blackwell, 1986), p. 12.

31. Michael Shapiro, *Methods and Nations: Cultural Governance and the Indigenous Subject* (New York, NY: Routledge, 2004), p. 45.

32. Ibid., p. 45.

33. Eric Hobsbawm, "Introduction: Inventing Traditions", in E. Hobsbawm and T. Ranger (eds), *The Invention of Tradition* (Cambridge: Cambridge University Press, 1983), p. 14; emphasis added.

34. Assaf Sagiv, "Zionism and the Myth of the Motherland", *Azure* 5 (1998), par. 27.

35. David Ben-Gurion quoted in Sagiv, "Zionism", par. 33.

36. Ibid., par. 33.

37. Eliezer Schweid, *The Land of Israel: National Home or Land of Destiny?*, D. Greniman (tr), (Cranbury, NJ: Associated University Presses, 1985), p. 193.

38. Daniel Boyarin and Jonathan Boyarin, "Diaspora: Generation and the Ground of Jewish Identity", *Critical Inquiry* 19.4 (1993), p. 718.

39. Stratton, "(Dis)placing the Jews", p. 314.

40. Benny Morris, *One State, Two States: Resolving the Israel/Palestine Conflict* (New Haven, CT: Yale University Press, 2009); Ilan Pappé, *The Ethnic Cleansing of Palestine* (Oxford: One World, 2006).

41. Jeff Halper, *An Israeli in Palestine: Resisting Dispossession, Redeeming Israel* (London; Ann Arbor, MI: Pluto Press, 2008); Uri Davis, *Apartheid Israel: Possibilities for the Struggle Within* (London: Zed Books, 2003).

42. *Terra nullius* is a Latin expression that translates as "land belonging to no one" or "no man's land". The British settlers to Australia enforced this concept, allowing them to settle on the land without consulting with indigenous populations. Unlike in parts of North America, Africa and New Zealand, in Australia the British colonial powers did not sign treaties with the indigenous communities. In 1992 the High Court of Australia, during the Aboriginal rights Mabo case, issued a judgment that repealed *terra nullius*.

43. Apart from denying the existence of the Palestinians and segregating them from Israeli society, Israel has also sought to define its internal national body. It has done so by being selective about what kind of Jewish national it is willing to accept. William Safran points out that "Israel (despite its Law of Return) is somewhat ambivalent about a massive influx of Soviet or American Jews – the former, because of the problem of integrating them professionally, and the latter, because they are too 'Anglo-Saxon'". See Safran, "Diasporas in Modern Societies", p. 94.

44. Homi Bhabha, "Introduction: Narrating the Nation", in H. Bhabha (ed), *Nation and Narration* (New York, NY: Routledge, 1990), p. 4.

45. Ibid., p. 5.

46. Issa Boullata, "Review: *Constructing Lebanon: A Century of Literary Narratives* by Elise Salem", *Digest of Middle East Studies* 12.2 (2003), p. 79.

47. Salem, *Constructing Lebanon*, p. 10.

48. Ibid., p. 152.

49. Ibid., p. 200. Maalouf's *The Rock of Tanios* was originally published in French as *Le Rocher de Tanios* (Paris: Bernard Grasset, 1993) and translated in 1994 as *The Rock of Tanios* by Dorothy Blair. In same year of its French publication Maalouf became the recipient of the prestigious French literary prize, the Prix Goncourt.

50. Boyarin and Boyarin, "Diaspora", p. 723.

Chapter 8   One Land or Two? Israel and Palestine in Amin Maalouf's *Ports of Call*

1. Jamal En-nehas, "Review: Amin Maalouf, *Les Échelles du Levant*", *World Literature Today* 71.2 (1997), p. 341.

2. Ibid., p. 341.

3. Lucy Dallas, "The Hero from Beirut", *Times Literary Supplement* 5036 (1999), p. 23.

4. Ibid., p. 23.

5. Ibid., p. 23.

6. Amin Maalouf, *Ports of Call*, A. Manguel (tr), (London: The Harvill Press, 1999), p. 72.

7. Dallas, "The Hero from Beirut", p. 23.

8. Maalouf, *Ports of Call*, p. 137.

9. Ibid., p. 125.

10. Ibid., p. 137.

11. Gil Hochberg, *In Spite of Partition: Jews, Arabs and the Limits of Separatist Imagination* (Princeton, NJ: Princeton University Press, 2007), p. 122.

12. Ali Abunimah, *One Country: A Bold Proposal to End the Israeli–Palestinian Impasse* (New York, NY: Metropolitan Books, 2006), p. 19.

13. Ilan Pappé, *A History of Modern Palestine: One Land, Two Peoples* (Cambridge: Cambridge University Press, 2004), p. 106.

14. Abunimah, *One Country*, p. 21; Ghada Karmi, *Married to Another Man: Israel's Dilemma in Palestine* (London: Pluto Press, 2007), p. 221; Pappé, *A History of Modern Palestine*, p. 143.

15. Karmi, *Married to Another Man*, p. 220.

16. Ibid., pp. 220–1.

17. For detailed information on various peace proposals see Abunimah, *One Country*, pp. 19–54, Karmi, *Married to Another Man,* pp. 218–22 and Pappé, *A History of Modern Palestine*, pp. 123–84.

18. Barak Obama, "Remarks by the President on the Middle East and North Africa", *The White House*, 19 May 2011. Available at www.whitehouse.gov/the-press-office/2011/05/19/remarks-president-middle-east-and-north-africa (accessed 20 November 2011).

19. Abunimah, *One Country*, p. 20.

20. Virginia Tilley, *The One-State Solution: A Breakthrough for Peace in the Israeli–Palestinian Deadlock* (Ann Arbor, MI: The University of Michigan Press, 2005), p. 1.

21. Ibid., p. 1.

22. Ibid., p. 3.

23. Ibid., p. 3.

24. Ibid., pp. 3–5.

25. The security wall is also a project of "soft transfer". It will shield Israel from the security and labour pressures it is producing within Palestinian society and hopefully entice the Arab population, suffering under these conditions, to relocate to Jordan and other Arab states. See Tilley, *The One-State Solution*, pp. 5–6.

26. Hochberg, *In Spite of Partition*, pp. 4–5.

27. Tilley, *The One-State Solution*, p. 6.

28. Hochberg, *In Spite of Partition*, p. 6.
29. Edward Said, "Arabs and Jews", *Journal of Palestine Studies* 3.2 (1974), p. 3; emphasis added.
30. Julia Kristeva, *Strangers to Ourselves* (New York, NY: Columbia University Press, 1991), p. 181.
31. Ibid., p. 1.
32. Ibid., p. 1.
33. Amin Maalouf, *On Identity*, B. Bray (tr), (London: The Harvill Press, 2000), p. 3; Amin Maalouf, *Origins: A Memoir*, C. Temerson (tr), (New York, NY: Farrar, Straus and Giroux, 2008), np.
34. Maalouf, *On Identity*, p. 3.
35. Ibid., p. 3.
36. For arguments related to the Jewish peoples autochthonous origins see Daniel Boyarin and Jonathan Boyarin, "Diaspora: Generation and the Ground of Jewish Identity", *Critical Inquiry* 19.4 (1993), pp. 693–725 and Eliezer Schweid, "The Rejection of the Diaspora in Zionist Thought: Two Approaches", *Studies in Zionism* 5.1 (1984), pp. 73–70. For arguments made in relation to Palestinian indigeneity see Ilan Pappé, *The Ethnic Cleansing of Palestine* (Oxford: One World, 2006) and Tilley, *The One-State Solution*.
37. Hochberg, *In Spite of Partition*, p. 123.
38. Ibid., p. 123.
39. Maalouf, *Ports of Call*, p. 66.
40. Ibid., p. 70.
41. Ibid., p. 97.
42. Ibid., p. 16.
43. Ibid., p. 30.
44. Vigen Guroian, "The Politics and Morality of Genocide", in R. G. Hovannisian (ed), *The Armenian Genocide: History, Politics, Ethics* (New York, NY: Palgrave Macmillan, 1992), p. 337.
45. Maalouf, *Ports of Call*, p. 26.
46. Ibid., p. 31.
47. Ibid., p. 31.
48. Ibid., p. 60.
49. Ibid., p. 60.
50. Jose Saldívar, *Border Matters: Remapping American Cultural Studies* (Berkeley, CA: University of California Press, 1997), p. ix.
51. Maalouf, *Ports of Call*, p. 123.
52. Ibid., p. 116.
53. Ibid., pp. 123, 137.
54. Ibid., p. 123.
55. Hochberg, *In Spite of Partition*, p. 121.
56. Ibid., pp. 122–3.
57. Maalouf, *Ports of Call*, pp. 140, 141.
58. Ibid., p. 137.

59. Ibid., p. 136.
60. Ibid., p. 136.
61. Ibid., p. 47.
62. Ibid., pp. 54–5.
63. Ibid., p. 56.
64. Ibid., pp. 56–7.
65. Ibid., p. 57.
66. Ibid., p. 60.
67. Ibid., p. 60.
68. Ibid., p. 60.
69. Edward Said, "Reflections on Exile", in E. Said, *Reflections on Exile and Other Essays* (Cambridge, MA: Harvard University Press, 2002), p. 177.
70. Maalouf, *Ports of Call*, p. 89.
71. Ibid., p. 117.
72. Ibid., p. 117.
73. Ibid., p. 118.
74. Ibid., p. 119.
75. Ibid., p. 118.
76. David Green, "Levantism Finds its Place in Modern Israel", *Ha'aretz*, 25 August 2011. Available at www.haaretz.com/culture/books/levantism-finds-its-place-in-modern-israel-1.380634 (accessed 25 November 2011).
77. Hochberg, *In Spite of Partition*, p. 120.
78. Maalouf, *Ports of Call*, p. 106.
79. Ibid., p. 106.
80. Ibid., p. 106.
81. Ibid., p. 108.
82. Ibid., p. 120.
83. Ibid., p. 130.
84. Ibid., p. 130.
85. Ibid., p. 130.
86. Said, "Arabs and Jews", p. 3.
87. Ilan Pappé, "The Exilic Homeland of Edward W. Said", *Interventions* 8.1 (2006), p. 18.
88. For further information on the Capitulations see Maurits H. van den Boogert, *The Capitulations and the Ottoman Legal System: Qadis, Consuls, and Beraths in the 18th Century* (Leiden: Brill, 2005) and Maurits H. van den Boogert and Kate Fleet (eds), *The Ottoman Capitulations: Text and Context* (Rome: Istituto per l'Oriente C.A. Nallino, 2004).
89. Maalouf, *Ports of Call*, p. 35.
90. Hochberg, *In Spite of Partition*, p. 46.
91. Ibid., p. 46.
92. Jacqueline Shohet Kahanoff, "Childhood in Egypt", in D. Starr and S. Somekh (eds), *Mongrels or Marvels: The Levantine Writings of Jacqueline Shohet Kahanoff* (Stanford, CA: Stanford University Press, 2011), p. 1. Orig. pub. 1958.

93. Deborah Starr and Sasson Somekh, "Editors' Introduction: Jacqueline Shohet Kahanoff – A Cosmopolitan Levantine", in D. Starr and S. Somekh (eds), *Mongrels or Marvels: The Levantine Writings of Jacqueline Shohet Kahanoff* (Stanford, CA: Stanford University Press, 2011), p. xii.

94. Jacqueline Shohet Kahanoff, "Afterword: From East the Sun", in D. Starr and S. Somekh (eds), *Mongrels or Marvels: The Levantine Writings of Jacqueline Shohet Kahanoff* (Stanford, CA: Stanford University Press, 2011), p. 246. Orig. pub. 1968.

95. Hochberg, *In Spite of Partition*, p. 52.

96. Nissim Rejwan, *Israel in Search of Identity: Reading the Formative Years* (Gainesville, FL: University of Florida Press, 1999).

97. Kahanoff, "Afterword: From East the Sun", p. 246.

98. Ibid., p. 246.

99. David Shasha, "A Jewish Voice Left Silent: Trying to Articulate the Levantine Option", *The American Muslim* (2003), par. 27. Available at http://theameri canmuslim.org/tam.php/features/articles/a_jewish_voice_left_silent_tryi ng_to_articulate_the_levantine_option/ (accessed 25 November 2011).

100. Ibid., par. 9.

101. Ibid., par. 24.

102. Ibid., pars. 22, 24.

103. Ibid., par. 27.

104. Maalouf, *Ports of Call*, p. 29.

105. Ibid., p. 44.

106. Ibid., p. 190.

107. Ibid., p. 190.

108. Edward Said, *After the Last Sky* (New York, NY: Pantheon Books, 1986), p. 14.

109. Ibid., p. 14.

110. Dallas, "The Hero from Beirut", p. 23; En-nehas, "Review: Amin Maalouf", p. 342.

111. Maalouf, *Ports of Call*, p. 190.

Conclusion   Place and Diaspora Literature

1. Theodor Adorno, *Minima Moralia: Reflections from Damaged Life* (London: New Left Books, 1974), p. 87.

2. Bill Ashcroft, *Caliban's Voice: The Transformation of English in Post-Colonial Literatures* (New York, NY: Routledge, 2009), p. 75.

3. Avtar Brah, *Cartographies of Diaspora: Contesting Identities* (London; New York, NY: Routledge, 1996), p. 177.

4. Nico Israel, *Outlandish: Writing Between Exile and Diaspora* (Stanford, CA: Stanford University Press, 2000), p. 3.

5. Hamid Naficy, *An Accented Cinema: Exilic and Diasporic Film Making* (Princeton, NJ: Princeton University Press, 2001), p. 14.

6. Ibid., p. 14.

7. Israel, *Outlandish*, p. 3.

8. Sophia McClennen, "Exilic Perspectives on 'Alien Nations'", *CLCWeb Comparative Literature and Culture: A WWWeb Journal* 7.1 (2005), par.5. Available at http://dx.doi.org/10.7771/1481-4374.1257 (accessed 5 October 2011).

9. Syrine Hout, "*The Last Migration*: The First Contemporary Example of Lebanese Diasporic Literature", *Journal of Postcolonial Writing* 43.3 (2007), p. 287. This article, initially published in 2007, has since been republished, with some minor revision, in two edited collections in 2009 and 2010. Given that it has been published several times and makes a substantial claim in relation to Lebanese diaspora literature – isolating one novel as the first example of such fiction – the absence of a version of this article from Hout's 2012 monograph is curious.

10. While Hout draws examples from various novels, the discussion here will centre on Jarrar and Hanania because of their inclusion in this book as diasporic texts.

11. Hout, "*The Last Migration*", p. 288.

12. Ibid., p. 288.

13. Ibid., pp. 288, 290.

14. Ibid., pp. 289, 291.

15. Nada Awar Jarrar, *Somewhere, Home* (2003; London: Vintage; 2004), p. 189.

16. Hout, "*The Last Migration*", p. 289.

17. Lily Cho, "The Turn to Diaspora", *Topia* 17 (2007), p. 14.

18. Samir Dayal, "Diaspora and Double Consciousness", *The Journal of the Midwest Modern Language Association* 29.1 (1996), p. 46.

19. Hout, "*The Last Migration*", p. 289.

20. Ibid., p. 289.

21. Jamal Abed, "Notes on the Art of Selling Cities: Urban Design in the New Downtown of Beirut", in J. Abed (ed), *Architecture Re-Introduced: New Projects in Societies in Charge* (Geneva: The Aga Khan Award for Architecture, 2004), p. 46.

22. Doreen Massey, *Space, Place and Gender* (Cambridge: Polity, 1994), p. 152.

23. Ibid., p. 121.

24. Rawi Hage, "To Roam a Borderless World", *The Globe and Mail*, 13 June 2008. Available at www.theglobeandmail.com/commentary/to-roam-a-borderless-world/article720197/ (accessed 31 August 2013).

25. Rawi Hage quoted in Canadian High Commission – London, "Special Profile: Rawi Hage. Power of the Pen", *Canada Focus*, no date. Available at www.dfait-maeci.gc.ca/missions/unitedkingdom-royaumeuni/Ezine/Focus/focus-SpecialProfile.htm (accessed 3 September 2012). Link no longer working.

26. Robert Fisk, "The Immortality of a Great, if Flawed, Historian", *The Independent*, 13 August 2011. Available at www.independent.co.uk/opinion/commentators/fisk/robert-fisk-the-immortality-of-a-great-if-flawed-historian-2336906 (accessed 13 August 2011); Gil Hochberg, *In Spite of Partition: Jews, Arabs and the Limits of Separatist Imagination* (Princeton, NJ: Princeton University Press, 2007), pp. 122–3.

27. Amin Maalouf, *Ports of Call*, A. Manguel (tr), (London: The Harvill Press, 1999), p. 60.

BIBLIOGRAPHY

Abdelhady, Dalia, "Beyond Home/Host Networks: Forms of Solidarity Among Lebanese Immigrants in a Global Era", *Identities: Global Studies in Culture and Power* 13.3 (2006), pp. 427–53.

——— "Cultural Production in the Lebanese Diaspora: Memory, Nostalgia and Displacement", *Journal of Political and Military Sociology* 35.1 (2007), pp. 39–62.

——— "Representing the Homeland: Lebanese Diasporic Notions of Home and Return in a Global Context", *Cultural Dynamics* 20.1 (2008), pp. 53–72.

——— *The Lebanese Diaspora: The Arab Immigrant Experience in Montreal, New York, and Paris* (New York, NY: University Press, 2011).

Abed, Jamal, "Notes on the Art of Selling Cities: Urban Design in the New Downtown of Beirut", in J. Abed (ed), *Architecture Re-Introduced: New Projects in Societies in Charge* (Geneva: The Aga Khan Award for Architecture, 2004), pp. 45–54.

Abi Samra, Muhammad, "Assi Rahbani in Fairouz's Voice", *An-Nahar* (Beirut), 22 May 1999, pp. 6–9.

Abunimah, Ali, *One Country: A Bold Proposal to End the Israeli-Palestinian Impasse* (New York, NY: Metropolitan Books, 2006).

——— "Did Obama's Big Speech Offer Any Hope for Palestinians", *Electronic Intifada* (2011). Available at http://electronicintifada.net/blog/ali-abunimah/did-obamas-big-speech-offer-any-hope-palestine#.TtBnyWCBLJQ (accessed 20 November 2011).

Adorno, Theodor, *Minima Moralia: Reflections from Damaged Life* (London: New Left Books, 1974).

——— "Commitment", *New Left Review* I 87–8 (1974), pp. 75–89.

Alameddine, Rabih, *Koolaids: The Art of War* (New York, NY: Picador, 1998).

——— *I, the Divine: A Novel in First Chapters* (London: Phoenix, 2003).

——— *The Hakawati* (New York, NY: Knopf, 2008).

Anderson, Benedict, *Imagined Communities: Reflections on the Origin and Spread of Nationalism* (London; New York, NY: Verso, 1991).

────── "Western Nationalism and Eastern Nationalism: Is There a Difference That Matters?", *New Left Review* 9 (2001), pp. 31–42.

Anthias, Floya, "Evaluating 'Diaspora': Beyond Ethnicity?", *Sociology* 32.3 (1998), pp. 557–80.

Ashcroft, Bill, *Post-Colonial Transformation* (London; New York, NY: Routledge, 2001).

────── *Caliban's Voice: The Transformation of English in Post-Colonial Literatures* (New York, NY: Routledge, 2009).

Atwood, Margaret, "Approximate Homes", in C. Rooke (ed), *Writing Home* (Toronto: McClelland and Stewart, 1997), pp. 1–8.

Axel, Brian, "National Interruption: Diaspora Theory and Multiculturalism in the UK", *Cultural Dynamics* 14. 3 (2002), pp. 235–56.

Bakhtin, M. Mikhail, *The Dialogic Imagination: Four Essays*. M. Holquist (ed), C. Emerson and M. Holquist (trs), (Austin, TX: University of Texas Press, 1981).

Ballaster, Ros, "Playing the Second String: The Role of Dinarzade in Eighteenth-Century English Fiction", in S. Makdisi and F. Nussbaum (eds), *The Arabian Nights in Historical Context: Between East and West* (Oxford: Oxford University Press, 2008), pp. 83–102.

Bammer, Angelika, "Editorial", *New Formations* 17 (1992), pp. vii–xi.

Banerji, Mithu, "Back to Where They Belong – A Lyrical Debut Novel Tells of Three Civil War Exiles' Return", *The Observer* (London), 23 June 2003, p. 17.

Baum, Kelly, *Nobody's Property: Art, Land, Space, 2000–2010* (Princeton, NJ: Princeton University Art Museum, 2010).

Bhabha, Homi, "Introduction: Narrating the Nation", in H. Bhabha (ed), *Nation and Narration* (New York, NY: Routledge, 1990), pp. 1–7.

────── "The World and the Home", *Social Text* 31–32 (1992), pp. 141–53.

────── *The Location of Culture* (London; New York, NY: Routledge, 2004).

Bigsby, Christopher, "The Need to Tell Stories", in E. Ingersoll (ed), *Doris Lessing: Conversations* (Princeton, NJ: Ontario Review Press, 1994), pp. 70–85.

Blunt, Alison, *Domicile and Diaspora* (Malden, MA: Blackwell Publishers, 2005).

Blunt, Alison, and Dowling, Robyn, *Home* (London: Routledge, 2006).

van den Boogert, Maurits H., *The Capitulations and the Ottoman Legal System: Qadis, Consuls, and Beraths in the 18th Century* (Leiden: Brill, 2005).

van den Boogert, Maurits H. and Fleet, Kate (eds), *The Ottoman Capitulations: Text and Context* (Rome: Istituto per l'Oriente C.A. Nallino, 2004).

Boullata, Issa, *Modern Arabic Poets: 1950–1975* (London: Heineman, 1976).

────── "Review: *Constructing Lebanon: A Century of Literary Narratives* by Elise Salem", *Digest of Middle East Studies* 12.2 (2003), pp. 79–81.

Boyarin, Daniel, and Boyarin, Jonathan, "Diaspora: Generation and the Ground of Jewish Identity", *Critical Inquiry* 19.4 (1993), pp. 693–725.

Boym, Svetlana, *The Future of Nostalgia* (New York, NY: Basic Books, 2001).

Brah, Avtar, *Cartographies of Diaspora: Contesting Identities* (London; New York, NY: Routledge, 1996).

Braziel, Jana and Mannur, Anita, "Nation, Migration, Globalization: Points of Contention in Diaspora Studies", in J. Braziel and A. Mannur (eds), *Theorizing Diaspora: A Reader* (Malden, MA: Blackwell Publishers, 2003), pp. 1–22.

Brewer, John, *Ethnography* (Buckingham: Open University Press, 2000).

Brice, Chris, "Home is Where the Culture is", *The Advertiser* (Adelaide), 26 June 2004, p. 9.

Briganti, Chiara, and Mezei, Kathy, *Domestic Modernism, the Interwar Novel, and E.H. Young* (Hampshire: Ashgate, 2006).

Brown, David, *The State and Ethnic Politics in South-East Asia* (London: Routledge, 1994).

Brydon, Diana, "Canadian Writers Negotiating Home Within Global Imaginaries". Keynote address for *Moving Cultures, Shifting Identities* conference at Flinders University, Australia (2007). Available at http://myuminfo.umanitoba.ca/Documents/1169/Negotiating%20Home.pdf (accessed 23 March 2013).

Burton, Antoinette, *Dwelling in the Archive: Women Writing House, Home, and History in Late Colonial India* (Oxford: Oxford University Press, 2003).

Campi, Daniel, "Book Review: *De Niro's Game*", *Barcelona Metropolitan Magazine 1.0*, 2006. Available at www.barcelona-metropolitan.com (accessed 9 June 2009). Link no longer working.

Canadian High Commission – London, "Special Profile: Rawi Hage. Power of the Pen", *Canada Focus*, no date. Available at www.dfait-maeci.gc.ca/missions/unitedkingdom-royaumeuni/Ezine/Focus/focus-SpecialProfile.htm (accessed 3 September 2012). Link no longer working.

Carroll, David, *Albert Camus, the Algerian: Colonialism, Terrorism, Justice* (New York, NY: Columbia University Press, 2007).

de Certeau, Michel, *The Practice of Everyday Life* (Berkeley, CA: University of California Press, 1984).

Chaliand, Gérard and Rageau, Jean-Pierre, *The Penguin Atlas of Diasporas* (New York, NY: Viking Books, 1991).

Chambers, Iain, *Migrancy, Culture, Identity* (London: Routledge, 1994).

———— "Leaky Habits and Broken Grammar", in G. Robertson, M. Mash, L. Tickner, J. Bird, B. Curtis and T. Putnam (eds), *Travellers' Tales: Narratives of Home and Displacement* (London: Routledge, 1994), pp. 245–9.

Charlesworth, Ester, *Architects Without Frontiers: War, Reconstruction and Design Responsibility* (Oxford: Architectural Press, 2006).

Cherry, Colin, "The Telephone System: Creator of Mobility and Social Change", in I. de Sola Pool (ed), *The Social Impact of the Telephone* (Cambridge, MA: MIT Press, 1977), pp. 112–26.

Cho, Lily, "The Turn to Diaspora", *Topia* 17 (2007), pp. 11–30.

Clifford, James, "Diasporas", in J. Clifford, *Routes: Travels and Translation in the Late Twentieth Century* (Cambridge, MA: Harvard University Press, 1997), pp. 244–77.

Cohen, Robin, "Diasporas and the Nation-State: From Victims to Challengers", *International Affairs* 72.3 (1996), pp. 507–20.

———— *Global Diasporas: An Introduction* (Seattle, WA: University of Washington Press, 1997).

Cooke, Miriam, "Beirut Reborn: The Political Aesthetics of Auto-destruction", *The Yale Journal of Criticism* 15.2 (2002), pp. 393–424.

Cortas, Wadad Makdisi, *A World I Loved: The Story of an Arab Woman* (New York, NY: Nation Books, 2009).

Cox, Lloyd, "Nation-State and Nationalism", in G. Ritzer (ed), *Blackwell Encyclopedia of Sociology* (Malden, MA: Blackwell Publishing, 2007), pp. 3143–52.

Cresswell, Tim, *Place: A Short Introduction* (Malden, MA: Blackwell Publishing, 2004).

Cunningham, M. Wayne, "Ten Thousand Plaudits", *January Magazine*, May 2007. Available at www.januarymagazine.com/fiction/denirosgame.html (accessed 31 August 2009).

Dallas, Lucy, "The Hero from Beirut", *Times Literary Supplement* 5036 (1999), p. 23.

Darwish, Mahmoud, "The Earth is Closing on Us", in Adonis, M. Darwish and S. al-Qasim, *Victims of a Map: A Bilingual Anthology of Arabic Poetry*. A. al-Udhari (tr), (London: Saqi, 1984), p. 13.

Davie, Michael, "City as Excavation? Notes for the Excavation of Beirut: A Quest for National Identity?" Paper delivered at *City Debates Seminar* at the American University of Beirut, 3 June 2002.

Davis, Mike, *Planet of Slums: Urban Involution and the Informal Working Class* (London: Verso, 2006).

Davis, Uri, *Apartheid Israel: Possibilities for the Struggle Within* (London: Zed Books, 2003).

Dayal, Samir, "Diaspora and Double Consciousness", *The Journal of the Midwest Modern Language Association* 29.1 (1996), pp. 46–62.

Deleuze, Giles, and Guattari, Félix, *Kafka: Toward a Minor Literature* (Minneapolis, MN: University of Minnesota Press, 1986).

Derrida, Jacques, *Archive Fever: A Freudian Impression*. E. Prenowitz (tr), (Chicago, IL: Chicago University Press, 1996).

Devlin, Kieron, "A Conversation with Rabih Alameddine", *Blip Magazine*, 16 October 2002. Available at http://blipmagazine.net/backissues/2002/leilani-devlin-alameddine.html (accessed 26 August 2010).

Dooley, Gillian, "Review: *Somewhere, Home*", *Writer's Radio, Radio Adelaide*, 12 July 2004. Available at http://dspace.flinders.edu.au/jspui/bitstream/2328/474/1/SomewhereHome.pdf (accessed 20 August 2012).

Douglas, Mary, "The Idea of a Home", *Social Research* 58.1 (1991), pp. 287–307.

Dublin City Council, "Lord Mayor of Dublin Unveils Winner of International IMPAC Dublin Literary Award", *Dublin City Council Website*, 12 June 2008. Available at www.dublincity.ie/PRESS/PRESSRELEASES/PRESSRELEASES 2008/PRESSRELEASESJUNE2008/Pages/impac_dublin_literary_award_announced.aspx (accessed 31 August 2013).

Eliot, T. S., *The Waste Land* (1922; London: Hogarth Press, 1923).

Embalo, Brigit, "The City, Mythical Images and their Deconstructions: The Image of Beirut in Contemporary Works of Arab Fiction", in A. Neuwirth, B. Embalo, S. Gunther and M. Jarrar (eds), *Myths, Historical Archetypes, and Symbolic Figures in Arabic Literature: Towards a New Hermeneutic Approach* (Beirut: In Kommission bei Franz Steiner Verlag Stuttgart, 1999), pp. 583–603.

En-nehas, Jamal, "Review: Amin Maalouf, *Les Échelles du Levant*", *World Literature Today* 71.2 (1997), pp. 341–2.

Entelis, John P., "Belief-System and Ideology Formation in the Lebanese Katâ'ib Party", *International Journal of Middle East Studies* 4.2 (1973), pp. 148–62.

Etzioni, Amitai, *How Patriotic is the Patriot Act? Freedom Versus Security in the Age of Terrorism* (New York, NY: Routledge, 2005).

Ezzati, Abul, "The Concept of Martyrdom in Islam", *Al-Serat: A Journal of Islamic Studies* xii (1986). Available at www.al-islam.org/al-serat/concept-ezzati.htm (accessed 31 August 2013).

Farah, May, "Lebanese Writer Returns to Her *Somewhere, Home*", *The Daily Star* (Beirut), 12 April 2003, p. 6.

Fawaz, Mona, Harb, Mona, and Gharbieh, Ahmad, "Living Beirut's Security Zones: An Investigation of the Modalities and Practice of Urban Security", *City and Society* 24.2 (2002), pp. 137–95.

Fisk, Robert, "The Immortality of a Great, if Flawed, Historian", *The Independent*, 13 August 2011. Available at www.independent.co.uk/opinion/commentators/fisk/robert-fisk-the-immortality-of-a-great-if-flawed-historian-2336906 (accessed 13 August 2011).

Frankfurt City Library, "Alia Yunis Presents *The Night Counter*", *US Consulate Frankfurt Channel*, 24 November 2010. Available at www.youtube.com/watch?v=7o7s6QssY10 (accessed 12 May 2011).

Frazer, George, *The Golden Bough: A Study in Magic and Religion* (London: Macmillan, 1922).

Freud, Sigmund, "The 'Uncanny'", in S. Freud, *The Penguin Freud Library Volume 14: Art and Literature* (London: Penguin Books, 1985), pp. 339–76. Orig. pub. 1919.

Gana, Nouri, "Rawi Hage: *De Niro's Game*", *The International Fiction Review* 34 (2007), pp. 196–8.

Gauch, Suzanne, *Liberating Shahrazad: Feminism, Postcolonialism, and Islam* (Minneapolis, MN: University of Minnesota Press, 2007).

Gavin, Angus, and Maluf, Ramez, *Beirut Reborn: The Restoration and Development of the Central District* (London: Academy Editions, 1996).

Gellner, Ernest, *Nations and Nationalism* (Oxford: Blackwell, 1983).

Genette, Gérand, *Narrative Discourse*. J.E. Lewin (tr), (Oxford: Blackwell, 1980).

George, Rosemary, *The Politics of Home: Postcolonial Reformations and Twentieth-Century Fiction* (Cambridge: Cambridge University Press, 1996).

Georges, Robert, and Jones, Michael Owen, *Folkloristics: An Introduction* (Bloomington, IN: Indiana University Press, 1995).

Georgis, Dina, "Masculinities and the Aesthetics of Love: Reading Terrorism in *De Niro's Game* and *Paradise Now*", *Studies in Gender and Sexuality* 12.2 (2011), pp. 134–48.

Gerhardt, Mia, *The Art of Story-Telling: A Literary Study of The Thousand and One Nights* (Leiden: E. J. Brill, 1963).

Ghosh, Amitav, "The Diaspora in Indian Culture", in A. Ghosh, *The Imam and the Indian: Prose Pieces* (Delhi: Orient Longman, 2002), pp. 243–50.

Gillespie, Kate, Riddle, Liesl, Sayre, Edward, and Sturges, David, "Diaspora Interest in Homeland Investment", *The Journal of International Business Studies* 30.3 (1999), pp. 623–34.

Gilroy, Paul, *The Black Atlantic: Modernity and Double Consciousness* (Cambridge, MA: Harvard University Press, 1993).

Gohar, Saddik, "Towards a Hybrid Poetics", *InterCulture: An Interdisciplinary Journal* 4.2 (2007), pp. 1–19.

Green, David, "Levantism Finds its Place in Modern Israel", *Ha'aretz*, 25 August 2011. Available at www.haaretz.com/culture/books/levantism-finds-its-place-in-modern-israel-1.380634 (accessed 25 November 2011).

Green, Nancy, *Jewish Workers in the Modern Diaspora* (Berkeley, CA: University of California Press, 1998).

Gruen, Erich, *Diaspora: Jews Amidst Greeks and Romans* (Cambridge, MA: Harvard University Press, 2002).

Gulick, John, *Tripoli: A Modern Arab City* (Cambridge, MA: Harvard University Press, 1967).

Guroian, Vigen, "The Politics and Morality of Genocide", in R. G. Hovannisian (ed), *The Armenian Genocide: History, Politics, Ethics* (New York, NY: Palgrave Macmillan, 1992), pp. 311–39.

Hage, Ghassan, "Religious Fundamentalism as a Political Strategy: The Evolution of the Lebanese Forces' Religious Discourse during the Lebanese Civil War", *Critique of Anthropology* 12.27 (1992), pp. 27–45.

—— "Nationalist Anxiety and the Fear of Losing Your Other", *Australian Journal of Anthropology* 7.2 (1996), pp. 121–41.

—— "At Home in the Entrails of the West: Multiculturalism, Ethnic Food and Migrant Home-building", in H. Grace, G. Hage, L. Johnson, J. Langsworth and M. Symonds (eds), *Home/World: Space, Community and Marginality in Sydney's West* (Annandale, NSW: Pluto Press, 1997), pp. 99–153.

—— "Under the Global Olive Tree: A Review of Amin Maalouf's *Origines*", *Griffith Review* 6 (2004), pp. 213–21.

—— "With the Fig, the Olive and the Pomegranate Trees: Thoughts on Australian Belonging", in P. Tabar and J. Skulte-Ouaiss (eds), *Politics, Culture and the Lebanese Diaspora* (Newcastle: Cambridge Scholars Press, 2010), pp. 151–60.

El Hage, Jad, *The Last Migration: A Novel of Diaspora and Love* (Melbourne: Panache, 2002).

Hage, Rawi, *De Niro's Game* (Canada: Anansi, 2006).

—— "To Roam a Borderless World", *The Globe and Mail*, 13 June 2008. Available at www.theglobeandmail.com/commentary/to-roam-a-borderless-world/arti cle720197/ (accessed 31 August 2013).

Hall, Stuart, "Cultural Identity and Diaspora", in P. Williams and L. Chrisman (eds), *Colonial Discourse and Post-Colonial Theory: A Reader* (New York, NY: Columbia University Press, 1994), pp. 392–403.

—— "New Cultures for Old", in D. Massey and P. Jess (eds), *A Place in the World? Places, Cultures and Globalization* (Oxford: Oxford University Press, 1995), pp. 175–214.

Halper, Jeff, *An Israeli in Palestine: Resisting Dispossession, Redeeming Israel* (London; Ann Arbor, MI: Pluto Press, 2008).

Hanania, Tony, *Unreal City* (1999; London: Bloomsbury, 2000).

Hanf, Theodor, *Coexistence in Wartime Lebanon: Decline of a State and Rise of a Nation* (London: I.B.Tauris, 1993).

Hassan, Salah, "UnStated: Narrating War in Lebanon", *PMLA* 123.5 (2008), pp. 1621–9.

Haugbolle, Sune, *War and Memory in Lebanon* (Cambridge: Cambridge University Press, 2010).

—— "The Secular Saint: Iconography and Ideology in the Cult of Bashir Jumayil", in A. Bandak and M. Bille (eds), *Politics of Worship in the Contemporary Middle East: Sainthood in Fragile States* (Leiden: Brill, 2013), pp. 191–211.

Herzl, Theodor, *The Jewish State* (Minneapolis, MN: Filiquarian Publishing, 2006). Orig. pub. 1896.

Hobsbawm, Eric, "Introduction: Inventing Traditions", in E. Hobsbawm and T. Ranger (eds), *The Invention of Tradition* (Cambridge: Cambridge University Press, 1983), pp. 1–15.

—— *Nations and Nationalism Since 1780* (Cambridge: Cambridge University Press, 1990).

—— "Introduction", *Social Research* 58.1 (1991), pp. 65–8.

Hochberg, Gil, *In Spite of Partition: Jews, Arabs and the Limits of Separatist Imagination* (Princeton, NJ: Princeton University Press, 2007).

Holman, Emily, "Humorous, Humane and Readable. But Charming?", *The Daily Star* (Beirut), 2 December 2009. Available at www.dailystar.com.lb/Culture/Arts/Dec/02/Humorous-humane-and-readable-But-charming.ashx#axzz1i ZNuuPox (accessed 11 October 2010).

hooks, bell, *Yearning: Race, Gender, and Cultural Politics* (London: Turnaround, 1991).

al-Hout, Bayan, *Sabra and Shatila: September 1982* (London: Pluto Press, 2004).

Hout, Syrine, "Memory, Home, and Exile in Contemporary Anglophone Lebanese Fiction", *Critique* 46.3 (2005), pp. 219–33.

—— "The Predicament of In-Betweenness in the Contemporary Lebanese Exilic Novel in English", in Y. Suleiman and I. Muhawi (eds), *Literature and Nation in the Middle East* (Edinburgh: Edinburgh University Press, 2006), pp. 190–207.

—— "*The Last Migration*: The First Contemporary Example of Lebanese Diasporic Literature", *Journal of Postcolonial Writing* 43.3 (2007), pp. 286–96.

—— "*The Last Migration*: The First Contemporary Example of Lebanese Diasporic Literature", in L. Al Maleh (ed), *Arab Voices in Diaspora: Critical Perspectives on Anglophone Arab Literature* (Amsterdam: Rodopi, 2009), pp. 143–62.

—— "*The Last Migration*: The First Contemporary Example of Lebanese Diasporic Literature", in P. Tabar and J. Skulte-Ouaiss (eds), *Politics, Culture and the Lebanese Diaspora* (Newcastle: Cambridge Scholars Press, 2010), pp. 358–72.

—— *Post-War Anglophone Lebanese Fiction: Home Matters in the Diaspora* (Edinburgh: Edinburgh University Press, 2012).

Hudson, Michael, *The Precarious Republic: Political Modernization in Lebanon* (New York, NY: Random House, 1968).

Humphrey, Michael, "Lebanese Identities: Between Cities, Nations and Transnations", *Arab Studies Quarterly* 26.1 (2004), pp. 31–50.

Hutchby, Ian, *Conversations and Technology: From the Telephone to the Internet* (Cambridge: Polity Press, 2001).

Hutchinson, John, *The Dynamic of Cultural Nationalism: The Gaelic Revival and the Creation of the Irish Nation State* (London: Allen and Unwin, 1987).

—— *Modern Nationalism* (London: Fontana Press, 1994).

Hutchinson, John, and Smith, Anthony D., "Introduction", in J. Hutchinson and A. D. Smith (eds), *Nationalism* (Oxford: Oxford University Press, 1994), pp. 1–14.

Irwin, Robert, *The Arabian Nights: A Companion* (London: Allen Lane, 1994).

Israel, Nico, *Outlandish: Writing Between Exile and Diaspora* (Stanford, CA: Stanford University Press, 2000).

Jabbra, Nancy W., and Jabbra, Joseph G., "Education and Political Development in the Middle East", in S. G. Hajjar (ed), *The Middle East: From Transition to Development* (Leiden: E. J. Brill, 1985), pp. 82–98.

Jarrar, Maher, "The Martyrdom of Passionate Lovers: Holy War as a Sacred Wedding", in A. Neuwirth, B. Embalo, S. Gunther and M. Jarrar (eds), *Myths, Historical Archetypes and Symbolic Figures in Arabic Literature: Towards a New Hermeneutic Approach* (Beirut: In Kommission bei Franz Steiner Verlag Stuttgart, 1999), pp. 87–107.

———— "*The Arabian Nights* and the Contemporary Arabic Novel", in S. Makdisi and F. Nussbaum (eds), *The Arabian Nights in Historical Context: Between East and West* (Oxford: Oxford University Press, 2008), pp. 297–316.

Jarrar, Nada Awar, *Somewhere, Home* (2003; London: Vintage; 2004).

———— "Family at War", *The Times*, 27 July 2006. Available at www.timesonline.co. uk/article/0,7-2286676_2,00.html (accessed 2 August 2006).

Kalra, Virinder S., Kaur, Raminder, and Hutnyk, John, *Diaspora and Hybridity* (London; Thousand Oaks, CA: SAGE Publications, 2005).

Kahanoff, Jacqueline Shohet, "Childhood in Egypt", in D. Starr and S. Somekh (eds), *Mongrels or Marvels: The Levantine Writings of Jacqueline Shohet Kahanoff* (Stanford, CA: Stanford University Press, 2011), pp. 1–13. Orig. pub. 1958.

———— "Afterword: From East the Sun", in D. Starr and S. Somekh (eds), *Mongrels or Marvels: The Levantine Writings of Jacqueline Shohet Kahanoff* (Stanford, CA: Stanford University Press, 2011), pp. 243–60. Orig. pub. 1968.

Karmi, Ghada, *Married to Another Man: Israel's Dilemma in Palestine* (London: Pluto Press, 2007).

Karpat, Kamal, "The Ottoman Emigration to America, 1860–1914", *International Journal of Middle East Studies* 17 (1985), pp. 175–209.

Kassir, Samir, *Beirut*. M.B. DeBovoise (tr), (Berkeley, CA: University of California Press, 2011).

Kehe, Marjorie, "The Night Counter", *The Christian Science Monitor*, 1 August 2009. Available at www.csmonitor.com/Books/Book-Reviews/2009/0801/the-night-counter (accessed 1 October 2009).

Khalaf, Samir, *Lebanon's Predicament* (New York, NY: Columbia University Press, 1987).

———— "Urban Design and the Recovery of Beirut", in S. Khalaf and P. S. Khoury (eds), *Recovering Beirut: Urban Design and Post-War Reconstruction* (Leiden: E. J. Brill, 1993), pp. 11–62.

———— "Contested Space and the Forging of New Cultural Identities", in P. Rowe and H. Sarkis (eds), *Projecting Beirut: Episodes in the Construction and Reconstruction of a Modern City* (Munich; London; New York, NY: Prestel, 1998), pp. 140–64.

———— *Civil and Uncivil Violence in Lebanon: A History of the Internationalization of Communal Conflict* (New York, NY: Columbia University Press, 2002).

———— *Heart of Beirut: Reclaiming the Bourj* (London: Saqi, 2006).

Khalaf, Samir, and Denoeux, Guilain, "Urban Networks and Political Conflict in Lebanon", in N. Shehadi and D. H. Mills (eds), *Lebanon: A History of Conflict and Consensus* (London: I.B.Tauris, 1988), pp. 181–200.

Khalaf, Samir, and Kongstad, Per, *Hamra of Beirut: A Case of Rapid Urbanization* (Leiden: E. J. Brill, 1973).

——— "Urbanization and Urbanism in Beirut: Some Preliminary Results", in L. Carl Brown (ed), *From Madina to Metropolis: Heritage and Change in the Near Eastern City* (Princeton, NJ: The Darwin Press, 1973), pp. 116–49.

Khalil, Iman, "Writing Civil War: The Lebanese Experience in Juseuf Naoum's German Short Stories", *The German Quarterly* 67.4 (1994), pp. 549–60.

Khalili, Laleh, "Places of Memory and Mourning: Palestinian Commemoration in the Refugee Camps of Lebanon", *Comparative Studies of South Asia, Africa and the Middle East* 25.1 (2005), pp. 30–45.

Khashan, Hilal, "The Political Values of Lebanese Maronite College Students", *Journal of Conflict Resolution* 34 (1990), pp. 723–44.

Khater, Akram, *Inventing Home: Emigration, Gender, and the Middle Class in Lebanon, 1870–1920* (Berkeley, CA: University of California Press, 2001).

Khuri, Fuad, *From Village to Suburb: Order and Change in Greater Beirut* (Chicago, IL: University of Chicago Press, 1975).

King, Charles, and Melvin, Neil, "Diaspora Politics: Ethnic Linkages, Foreign Policy, and Security in Eurasia", *International Security* 24.3 (1999), pp. 108–38.

Kitab Book Show, "Alia Yunis – Part 1", 1 December 2009. Available at www.youtube.com/watch?v=filEKvStxxk&feature=related (accessed 12 May 2011).

Kleiner-Liebau, Désirée, *Migration and the Construction of National Identity in Spain* (Madrid: Iberoamericana, 2009).

Kristeva, Julia, *Strangers to Ourselves* (New York, NY: Columbia University Press, 1991).

Kysar, Kathryn, "1,001 Nights with Modern Family Twist", *StarTribune*, 8 August 2009. Available at www.startribune.com/entertainment/books/52617702.html (accessed 11 October 2009).

Labaki, Boutros, "Lebanese Migration During the War: 1975–1989", in A. Hourani and N. Shehadi (eds), *Lebanese Migration in the World: A Century of Emigration* (London: I.B.Tauris, 1992), pp. 605–26.

Lamb, Franklin, "Why Lebanon's Palestinians are Hopeful about an Election in Which They Cannot Vote: The Palestinians 26 Years After the Massacre at Sabra-Shatila – Part Three", *thepeoplesvoice.org*, 25 September 2008. Available at www.thepeoplesvoice.org/cgibin/blogs/voices.php/2008/09/25/p28996 (accessed 13 December 2011).

Lawson, Stephanie, *Culture and Context in World Politics* (Basingstoke: Palgrave Macmillan, 2006).

Lehan, Richard, *The City in Literature: An Intellectual and Cultural History* (Berkeley, CA: University of California Press, 1998).

L'Estrange, Sarah, "The Book Show: Rawi Hage's *De Niro's Game*", *ABC Radio National*, 12 June 2007. Available at www.abc.net.au/radionational/programs/bookshow/rawi-hages-de-niros-game/3248206#transcript (accessed 4 May 2009).

Lijphart, Arend, "Consociational Democracy", *World Politics* 21.2 (1969), pp. 207–25.

——— *Democracy in Plural Societies: A Comparative Exploration* (New Haven, CT: Yale University Press, 1977).

Long, Michael, "Eliot, Pound, Joyce: 'unreal city'", in E. Timms and D. Kelley (eds), *Unreal City: Urban Experience in Modern European Literature and Art* (New York, NY: St. Martin's Press, 1985), pp. 144–57.

Maalouf, Amin, *The Rock of Tanios*. D. Blair (tr), (London: Abacus, 1994).

——— *Ports of Call*. A. Manguel (tr), (London: The Harvill Press, 1999).

————— *On Identity*. B. Bray (tr), (London: The Harvill Press, 2000).

————— *Origins: A Memoir*. C. Temerson (tr), (New York, NY: Farrar, Straus and Giroux, 2008).

Maasri, Zeina, "The Aesthetics of Belonging: Transformations in Hizbullah's Political Posters", *Middle East Journal of Culture and Communication* 5 (2012), pp. 146–89.

Makdisi, Jean Said, *Beirut Fragments: A War Memoir* (New York, NY: Persea Books, 1990).

Makdisi, Saree, "Beirut, City Without History?", in P. Silverstein and U. Makdisi (eds), *Memory and Violence in the Middle East and North Africa* (Bloomington, IN: Indiana University Press, 2006), pp. 201–14.

Makdisi, Saree, and Nussbaum, Felicity, "Introduction", in S. Makdisi and F. Nussbaum (eds), *The Arabian Nights in Historical Context: Between East and West* (Oxford: Oxford University Press, 2008), pp. 1–24.

Makdisi, Samir, and Sadaka, Richard, "The Lebanese Civil War, 1975–1990", *American University of Beirut, Institute of Financial Economics: Lecture and Working Paper* Series 3 (Beirut: American University of Beirut Press, 2003).

Makdisi, Ussama, "From Sectarianism to Lebanese Nationalism: Has the Lebanese War Unequivocally Ended?", *Adab* 11–12 (2001), p. 49.

Malti-Douglas, Fedwa, "Shahrazād feminist", in R. G. Hovannisian and G. Sabagh (eds), *The Thousand and One Nights in Arabic Literature and Society* (Cambridge: Cambridge University Press, 1997), pp. 40–55.

Massey, Doreen, "A Place Called Home?", *New Formations* 17 (1992), pp. 3–15.

————— *Space, Place and Gender* (Cambridge: Polity, 1994).

Massey, Doreen, and Jess, Pat, "Introduction", in D. Massey and P. Jess (eds), *A Place in the World? Places, Cultures and Globalization* (Oxford: Oxford University Press, 1995), pp. 1–4.

Mawad, Dalal, "Lebanon's History Awaits its Textbook", *The Daily Star* (Beirut), 20 November 2009. Available at www.dailystar.com.lb/Opinion/Commentary/Nov/20/Lebanons-history-awaits-its-textbook.ashx#axzz1iQL3iRv2 (accessed 11 October 2010).

McClennen, Sophia, "Exilic Perspectives on 'Alien Nations'", *CLCWeb Comparative Literature and Culture: A WWWeb Journal* 7.1 (2005). Available at http://dx.doi.org/10.7771/1481-4374.1257 (accessed 5 October 2011).

Meinecke, Friedrich, *Cosmopolitanism and the National State* (Princeton, NJ: Princeton University Press, 1970). Orig. pub. 1907.

Mezei, Kathy, and Briganti, Chiara, "Reading the House: A Literary Perspective", *Signs* 27.3 (2002), pp. 837–46.

Mirapuri, Dawn, "Meditations on Memory and Belonging: Nada Awar Jarrar's *Somewhere, Home*", in L. Al Maleh (ed), *Arab Voices in Diaspora: Critical Perspectives on Anglophone Arab Literature* (Amsterdam: Rodopi, 2009), pp. 463–86.

Mishra, Sudesh, *Diaspora Criticism* (Edinburgh: Edinburgh University Press, 2006).

Moosa, Matti, *The Maronites in History* (Syracuse, NY: Syracuse University Press, 1986).

Moreh, Shmuel, *Modern Arabic Poetry 1800–1970: The Development of Its Forms and Themes Under the Influence of Western Literature* (Leiden: E. J. Brill, 1976).

————— *Studies in Modern Arabic Prose and Poetry* (Leiden: E. J. Brill, 1987).

Morris, Benny, *One State, Two States: Resolving the Israel/Palestine Conflict* (New Haven, CT: Yale University Press, 2009).

Mostafa, Dalia S., "Journeying through a Discourse of Violence: Elias Khoury's *Yalo* and Rawi Hage's *De Niro's Game*", *Middle East Critique* 20.1 (2011), pp. 21–45.

Muhawi, Ibrahim, "The Arabian Nights and the Question of Authorship", *Journal of Arabic Literature* 36.3 (2005), pp. 323–37.

Naficy, Hamid, *An Accented Cinema: Exilic and Diasporic Filmmaking* (Princeton, NJ: Princeton University Press, 2001).

Nagel, Caroline, "Ethnic Conflict and Urban Redevelopment in Downtown Beirut", *Growth and Change* 31.2 (2000), pp. 211–34.

Nasr, Salim, "The Political Economy of the Lebanese Conflict", in N. Shehadi and B. Harney (eds), *Politics and the Economy in Lebanon* (Oxford: Center for Lebanese Studies, 1989), pp. 43–50.

Neuwirth, Angelika, "Introduction", in A. Neuwirth, B. Embalo, S. Gunther and M. Jarrar (eds), *Myths, Historical Archetypes and Symbolic Figures in Arabic Literature: Towards a New Hermeneutic Approach* (Beirut: In Kommission bei Franz Steiner Verlag Stuttgart, 1999), pp. ix–xxii.

Nimni, Ephraim (ed), *The Challenge of Post-Zionism: Alternatives to Israeli Fundamentalist Politics* (London: Zed Books, 2003).

Obama, Barak, "Remarks by the President on the Middle East and North Africa", *The White House*, 19 May 2011. Available at www.whitehouse.gov/the-press-office/2011/05/19/remarks-president-middle-east-and-north-africa (accessed 20 November 2011).

O'Brien, Conor Cruise, *Camus* (London: Fontana, 1970).

Ofeish, Sami, and Ghandour, Sabah, "Transgressive Subjects: Gender, War, and Colonialism in Etel Adnan's *Sitt Marie Rose*", in L. S. Majaj and A. Amireh (eds), *Etel Adnan: Critical Essays on the Arab American Writer and Artist* (North Carolina, NC: McFarland & Company Inc. Publishers, 2002), pp. 122–36.

Padel, Ruth, "Illicit Love in a War-Torn Land", *The Daily Telegraph*, 6 March 1999. Available at www.telegraph.co.uk/culture/4716981/Illicit-love-in-a-war-torn-land.html (accessed 31 August 2013).

Pappé, Ilan, *A History of Modern Palestine: One Land, Two Peoples* (Cambridge: Cambridge University Press, 2004).

———— *The Ethnic Cleansing of Palestine* (Oxford: One World, 2006).

———— "The Exilic Homeland of Edward W. Said", *Interventions* 8.1 (2006), pp. 9–23.

Park, Robert, "The City: Suggestions for the Investigation of Human Behavior in the Urban Environment", *The American Journal of Sociology* 20.5 (1915), pp. 577–612.

———— "Chapter I: The City: Suggestions for the Investigation of Human Behavior in the Urban Environment", in R. Park and E. Burgess, *The City* (Chicago, IL: University of Chicago Press, 1925), pp. 1–46.

Paye, Jean-Claude, *Global War on Liberty*. J. Membrez (tr), (New York, NY: Telos Press Publishing, 2007).

Phares, Walid, "Whose Lebanon? Parallels of Arab Occupation", *B'tzedek Online*, 1998. Available at www.btzedek.co.il/lebanon.htm (accessed 12 April 2008). Link no longer working.

Porteous, Douglas J., "Home: The Territorial Core", *Geographical Review* 66.4 (1976), pp. 383–90.

——— *Lebanese Christian Nationalism: The Rise and Fall of an Ethnic Resistance* (Boulder, CO: Lynne Rienner Publishers, 1995).

Potter, Russel, "Black Modernisms/Black Postmodernisms", *Postmodern Culture* 5.1 (1994). Available at http://pmc.iath.virginia.edu/text-only/issue.994/review-1. 994 (accessed 28 October 2013).

Pugh-Thomas, Claudia, "Book: War on the Home Front", *The Independent*, 20 March 1999. Available at www.independent.co.uk/arts-entertainment/book-war-on-the-home-front-1081802.html (accessed 11 October 2011).

Quayson, Ato, and Daswani, Girish, "Introduction – Diaspora and Transnationalism: Scapes, Scales, and Scopes", in A. Quayson and G. Daswani (eds), *A Companion to Diaspora and Transnationalism* (Malden, MA: Blackwell Publishers, 2013), pp. 1–26.

Quilty, Jim, "Confronting Demons to Banish them like Sabra and Shatilla, 'Massaker' is a Political Creature and Should be Handled as Such", *The Daily Star* (Beirut), 21 October 2005. Available at www.dailystar.com.lb/Culture/Arts/Oct/21/Confronting-demons-to-banish-them-like-Sabra-and-Shatilla-Massaker-is-a-political-creature-and-should.ashx#axzz1aHS4VFcH (accessed 11 October 2011).

Rahman, Najat, "Apocalyptic Narrative Recalls and the Human: Rawi Hage's *De Niro's Game*", *University of Toronto Quarterly* 78.2 (2009), pp. 800–14.

Rapport, Nigel and Dawson, Andrew, "The Topic and the Book", in N. Rapport and A. Dawson (eds), *Migrants of Identity: Perceptions of Home in a World of Movement* (Oxford, UK; New York, NY: Berg, 1998), pp. 3–17.

——— "Home and Movement – A Polemic", in N. Rapport and A. Dawson (eds), *Migrants of Identity: Perceptions of Home in a World of Movement* (Oxford, UK; New York, NY: Berg, 1998), pp. 19–38.

Reinhart, Tanya, *Israel/Palestine: How to End the War of 1948* (New York, NY: Seven Stories Press, 2005).

Reis, Michelle, "Theorizing Diaspora: Perspectives on 'Classical' and 'Contemporary' Diaspora", *International Migration* 42.2 (2004), pp. 41–56.

Rejwan, Nissim, *Israel in Search of Identity: Reading the Formative Years* (Gainesville, FL: University of Florida Press, 1999).

Renzetti, Elizabeth, "The Search for Rawi Hage", *The Globe and Mail*, 4 August 2008/. Available at www.theglobeandmail.com/news/arts/the-search-for-rawi-hage/article308056/ (accessed 23 April 2009).

Rouse, Roger, "Mexican Migration and the Social Space of Postmodernism", *Diaspora: A Journal of Transnational Studies* 1.1 (1991), pp. 8–20.

Rose, Gillian, *Feminism and Geography: The Limits of Geographical Knowledge* (Cambridge: Polity, 1993).

Rose, Jacqueline, *Proust Among the Nations: From Dreyfus to the Middle East* (Chicago, IL: University of Chicago Press, 2011).

Rushdie, Salman, *Shame* (London: Cape, 1983).

Rykwert, Joseph, "House and Home", *Social Research* 58.1 (1991), pp. 51–62.

Safran, William, "Diasporas in Modern Societies: Myths of Homeland and Return", *Diaspora: A Journal of Transnational Studies* 1.1 (1991), pp. 83–95.

——— "Comparing Diasporas: A Review", *Diaspora: A Journal of Transnational Studies* 8.3 (1999), pp. 255–91.

———— "The Jewish Diaspora in a Comparative and Theoretical Perspective", *Israel Studies* 10.1 (2005), pp. 36–60.

Sagiv, Assaf, "Zionism and the Myth of the Motherland", *Azure* 5 (1998).

Said, Edward, "Arabs and Jews", *Journal of Palestine Studies* 3.2 (1974), pp. 3–14.

———— *The World, the Text, and the Critic* (Cambridge, MA: Harvard University Press, 1983).

———— *After the Last Sky* (New York, NY: Pantheon Books, 1986).

———— "Identity, Authority, and Freedom: The Potentate and the Traveller", *Transition* 54 (1991), pp. 4–18.

———— *The Question of Palestine* (New York, NY: Vintage Books, 1992).

———— *Culture and Imperialism* (New York, NY: Viking, 1994).

———— *The Politics of Dispossession* (London: Vintage, 1995).

———— *Representations of the Intellectual: The Reith Lectures* (1994; New York, NY: Vintage Books, 1996).

———— "Truth and Reconciliation", *Al-Ahram Weekly* 412, 14–20 January 1999.

———— "What Can Separation Mean?", *Al-Ahram Weekly* 455, 11–17 November, 1999.

———— "The Only Alternative", *Al-Ahram Weekly* 523, 1–7 March, 2001.

———— "Reflections on Exile", in E. Said, *Reflections on Exile and Other Essays* (Cambridge, MA: Harvard University Press, 2002), pp. 173–86.

Salamey, Imad, and Tabar, Paul, "Consociational Democracy and Urban Sustainability: Transforming the Confessional Divides in Beirut", *Ethnopolitics* 7.2–3 (2008), pp. 239–63.

Saldívar, Jose, *Border Matters: Remapping American Cultural Studies* (Berkeley, CA: University of California Press, 1997).

Salem, Elise, *Constructing Lebanon: A Century of Literary Narratives* (Gainesville, FL: University Press of Florida, 2003).

Salibi, Kamal, *Maronite Historians of Mediaeval Lebanon* (Beirut: American University of Beirut, 1959).

———— *A House of Many Mansions: The History of Lebanon Reconsidered* (London: I.B.Tauris, 1998).

———— "Introduction: The Historical Perspective", in N. Shehadi and D. H. Mills (eds), *Lebanon: A History of Conflict and Consensus* (London: I.B.Tauris, 1988), pp. 3–13.

Sallis, Eva, *Sheherazade Through the Looking Glass: The Metamorphosis of the Thousand and One Nights* (England: Curzon, 1999).

Sand, Shlomo, *The Invention of the Jewish People*. Y. Lotan (tr), (London; New York, NY: Verso, 2009).

Sarkis, Hashim, "Territorial Claims: Architecture and Post-War Attitudes Toward the Built Environment", in S. Khalaf and P. S. Khoury (eds), *Recovering Beirut: Urban Design and Post-War Reconstruction* (Leiden: E. J. Brill, 1993), pp. 101–27.

———— "Beirut, the Novel", *Parachute: Contemporary Art Magazine* 108 (2002), pp. 107–43.

Schweid, Eliezer, "The Rejection of the Diaspora in Zionist Thought: Two Approaches", *Studies in Zionism* 5.1 (1984), pp. 43–70.

———— *The Land of Israel: National Home or Land of Destiny*. D. Greniman (tr), (Cranbury, NJ: Associated University Presses, 1985).

See, Carolyn, "Book World: Carolyn See Reviews *The Night Counter* by Alia Yunis", *The Washington Post*, 14 August 2009. Available at www.washingtonpost.com/wpdyn/content/article/2009/08/13/AR2009081303267.html (accessed 10 October 2009).

Sennett, Richard, "An Introduction", in R. Sennett (ed), *Classic Essays on the Culture of Cities* (New York, NY: Appleton-Century-Crofts, 1969), pp. 3–19.

Shapiro, Michael, *Methods and Nations: Cultural Governance and the Indigenous Subject* (New York, NY: Routledge, 2004).

Sharpe, William, and Wallock, Leonard, "From 'Great Town' to 'Nonplace Urban Realm': Reading the Modern City", in W. Sharpe and L. Wallock (eds), *Visions of the Modern City: Essays in History, Art, and Literature* (1983; Baltimore, MD: Johns Hopkins University Press, 1987), pp. 1–50.

Shasha, David, "A Jewish Voice Left Silent: Trying to Articulate the Levantine Option", *The American Muslim*, 2003. Available at http://theamericanmuslim.org/tam.php/features/articles/a_jewish_voice_left_silent_trying_to_articulate_the_levantine_option/ (accessed 25 November 2011).

al-Shawaf, Rayyan, "*Somewhere, Home*: An Evocative Look at Our Need to Belong", *The Daily Star* (Beirut), 6 January 2004, p. 8.

Sheffer, Gabriel, *Diaspora Politics* (Cambridge: Cambridge University Press, 2003).

Showalter, Jr., English, *The Stranger: Humanity and the Absurd* (Boston, MA: Twayne Publishers, 1989).

Shuval, Judith, "Diaspora Migration: Definitional Ambiguities and a Theoretical Paradigm", *International Migration* 38.5 (2000), pp. 41–55.

Simmel, George, "The Metropolis and Mental Life", in R. Sennett (ed), *Classic Essays on the Culture of Cities* (New York, NY: Appleton-Century-Crofts, 1969), pp. 47–60. Orig. pub. 1903.

Smith, Anthony D., *The Ethnic Origins of Nations* (Oxford: Blackwell, 1986).

Somerville, Peter, "Homelessness and the Meaning of Home: Rooflessness or Rootlessness?", *International Journal of Urban and Regional Research* 16.4 (1992), pp. 529–39.

Starr, Deborah, and Somekh, Sasson, "Editors' Introduction: Jacqueline Shohet Kahanoff – A Cosmopolitan Levantine", in D. Starr and S. Somekh (eds), *Mongrels or Marvels: The Levantine Writings of Jacqueline Shohet Kahanoff* (Stanford, CA: Stanford University Press, 2011), pp. xi–xxix.

Stone, Christopher, *Popular Culture and Nationalism in Lebanon: The Fairouz and Rahbani Nation* (London: Routledge, 2008).

Stratton, Jon, "(Dis)placing the Jews: Historicizing the Idea of Diaspora", *Diaspora: A Journal of Transnational Studies* 6.3 (1997), pp. 301–29.

Suleiman, Michael, "Introduction: The Arab Immigrant Experience", in M. Suleiman (ed), *Arabs in America: Building a New Future* (Philadelphia, PA: Temple University Press, 1999), pp. 1–24.

Suleiman, Yasir, *The Arabic Language and National Identity: A Study in Ideology* (Edinburgh: Edinburgh University Press, 2003).

Swart, Genevieve, "10,000 Reasons to Revisit His Youth", *The Sydney Morning Herald*, 28 May 2007. Available at www.smh.com.au/news/books/10000-reasons-to-revisit-his-youth/2007/05/27/1180205060755.html?page=fullpage#contentSwap1 (accessed 9 June 2008).

Tabar, Paul, "'*Ashura* in Sydney: A Transformation of a Religious Ceremony in the Context of a Migrant Society", *Journal of Intercultural Studies* 23.3 (2002), pp. 285–305.

———— "Lebanese Diaspora: Hybrid, Complex and Contentious", in P. Tabar (ed), *Lebanese Diaspora: History, Racism and Belonging* (Beirut: Lebanese American University Press, 2005), pp. 7–12.

Tabet, Jad, "Towards a Master Plan for Beirut", in S. Khalaf and P. S. Khoury (eds), *Recovering Beirut: Urban Design and Post-War Reconstruction* (Leiden: E. J. Brill, 1993), pp. 81–100.

Terdiman, Richard, *Present Past: Modernity and the Memory Crisis* (Ithaca: NY, Cornell University Press, 1993).

Thody, Philip, "Camus's *L'Étranger* Revisited", *Critical Quarterly* 21.2 (1979), pp. 61–9.

Tilley, Virginia, *The One-State Solution: A Breakthrough for Peace in the Israeli-Palestinian Deadlock* (Ann Arbor, MI: The University of Michigan Press, 2005).

Toby Eady Associates, "Top Titles: *Somewhere, Home*", 7 July 2003. Available at www.tobyeadyassociates.co.uk/top_titles/somewhere_home.htm (accessed 25 June 2013). Link no longer working.

Tölölyan, Khachig, "The Nation-State and its Others: In Lieu of a Preface", *Diaspora: A Journal of Transnational Studies* 1.1 (1991), pp. 3–7.

Toufic, Jalal, *Undeserving Lebanon* (Beirut: Forthcoming Books, 2007). Available at http://www.jalaltoufic.com/downloads/Jalal_Toufic_Undeserving_Lebanon.pdf (accessed 10 May 2014).

Traboulsi, Fawaz, *A History of Modern Lebanon* (London: Pluto Press, 2007).

Tristram, Philippa, *Living Space in Fact and Fiction* (London: Routledge, 1989).

Tuan, Yu-Fu, *Space and Place: The Perspective of Experience* (London: Edward Arnold, 1977).

Vinten, Luke, "Out of His Head", *Times Literary Supplement* 5007 (1999), p. 22.

Walters, William, "Secure Borders, Safe Havens: Domopolitics", *Citizenship Studies* 3.3 (2004), pp. 237–60.

Ward, Patricia Sarrafian, *The Bullet Collection* (Saint Paul, MN: Graywolf Press, 2003).

Weber, Max, "The City (Non-Legitimate Domination)", in M. Weber, *Economy and Society: An Outline of Interpretive Sociology*. G. Roth and C. Wittich (eds), E. Fischoff, H. Gerth, A.M. Henderson, F. Kolegar, C.W. Mills, T. Parsons, M. Rheinstein, G. Roth, E. Shils and C. Wittich (trs), (Berkeley, CA: University of California Press, 1978), pp. 1212–372. Orig. pub. 1913.

Weston, Jessie L., *From Ritual to Romance* (Cambridge: The University Press, 1920).

Wettig, Hannah, "Is Latest Version of National History Fit to Print?", *The Daily Star* (Beirut), 2 August 2004. Available at www.dailystar.com.lb/News/Local-News/Aug/02/Is-latest-version-of-national-history-fit-to-print.ashx#axzz1aHS4VFcH (accessed 11 October 2011).

Williams, Raymond, *The Country and The City* (London: Chatto and Windus, 1973).

Wirth, Louis, "Urbanism as a Way of Life", *The American Journal of Sociology* 44.1 (1938), pp. 1–24.

Worth, Robert, "10 Years After a Mea Culpa, No Hint of a 'Me, Too'", *The New York Times*, 16 April 2010. Available at www.nytimes.com/2010/04/17/world/mi ddleeast/17lebanon.html (accessed 13 December 2011).

Yunis, Alia, *The Night Counter* (New York, NY: Shaye Areheart Book, 2009).

Zaarour, Rola, "Chasing the American Dream, Arabian Style", *Egypt Independent*, 10 January 2010. Available at www.almasryalyoum.com/en/node/10160 (accessed 12 October 2010).

INDEX

Abdelhady, Dalia, 23, 100, 112
Abdullah, Fatima (*The Night Counter*),
    108, 139–67, 213
Abdullah, Ibrahim (*The Night
    Counter*), 140, 146, 150, 156,
    160–2, 166
Abou-Nahra (*De Niro's Game*), 79, 80,
    86, 88, 89
Abu Musa (*Unreal City*), 45, 47–8, 58–9
Abunimah, Ali, 185–7
Al-Abyad, Bassam (*De Niro's Game*),
    20–1, 67–8, 70–2, 76–80,
    84–95
Adana, 191, 192, 204
Adnan (*Somewhere, Home*), 115–16
Adonis, 55–60
Adorno, Theodor, 22, 87–8, 207
Aida (*Somewhere, Home*), 112, 114–18,
    124–5, 133–5, 137–8, 209
Ain al-Rummaneh, 39
Alameddine, Rabih, 75, 132, 208
*Alf Layla wa Layla see Thousand and One
    Nights*
Ali, 61–2
Ali (*Unreal City*), 63, 65, 65
Alia (*Somewhere, Home*), 113, 125–30
alienation, 3, 18, 27, 34, 42, 44, 90,
    133, 160, 162
    urban, 49, 51, 63, 66, 67

Ameen (*Somewhere, Home*), 129
Amir (*The Night Counter*), 139–43,
    150, 160, 162–3, 165–6
Amou Mohammed (*Somewhere, Home*),
    115, 117–18, 125, 133–7
Anderson, Benedict, 20, 100
Anthias, Floya, 3, 8, 165
Arab culture, 80–1
Arab identity, 189, 200–1
Arab–Israeli conflict, 184–90
Arabic poetry, 119–20, 181
architecture, 46–7, 143–4
archives and archiving, 113, 125–33
archons, 128–9
Asad (*Unreal City*), 52–3, 59, 63
Ashcroft, Bill, 11, 21, 207
Atwood, Margaret, 14
Australia, 115–16
    settler-state, as, 179–80
autochthony, 177–9

Ballaster, Ros, 156, 157
Bammer, Angelika, 15, 100–1, 112,
    145
Bassam (*The Night Counter*), 147, 150,
    159
Beirut
    city, descriptions of, 1–2, 27, 41–2,
        44–55, 59–60, 72–3, 114–15

Beirut (cont.)
  Downtown, 24–5, 40–1
  history, 26, 36–7
  war, at, 33–4, 68, 69–96, 113–15,
    118
  war amnesia, 36–42, 73–81, 95, 137
  wasteland, as, 45–55
belonging, 107, 183, 192–3
Berdyczewski, Micha Josef, 173, 178
Berger, John, 148–9
Bertrand (*Ports of Call*), 195–7
Bey, 47–8, 50–1, 63–4
Bhabha, Homi, 18, 148, 180
black market economy, 50–1
Blunt, Alison, 102–3
Booth, Charles, 34
Boyarin, Daniel and Jonathan, 179,
    182, 192
Boym, Svetlana, 106–7
Brah, Avtar, 2, 99–100, 106–7
Braziel, Jana, 15–16
Brenda (*The Night Counter*), 147
Brenner, Yosef Haim, 173
Brice, Chris, 110–11, 127
Briganti, Chiara, 145, 146, 147, 148
Brittany (*The Night Counter*), 151–2
Brydon, Diana, 14, 104–5, 112, 172

Camus, Albert, 89–91
capitalism, 6, 26, 34–5, 42, 46, 48,
    50, 67
Capitulations, 201
Carla (*The Night Counter*), 151–2
Carmali, Mahmoud (*Ports of Call*)
    197–8
Chahine (*De Niro's Game*), 84
Chaiben, Joseph (*De Niro's Game*), 93
Chambers, Ian, 148–9, 153
Charlesworth, Ester, 39–40
Cherry, Colin, 158–9
Cho, Lily, 8–9, 22, 105, 112, 172
Christianity, 23–4, 26–7, 36–7, 39,
    68, 69–96, 121, 132, 151,
    202–3, 211
  icons, 89

Maronites *see* Maronite Christians
Muslims, confrontation with,
    82–3
civil war, 6, 20, 38, 42, 43, 69–73, 83,
    109–11, 118, 134, 204
Clifford, James, 4, 6, 8–9, 22, 105–6
    112, 158, 165
coexistence, 28, 198–206, 212
Cohen, Robin, 3, 8, 172
communication, 157–67
consociationalism, 38
cosmopolitanism, 34
Cresswell, Tim, 11–12
cultural homogeneity, 194–8, 212

Dallas, Lucy, 183–4
Darwish, Mahmoud, 53, 55, 133, 135,
    137
Daswani, Girish, 16
Dawson, Andrew, 103–5
Dayal, Samir, 9–10, 209
Decimal (*The Night Counter*), 147, 150,
    159
De Niro, Robert, 70
De Niro's Game, 20, 26–7, 33, 42, 67–
    8, 69–96, 118, 211
Deer Hunter, 70
Deir Zeitoon, 141, 143–5, 150–1
    161, 166–7
Deleuze, Gilles, 20–1
Derrida, Jacques, 125–8
deterritorialisation, 19–21
Detroit, 140, 149–50, 160–1, 165, 167
diaspora
  Armenian, 3, 172
  black Atlantic, 5, 7, 22, 107
  characteristics, 3–6, 99–100
  Chinese, 3, 172
  Cuban, 3
  Greek, 3, 100, 172
  home and *see* home
  Indian, 5
  Irish, 172
  Jewish, 3–5, 8, 100
  Lebanese, 23–9

lessons of, 182
literature, 2
Maghrebi, 3
Mexican, 106
music and, 7
nation and *see* nation
Palestinian, 3
place and *see* place, questions of
scholarship, 16, 96, 99
Turkish, 3
diasporic aesthetic/sensibility, 8–10,
    19, 28, 209
Dina (*Somewhere, Home*), 134
Dina (*The Night Counter*), 150–1,
    154–5, 163
dispersal, 4–5, 8, 99–100, 107, 209
displacement, 2–4, 9–10, 16, 21–2,
    117, 133, 135, 137, 148, 154–5,
    167, 173–5, 206–10
domestic violence, 13
domesticity, 27, 99, 101–4, 111,
    112–17, 142–3, 146, 153, 164,
    212–13 *see also* home
    telephonic, 157–67
domus, 112, 164–5
Dooley, Gillian, 117, 127
double consciousness, 8–10, 15, 19, 21
Douglas, Mary, 104
Downtown, 24–5, 40–1
Dreyfus Affair, 174
Druze Muslims, 37, 115, 120, 131–2

East Beirut, 26, 27, 39, 67, 68, 69–96,
    136, 211
Eid al-'Ashura, 62
El Hage, Jad, 208–9
Eliot, T. S., 45, 56, 66
Embalo, Brigit, 51–5
Emden, Clara (*Ports of Call*), 183–5,
    190–201, 204–6
Engels, Friedrich, 34
En-nahas, Jamal, 183
exclusion and inclusion, 20
exile, 9–10, 109, 208

exilic literature, 208
Palestinian, 133–8

family, 113–14, 145–8, 212–13
Al-Faransawi, George (*De Niro's Game*),
    20, 68, 71–2, 76–80, 84–6,
    88–9, 94–5
Fawzi-from-the-mountains (*Unreal
    City*), 47
FBI, 139, 141, 160, 162
fellahin, 46–8, 58, 65–6
female body, 52–3
fixity, 103–8
folklore, 120–1, 125
food, 14
foreigners, 18–19, 189–90
France, 90–2, 94–5, 211–12
    Nazi occupied, 184–5, 191, 195–7,
    199
Frayha, Anis, 120–1, 132
Frazer, Sir James George, 56–7
Freudian uncanny, 18–19

Gana, Nouri, 71, 77, 90
Gaza Strip, 186–7
Geagea, Samir, 74
Gemayel, Amin, 74
Gemayel, Bashir, 74, 83–4, 88, 93
Gibran, Khalil, 119, 181
Gilroy, Paul, 5, 7, 165
globalisation, 10–11, 16
Gohar, Saddik, 56–7
The Golden Bough, 56–7
Gordon, Ahron David, 173
Green Line, 38–9
Gruen, Erich, 173, 174
Guattari, Félix, 20–1

Ha'am, Ahad, 173
Hage, Ghassan, 6, 13–14, 82, 93, 165
Hage, Rawi, 20, 26–8, 42, 67–8,
    69–96, 132, 211–12
Haifa, 43, 184–5, 191, 193–4, 197,
    198, 201, 205

Hala and the King (1967), 121–2
Hala (*The Night Counter*), 147, 150, 159
Hall, Stuart, 5, 7, 10, 158, 165
Hanania, Tony, 1, 26–8, 42, 43–68,
    208–12
Harun (*Unreal City*), 52, 58–9, 63
Hazard, Sherri (*The Night Counter*),
    160–3, 165
heim and *heimat*, 15, 101–2, 114
heimlich, 18
Herzl, Theodor, 174
Hezbollah, 39–40, 61, 65, 136
historical narratives, management of,
    177–8
Hobeika, Elie, 74
Hobsbawm, Eric, 15, 101–2, 112, 114,
    177
Hochberg, Gil, 185, 188, 190–1, 193,
    199, 201, 203, 206, 211
home, 10–23, 130–3, 141–2, 212–13
    see also domesticity
    archive, as, 113, 125–33
    culture and, 110–11
    definitions, 100–1
    emotive constitution of, 107
    family, as, 113–14, 145–8, 212–13
    fixity and mobility, 103–8, 138,
        142–3, 148–67
    geographically shifting site, as
        115–17
    house as, 27, 101, 104, 108, 112–
        18, 122–8, 130, 134–5, 138,
        143–5, 147–8, 165
    nation as, 100–1
    nostalgia and, 114–15
    relationships and, 160–2
    women and, 12–13, 99–108
home-building, 13–14
homeland, 2–5, 10–23, 100, 175
hooks, bell, 13, 107
Hout, Syrine, 65, 70, 74, 77, 111–13,
    115–16, 208–10
human ecology, 36
Humphrey, Michael, 22–4, 26

Hussein, Imam, 61–2
Hutchby, Ian, 158–9
Hutchison, John, 15–17, 176

internal focalisation, 78
Ishtar, 57–8
Israel, 28
    Arab–Israeli conflict, 184–90
    Declaration of Independence, 179
    Israel–Palestine question, 28, 167,
        171, 178–9, 182, 183–206,
        211–12
    Law of Return, 180
    Maronite association with, 93–4
Israel, Nico, 9, 206, 208

Jaffer (*Unreal City*), 46, 50–2, 60, 62–3
Jarrar, Nada Awar, 26, 28, 99, 103, 108,
    109–38, 144–7, 208–9, 212
Jewish diaspora, 3–5, 8, 173–5
Jewish identity, 189, 200–1
Jewish state, 28, 178–9, 186–8 *see also*
    Israel
jihad, 64–5
Jihad al-Binaa, 51, 61, 67, 210

Kafka, Franz, 21
Kahanoff, Jacqueline, 202–3
Ketabdar, Ossyane (*Ports of Call*)
    183–5, 190–201, 204–6, 211
keys, 204–6
Khalaf, Samir, 24, 37, 73–4, 119–21
Khoury, Bernard, 136–7
Khoury, Elias, 75, 157
Kristeva, Julia, 18–19, 21, 189
kulturnation, 176

Laila (*The Night Counter*), 146,
    150, 159
land and identity, 190–4
language, 21–2, 202
    Arab, 81, 181
    bucolic, 123–4
    Levantinism and, 200

The Last Migration: A Novel of Diaspora and Love, 208–9

Laurent, Monsieur (*De Niro's Game*), 86

Layla (*Unreal City*), 44, 46, 51–5, 58–9, 62–3

Lebanese diaspora, 23–9
  Forces (LF), 74
  literature, 180–2, 208
  pastoral, 117–25
  politics, 38–40, 136

Leila (*Somewhere, Home*), 113, 126–8, 130

Lena (*The Night Counter*), 150, 159

L'Étranger, 89–91

Levantinism, 198–206, 211–12

Lijphart, Arend, 38

London, 34, 42, 44–5, 50, 52, 56, 59, 63–4, 66, 109, 208–11

Maalouf, Amin, 6, 8, 26, 28, 167, 171, 178, 180, 182, 183–206, 211–12

McWatt, Tessa, 14

Majalis, 86–7

Makdisi, Saree, 24–5, 40–1, 156–7

Mani, Claude (*De Niro's Game*), 94

Mani, Rhea (*De Niro's Game*), 94

Mannur, Anita, 15–16

Maronite Christians, 36–7, 39, 53, 81–95, 132
  militia, 53, 68, 70, 74, 76–80, 84, 86–9, 93–5
  political leaders *zuama*, 73–4
  war amnesia, 73–81, 95

Martel, Yann, 14

martyrdom, 64

Marwan (*The Night Counter*), 146, 164

Masri, Jamal (*The Night Counter*), 151

Massey, Doreen, 11–13, 16, 172, 210

Mayhew, Henry, 34

Maysa (*Somewhere, Home*), 112–16, 118, 123–32, 145

Meinecke, Friedrich, 176

memory crisis, 123

Meursault (*L'Étranger*), 90

Mexican migrants, 14–15, 105–6

Mezei, Kathy, 145, 146, 147, 148

Middle Passage, 22

migration, 11, 14, 23–8, 46, 100, 105–6, 110–11, 118–19, 122, 141, 149–50, 157–8, 164, 167, 180, 208–9

Mike (*The Night Counter*), 151–2

Miriam (*The Night Counter*), 150

mobility, 99, 103–8, 138, 142–3, 148–67
  insecurity about, 162–5

Moreh, Shmuel, 119

Mossad, 94

Muharram, 62

murafiq, 47

Musa-al-Tango (*Unreal City*), 47–8, 50, 63, 64

Nadia (*The Night Counter*), 150

Naficy, Hamid, 9, 207–8

nation
  definitions, 100–1
  diaspora and, 15–21, 27–8, 171–82
  home as, 100–1
  state and, 175–80

nation-state, 2, 10, 15–23, 27–8, 171–5, 192–3, 212
  cultural homogeneity and, 194–8, 212

national-ethnic order of separation, 185–8, 194–5

national identity
  land and, 190–4

National Pact *al Mithaq al Watani*, 24, 38, 80

nationalism, 16–17, 27–8, 85, 171
  Zionist, 176–80

Netanyahu, Benjamin, 188

Neuwirth, Angelika, 51, 53, 55

New Castle, 150–2

The Night Counter, 26–7, 99, 103, 108, 138, 139–67, 205, 213

Nussbaum, Felicity, 156, 157

oikos, 164
Olmert, Ehud, 188
Oslo Accords, 186
Ottoman Empire, 47, 82, 91, 131, 183,
    190–2, 201, 203–4

Palestine Arab and Jewish United
    Workers Committee, 199
Palestinians/Palestine, 21, 43, 50, 51,
    53, 55, 57, 75, 79–80, 82–3, 85,
    88–9, 93, 95, 115–16, 141, 151,
    154, 187–8
  diaspora, 3
  exile, 133–8
  Israel–Palestine question, 28, 167,
    171, 178–9, 182, 183–206,
    211–12
  massacre, 53, 74, 86, 88
  UN membership, 186–7
Pappe, Ilan, 5, 179, 186, 200
Patriot Act, 162
Paris, 21, 77, 90–5, 109, 199, 206
Park, Robert, 26–7, 35–6, 42, 72, 76,
    95–6
pastoral imagery, 117–25
Phalange, 74
Phares, Walid, 82–3, 93
place, questions of, 2–3, 10–23, 29, 213
  diaspora and, 2–3, 10–23, 207–13
  war, during, 33–4
plurilocality, 15
politics of location, 2
Porteous, Douglas J., 12–13
Ports of Call, 26, 28, 167, 171, 182,
    183–206, 211–12
Potter, Russell, 7
property developers, 49–50
Prophet Muhammad, 61–2
prostitution, 46, 52–4, 63

Qabbani, Nizar, 53, 55
Quayson, Ato, 16

Rahbani Brothers, 121–2, 132
Rambo (*De Niro's Game*), 86–7

Randa (*The Night Counter*), 150, 154–5,
    162
Rapport, Nigel, 103–5
redemption
  narratives of, 55–67
refugees, 8, 36, 49, 51–3, 59, 74, 88,
    115, 133–6, 150A, 154–5
Reis, Michele, 3–4
religious segregation, 36, 77–80,
    132
return, teleology of, 5–6
rhizomic network, 12
Road Map for Peace, 186
Rock (*The Night Counter*), 150–3
roots, 6–8, 165–7
  roots-as-movement, 157–67
Rose, Gillian, 12–13, 107
Rouse, Roger, 14, 105–6, 145, 158
Rushdie, Salman, 44, 65–6, 158
Rykwert, Joseph, 104, 112

Saad, Ashraf, 208–9
Sabra and Shatila, 51, 134, 136–7,
    150
  massacres, 21, 52, 74–5, 86, 88,
    136–7
Saeeda (*Somewhere, Home*), 113–14, 125,
    127–8, 130
Safran, William, 2–6, 8, 99–100,
    104–5, 174–6
Said (*De Niro's Game*), 84
Said, Edward, 9–10, 76–7, 91, 133,
    177, 188–9, 197, 200, 205–6
Salem, Elise, 180–1
Salibi, Kamal, 24, 83
Salwa (*Somewhere, Home*), 112, 115–16,
    118, 209
Sand, Shlomo, 175
Sara (*Somewhere, Home*), 134
Sarkis, Hashim, 75–6
Scheherazade, 140–1, 143, 151, 153–7,
    164, 166–7, 213
Schweid, Eliezer, 173–4, 178
sectarian identification, 20, 24, 36–8,
    71, 76–7, 95

segregation, 36, 39–40
  national-ethnic, 185–8, 194–5
  religious segregation, 36, 77–80, 132
shahada, 64
Shapiro, Michael, 17, 177
Sharon, Ariel, 188
Shasha, David, 202, 203–4
al-Shawaf, Rayyan, 109, 111–12,
  117–18, 126–7
Shi'a Muslims, 39, 61–4, 181
Simmel, George, 26–7, 34–5, 42, 44, 67
Solidere company, 24–5, 40–1, 61, 67,
  75, 210
Somerville, Peter, 101, 115
Somewhere, Home, 26–7, 99, 103, 108,
  109–38, 144–6, 208–9, 212–13
  structure, 112–17
Soraya (*The Night Counter*), 150, 163
South Lebanon, 27, 39, 43, 45–6, 59,
  61, 63, 66, 93
staatsnation, 176
Stone, Christopher, 119–21
storytelling, 140–3, 145–8, 153–7
Stratton, Jon, 175, 176, 179
suicide mission, 44, 55, 64, 66, 210

Tabar, Paul, 62, 100, 112
Ta'if Accords, 23, 24
Tammuz, 56, 57
telephonic domesticity, 157–67
Terdiman, Richard, 122, 124
Termerles, Stefan (*Ports of Call*), 191,
  193, 197–8
terrorism, 139–41, 162
Thousand and One Nights, 140–1, 146,
  149, 153, 155–7
Tilley, Virginia, 187
Tölölyan, Khachig, 8, 16, 172
torture, 86–8
travel and journeys, 5–7, 77, 149–55,
  162–3, 193
  communication of, 159
Tuan, Yi-Fu, 12

ummah, 85
uncanny, nature of, 18–19
unheimlich, 18–19
Unreal City, 1, 26–7, 33, 42, 43–68,
  208–10
  culture, 34–6, 67–8, 72–3
  development, 33–4, 37
  space, 72
    feminisation of, 51–55
  theory
    Chicago School of, 26, 35–6
    German School of, 26, 34–6, 42,
      67

Vienna, 101–2, 114
violence, 13, 87–8

Wadih (*Somewhere, Home*), 113, 124
Walters, William, 163–5
war amnesia, 36–42, 73–81,
  95, 137
The Waste Land, 45, 56–7, 66, 210
Weber, Max, 26–7, 34–5, 42, 44, 67,
  95, 176
West Bank, 186–7
West Beirut, 26, 39, 43–68, 71, 76,
  78, 79, 85, 94
Williams, Raymond, 118–19
Wirth, Louis, 26, 35–6, 42
women
  archivists, 126–8
  home, and, 12–13, 99–108
  proto-feminist agency, 156
  urban space, as, 51–55

xenophobia, 18

Yunis, Alia, 26–8, 99, 103, 108, 138,
  139–67, 205, 212–13

Zaarour, Rola, 140–1
Zade (*The Night Counter*), 146
Zionist ideology, 173–5, 179

www.ingramcontent.com/pod-product-compliance
Lightning Source LLC
Chambersburg PA
CBHW071458110726
47908CB00003B/658